A Paler Shade of Red:
The 2008 Presidential Election in the South

A Paler Shade of Red

* * *

The 2008 Presidential Election in the South

* * *

Edited by Branwell DuBose Kapeluck,
Laurence W. Moreland, and Robert P. Steed

The Citadel Symposium on Southern Politics

The Diane D. Blair Center of Southern Politics and Society

The University of Arkansas Press
Fayetteville
2009

ISBN-10 (cloth): 1-55728-914-X
ISBN-10 (paper): 1-55728-915-8
ISBN-13 (cloth): 978-1-55728-914-8
ISBN-13 (paper): 978-1-55728-915-5

13   12   11   10   09   5   4   3   2   1

Text design by Ellen Beeler

⊗ The paper used in this publication meets the minimum requirements of the
American National Standard for Permanence of Paper for Printed Library
Materials Z39.48-1984.

This project is supported in part by the Blair Center of Southern Politics and
Society.

Library of Congress Cataloging-in-Publication Data

A paler shade of red : the 2008 Presidential election in the South / edited by
Branwell DuBose Kapeluck, Laurence W. Moreland, and Robert P. Steed.
        p. cm.
  Includes bibliographical references and index.
  ISBN-13: 978-1-55728-914-8 (cloth : alk. paper)
  ISBN-10: 1-55728-914-X
  ISBN-13: 978-1-55728-915-5 (pbk. : alk. paper)
  ISBN-10: 1-55728-915-8
  1. Presidents—United States—Election—2008. 2. Southern States—
Politics and government—1951– I. Kapeluck, Branwell DuBose, 1969–
II. Moreland, Laurence W. III. Steed, Robert P.
  JK5262008 .P35 2009
  324.973'0931—dc22
                                                            2009029422

Contents

List of Illustrations vii

Acknowledgments xi

Foreword xiii

Introduction: Southern Elections, Southern Politics xvii
    Robert P. Steed and Laurence W. Moreland

Part I   The Setting and the Nominating Process

1   The Continued Convergence of Demographics and
Issues 3
    Scott E. Buchanan

2   The 2008 Presidential Nomination Process 17
    John A. Clark

Part II   Elections in the Deep South

3   Alabama: Electoral Continuity and Racial Voting 35
    Patrick R. Cotter

4   Georgia: Where Competitiveness Came Late 49
    Charles S. Bullock III

5   Louisiana: From Political Bellwether to Republican
Stronghold 67
    Robert E. Hogan and Eunice H. McCarney

6   Mississippi: Democrats Fight for Relevance in an
Increasingly Republican State 83
    David A. Breaux and Stephen D. Shaffer

7   South Carolina: A Paler Shade of Red? 95
    Cole Blease Graham

Part III Elections in the Rim South

8. Arkansas: He's Not One of (Most of) Us 119
    Jay Barth, Janine A. Parry, and Todd G. Shields

9. Florida: Obama Gives GOP the Blues 137
    Jonathan Knuckey

10. North Carolina: Change and Continuity in 2008 161
    Charles Prysby

11. Tennessee: Cracker Barrel Realignment 177
    *Ronald Keith Gaddie, with the assistance of
    Michael D. Jones*

12. Texas: After the Bush Era 195
    Brian Arbour and Mark McKenzie

13. Virginia: The New Math of Blue Virginia 215
    John J. McGlennon

Conclusion: Don't Whistle Past Dixie Yet 235
    H. Gibbs Knotts

Notes 251

Contributors 279

Index 283

Illustrations

Tables

1.1. Demographic Support for John McCain (in percent) 5
1.2. Support for John McCain by Race and Gender (in percent) 8
1.3. Issue Positions by State (in percent) 10
1.4. Issue Positions and Support for John McCain (in percent) 11
2.1. Schedule of 2008 Nomination Contests 20
2.2. Republican Primary Outcomes in the South (in percent) 24
2.3. Democratic Primary Outcomes in the South (in percent) 27
3.1. Results of the 2008 Election in Alabama 39
3.2. Voting in Recent Alabama Presidential Elections by County
     Characteristics (in percent) 42
3.3. Alabama Exit Poll Results for the 1996, 2000, 2004, and 2008
     Presidential Elections (in percent) 44
3.4. Exit Poll Results for the 2008 Presidential Election—Alabama
     and the United States (in percent) 46
4.1. Comparison of the 2008 Georgia Vote with 2004 56
4.2. Comparisons of the 2008 Presidential Electorate in Georgia with the
     National Electorate 59
5.1. Support for Presidential Candidates in Louisiana and Nationally
     Among Various Categories of Voters (in percent) 76
5.2. Support for Presidential Candidates in Louisiana and Nationally
     Among Voters with Differing Political Viewpoints (in percent) 78
6.1. 2008 Election Returns in Mississippi Federal Elections (in percent) 93
6.2. Voter Ideologies and Perceptions of Candidates' Ideologies
     (in percent) 95
6.3. Demographic and Attitudinal Sources of 2008 Presidential Vote
     (in percent) 96
7.1. Party Identification, by Selected Dates and Average for Thirty-eight
     Survey Periods, Fall 1989 through Spring 2006 (in percent) 100
7.2. Results of 2000 South Carolina Presidential and Congressional
     Elections (in percent) 104
7.3. 2008 Urban/Rural Regions in South Carolina by County and
     County Proportion of Total State Vote (in percent) 107
7.4. Exit Poll Results Reporting Demographic Factors in the 2008
     Presidential Vote (in percent) 109
8.1. Primary Voter Turnout in Arkansas in Presidential Election Years,
     1976–2008 123

8.2. Selected Polls in Arkansas, Presidential Race 2008 125
8.3. Results of the 2008 Arkansas Presidential and Congressional
Elections (in percent) 126
8.4. Republican Vote in Arkansas, 2000, 2004, and 2008 by County
(in percent) 127
8.5. Poll Results of Arkansas Voters, 2008 (in percent) 130
8.6. General Election Voter Turnout in Arkansas, 1972–2008 134
8.7. Registered Voter Turnout and Presidential Vote in the Ten Most
Populous Arkansas Counties, 2008 135
9.1. Results of 2008 Florida Presidential Election and Selected
Congressional Districts 148
9.2. Partisan Change in Florida's "Mega" Counties in Presidential
Elections, 1988–2008 (in percent) 149
9.3. Florida 2008 Presidential Election Vote by Region 150
9.4. Florida Exit Poll Results Reporting Demographic and Political
Factors in the 2008 Presidential Vote (in percent) 152
10.1. North Carolina Election Results, Presidential Years, 1992–2008
(in percent) 162
10.2. Presidential Vote in North Carolina and the Nation, 1988–2008
(in percent) 166
10.3. North Carolina Voting by Selected Political Orientations, 2008
(in percent) 168
10.4. North Carolina Voting by Selected Demographic and Social
Variables, 2008 (in percent) 169
10.5. Congressional Election Outcomes in North Carolina, 2006–2008
(in percent) 171
11.1. How Often Do You Attend Religious Services? (in percent) 183
11.2. Poll Tracks in Tennessee, President, 2008 (in percent) 185
11.3. Comparing Obama's Tennessee Performance to the Rest of the
South (in percent) 187
11.4. NEP Exit Poll Estimates of White and Black Voter Preferences,
1992–2008 (in percent) 188
11.5. WLS Estimates of the 2004 and 2008 Democratic Presidential
Vote, and the Structure of Shifting Preferences in Tennessee 190
12.1 The Vote in Texas 197
12.2 Which One of These Five Issues is the Most Important Facing the
Country? 200
12.3 Vote Share of Presidential Candidates and District Judges, 2008
(in percent) 209
12.4. Exit Poll Results, 2008 (in percent) 211
13.1. Virginia Election Results 224
13.2. Virginia Exit Poll Results, 2008 (in percent) 225
13.3. Turnout and Vote in Selected Virginia Localities (in percent) 229

Figures

11.1. Counties Voting More Republican for President in 2008 than 2004 . . .189

12.1. Republican Vote Trend in Texas, 1948–2008 203

12.2. Republican Presidential Vote Trend by Place, 1976–2008 205

12.3. Republican Vote Trend for Urban Counties, 1976–2008 207

C.1. Growing Gap in Republican Presidential Support 238

C.2. Narrowing the Gap in Voter Turnout 239

C.3. 2008 Voter Turnout in Southern States 240

C.4. Republican Congressional Success in the South 241

C.5. Population Growth in Southern States 243

C.6. Racial Diversity in Southern States 244

C.7. Evidence of Racially Based Voting 246

C.8. Obama White Vote and Racial Context 247

Acknowledgments

This volume is the seventh in a series of analysis of elections in the South beginning in 1984 and continuing in 1988, 1992, 1996, and 2000. A state-by-state study of the 2004 presidential election was not published in edited book form, but did appear in a special double issue of the *American Review of Politics*. While the presidential election has been the focus of each volume, other important aspects of contemporary southern electoral politics have also been addressed, including congressional and state elections and the overall status of party development and competition in each southern state. This volume continues the general organizational plan of the previous publications, including an introductory chapter, a chapter on presidential primaries, a chapter on issues in the 2008 presidential election, as well as chapters on each southern state and a conclusion summarizing lessons from the 2008 election cycle.

This study of the 2008 presidential election in the South benefitted greatly from the institutional and financial support of the Diane D. Blair Center for the Study of Southern Politics and Society. We are grateful for the interest expressed by the Blair Center's director, Todd Shields, in continuing this project.

We are also appreciative of the support of those who have made this book possible or who have contributed to the atmosphere in which this work was created. The Citadel Foundation provided indispensable financial support for The Citadel Symposium on Southern Politics, a biennial conference that for over two decades has brought together a community of scholars engaged in the study of southern politics and which has, in the process, helped to develop the network of contributors involved in this study.

Finally, we wish to thank Lawrence J. Malley, the director of the University of Arkansas Press, and Sarah E. White, the copy editor, for their support, patience, and guidance during the publication process.

Foreword

Southern Politics and the 2008 Presidential Election

The contemporary American South is one of the most rapidly changing regions in the country. Fundamental changes in population, economics, and partisanship have altered the political landscape of not only the region but the entire nation. Prior to the civil rights movement, the "solid south" stood as a monument to de jure segregation, the politics of race, and the power of the Democratic Party over local, state, and national elections. Following the civil rights movement, however, the South's transformation from the once solidly Democratic South to a consistently Republican region represents one of the most dramatic political changes in American political history. The wide-ranging effects of these developments on electoral behavior and public policy are difficult to assess, but it is unquestionable that the New South remains as important to American politics as the old. With 153 Electoral College votes, a solid South represents over half the necessary 270 electoral votes necessary to win the presidency. More than a decade ago, Black and Black concluded that "as the united South goes: so goes the nation" (1992, 344). Given the historical forces that have moved the South to act as a unified voting block, it is no coincidence that many of our recent presidents have hailed from one of the former Confederate states. In 2008, the surprising success of the first African American presidential candidate and the Democratic Party across several southern states suggests that the Republican dominance of the region may be in decline. Not only did several southern states support a northern liberal Democratic candidate, they supported the nation's first African American presidential nominee. In a region better known for Jim Crow segregation than racial tolerance, such outcomes beg for scholarly investigation.

Since the 1984 presidential election between then president Ronald Reagan and former vice president Walter Mondale, our colleagues at The Citadel have drawn attention to the importance of the South in presidential elections. Every four years, these scholars have facilitated important insights into presidential elections and this book series has not only advanced our systematic understanding of southern politics but has served as a catalyst for countless articles and books focusing on the politics of the region. In this 2008 edition of the series, so aptly titled *A Paler*

Shade of Red, we understand more clearly how Senator Obama and the Democratic Party successfully broke up the "Republican South." Despite the "fifty state" campaign rhetoric from the Obama campaign, we find an extremely strategic and unique campaign strategy focusing resources on a few southern states while virtually ignoring others. Further, Obama's emphasis on mobilizing new voters, particularly among minorities and young people, promises to have fundamentally, and perhaps permanently, changed the face of the southern electorate. Fittingly enough, Diane D. Blair was an important contributor to this series in the past. Consequently, it is not only appropriate but is also an exciting opportunity for the Blair Center of Southern Politics and Society to collaborate and sponsor this research endeavor.

The Diane D. Blair Center of Southern Politics and Society

The Blair Center was established by a congressionally appropriated endowment granted in the fall of 2001. The center is a part of only a handful of research centers across the nation established by congressional appropriation and one of the only centers established to honor an individual who was not a former member of Congress. The Blair Center is dedicated to supporting interdisciplinary scholarship, study, and outreach relevant to Arkansas and the southern states.

Diane Divers Blair was born October 25, 1938, and was raised in Washington, D.C. She received her BA from Cornell University in 1959 and worked in Washington, D.C., for the President's Committee on Government Contracts, a Senate committee on unemployment, and as legislative secretary and speechwriter for Sen. Stuart Symington of Missouri. She moved to Arkansas in 1963 and received her master's degree in political science from the University of Arkansas in 1967. She debated Phyllis Schlafly before the Arkansas legislature on Valentine's Day 1975 on behalf of the Equal Rights Amendment, and in 1992 she was selected to cast one of Arkansas ballots in the Electoral College.

Mrs. Blair taught at the University of Arkansas for thirty years, established a record of accomplishment simply unparalleled in its combination of serious scholarship and practical involvement in both local and national politics. In May 2000, Mrs. Blair was awarded an honorary doctor of laws by the University of Arkansas, and she was twice nominated to the board of the Corporation for Public Broadcasting by Pres. William Jefferson Clinton and twice confirmed to that position by the Senate. She served two terms as chair of the Corporation for Public Broadcasting, and the corporation has now named its governing board after her. She was appointed by Gov. Dale Bumpers in 1971 to serve as chair of the Governor's Commission on the Status of Women, by Gov. David Pryor in 1976 to chair the Commission on Public Employee Rights, and by Gov. Bill Clinton in 1979 to serve as a member of the Arkansas Educational Television Network commission, on which she served until 1993 and chaired from 1986–87. In 1992 she took leave from the University of Arkansas to serve as senior researcher for the Clinton presidential campaign and again took leave in 1996 when she served as senior advisor to the Clinton-Gore reelection campaign.

In addition to establishing a breakneck record of service to her state and nation, Diane was also an accomplished scholar, teacher, and mentor. She published two books, the first an analysis of Sen. Hattie Caraway, the first woman elected to the U.S. Senate, entitled *Silent Hattie Speaks: The Personal Journal of Senator Hattie Caraway* (Greenwood Press, 1979). Her second book was titled *Arkansas Politics and Government: Do the People Rule?* (University of Nebraska Press, 1988), a book that continues to serve as a primary text in Arkansas high schools, colleges, and universities. In addition, she authored fourteen chapters in edited volumes and authored or coauthored over ninety articles in various publications. Her research interests focused primarily on women and politics, state and local government, and the politics of Arkansas and the South.

Diane was three times named Outstanding Faculty Member by University of Arkansas students, and in 1982 she was one of the first recipients of the Fulbright College Master Teacher Award. In 1995 she was honored by the Midwest Political Science Association for her body of work in political science, and the Southern Political Science Association now has a competitive annual award in her name given to a scholar, chosen by committee, who successfully combines rigorous analyses of contemporary politics with a commitment to political activism. Future activities of the Blair Center will continue to honor Mrs. Blair through a commitment to excellence in research and teaching of the importance of southern politics and society as well as through a commitment to service in the state and region.

Todd Shields, PhD
Director
The Diane D. Blair Center of
Southern Politics and Society

Introduction

Southern Elections, Southern Politics

Robert P. Steed and Laurence W. Moreland

Scholars have developed many ways to gauge political change in the South and to describe that region's contemporary political system. One approach is to examine electoral patterns inasmuch as these provide useful insights into the nature of partisan developments, group interaction and related power struggles, and evolving social and legal context. From the perspective of the South's role in national politics, attention to the region's role in presidential elections has been especially important.

Somewhat surprisingly, this scholarly attention to presidential elections in the South has a relatively short history. While most earlier studies of southern politics addressed presidential elections as a part of the larger analysis, these elections were seldom the focus of the work. A large part of the explanation was rooted in the region's one-partyism inasmuch as this rendered most discussion of presidential politics relatively meaningless—the South voted heavily and consistently Democratic so there was little point in further analysis. Only in those rare instances of a break in this pattern did interest increase. For example, V. O. Key Jr., in his landmark *Southern Politics in State and Nation*[1] included one chapter (of thirty-one) addressing the presidential elections of 1928 and 1948 because those two were characterized by a break in the region's Democratic solidarity; the otherwise scattered discussion of presidential politics in the South was included mainly to demonstrate other elements of the analysis (such as turnout differences from one level of election to another).

When the Democratic Solid South began to crack in the aftermath of the Dixiecrat Revolt of 1948, presidential electoral patterns began to receive more scholarly attention. Donald Strong's brief analysis of

Eisenhower's success in gaining southern votes in 1952 pointed to the growing middle-class urban/suburban electorate as a potential source of Republican growth (and, thereby, partisan transformation) in the region.[2] Similarly, other research into party change in the South over the next two decades included discussions of voting patterns in presidential elections.[3]

Still, by the early 1980s the connections between presidential politics and southern politics had not been thoroughly examined. As William Havard pointed out a quarter of a century ago, "Presidential electoral politics has, of course, been the subject of much analysis and comment, but the political relations between the [South] and the presidential institution in all of its functions—both symbolic and practical—have been carried out in a time of great change seem to have been scanted, so far as systematic analysis is concerned. The apparent absence of even scholarly interest in studying the relations between the enigmatic South and the nation's chief executive . . . is a hiatus that cannot easily be either explained or filled."[4]

In part to address this gap in the literature on southern politics, and in part because, as others had already recognized, analysis of presidential politics in the South offered an opportunity to explore political change in the region at a time of rapid and dramatic transformation, we (together with our late colleague, Tod A. Baker) brought together a group of outstanding scholars to develop a manuscript on the 1984 presidential election in the South. The original plan was to have a series of chapters discussing the presidential election campaign and results in each of the eleven states of the former Confederacy, modeled roughly after V.O. Key's state-by-state approach in *Southern Politics in State and Nation*. This project, organized in conjunction with the 1984 Citadel Symposium on Southern Politics, was expanded between conception and completion to include some analyses of other important elections in the states as well and a conclusion that addressed the 1984 elections on a region-wide scale.

We were fortunate to have the manuscript accepted for publication by Praeger and even more fortunate that Praeger found the project sufficiently interesting to continue publication of subsequent manuscripts on the 1988, 1992, 1996, and 2000 elections in the South. Our working relationship with Praeger was highly positive throughout this period, and we deeply appreciate that publisher's willingness to develop a continuing series of analyses for these five elections.

When Praeger (Greenwood) discontinued publishing the series after 2000 when it changed its editorial focus, the series was carried through the 2004 election cycle in the form of a special edition of the *American Review of Politics.*

We are extremely pleased that the University of Arkansas Press, in conjunction with the Diane D. Blair Center of Southern Politics and Society at the University of Arkansas, has now joined us in continuing this series with the publication of *A Paler Shade of Red: The 2008 Presidential Election in the South.* This association is especially rewarding because Diane Blair was a good friend and colleague who contributed informative and interesting chapters on Arkansas politics and elections to a number of the earlier books in the series. We always enjoyed working with her, and we are honored to be involved in a project that is so strongly supported by the Blair Center. We are also pleased that our colleague at The Citadel, Prof. DuBose Kapeluck, has joined us in this 2008 presidential election project.

In the years since the publication of the first book in the series, *The 1984 Presidential Election in the South: Patterns of Southern Party Politics,* the literature on presidential electoral politics in the South has expanded significantly.[5] In addition to the current series of books on specific elections, important works by Earl and Merle Black,[6] Joseph Aistrup,[7] Alexander Lamis,[8] and David Lublin,[9] to name a few, have underscored the importance of such a focus. Moreover, broader works on southern politics have continued to explore presidential electoral politics as valuable indicators of past change and future directions.[10]

As with the earlier publications, and in keeping with the point of view found in the rich literature briefly described above, we strongly feel that an analysis of electoral politics offers powerful insight into the nature of politics in the South. We see this book as part of ongoing efforts to track southern political change and to map the contemporary features of the region's political terrain.

In many ways, the 2008 presidential election was unusual. First, and foremost, an African American won the nomination of a major party for the first time in the nation's history in a hard-fought contest that also featured, again for the first time, a woman who was seriously competitive. In the historical context of southern politics, this event was especially significant in the region given the central importance of race (from slavery through the Civil War and Reconstruction, the implementation of the Jim Crow system, the civil rights movement and its aftermath). Indeed, one key question throughout the election period concerned whether this would be an advantage in the South, with its significant African American population, or whether this would be a disadvantage in a region where the white majority usually displayed strong conservative (and Republican) tendencies, often with vestiges of race-related undertones.

Second, the 2008 presidential election marked the first time since 1988, and only the third time since 1972, that a southerner had not been the nominee of at least one of the two major political parties (1984 and 1988 being the other two exceptions in this period). Given that partisan patterns in the South had changed dramatically during this time and that Democratic prospects in the region seemed to be strongly connected to the presence of a southerner on the ticket, a race without a southerner on either ticket increased uncertainty as to how the campaign would develop. Would the Democrats concede the region to the Republicans? Would the Democrats target a few states in the hope of peeling a couple away from the Republicans even though their candidate had no southern base comparable to that enjoyed by Clinton and Gore when they used this strategy with some success in 1992 and 1996? Or would the Democrats run a vigorous campaign throughout the South in the hope that a favorable combination of circumstances—an unpopular Republican president, an energized Democratic candidate with a compelling message of change, a well-respected but less-than-energetic Republican candidate, a huge campaign war chest, and, eventually, a national economic crisis—could overcome a recent pattern of Republican voting in a wide open race?

Third, in light of the closeness of the two most recent presidential elections, the question of southern electoral solidarity assumed particular importance. John McCain's ability to carry the entire region or Barack Obama's ability to break that solidarity were critical elements of their respective campaign strategies. As Obama's electoral momentum increased in the last weeks of the campaign, holding the South became even more crucial for McCain. At the same time, the Obama campaign, seeing a growing opportunity to close the door on McCain's presidential aspirations, intensified its effort in selected southern states. As a result, the South came to be an important part of the general election campaign in ways not often seen over the past quarter century.

Finally, the 2008 presidential election played out in a broader electoral context involving the distinct possibility that Democrats would not only retain their majorities in both houses of Congress, but that they had a good chance of picking up enough Senate seats to obtain a nominal filibuster-proof majority. The strength of Obama's campaign in the South would be a factor inasmuch as some of the key contested Senate seats were in the South (such as Georgia, North Carolina). Even if Obama failed to carry a given state, a stronger than usual campaign and final showing could help tip the balance in a close Senate election.

In short, there was great potential from the outset for the 2008 elections in the South to be both interesting and significant nationally as well as regionally. This book presents detailed analyses of how the presidential election, from the nomination struggle through the casting of votes in November, played out in the South. Additionally, there are examinations of important elections other than the presidential race. Most of the chapters are devoted to discussions of single states (covering all eleven states of the former Confederacy), but there are three chapters that take a regional perspective so as to help provide a broader framework for understanding both the flow and significance of developments at the state level. The goal, as with the previous publications in this series, is to use the details of the state-by-state analyses to develop a more general understanding of broader political patterns in the South and of the South's role in the national political arena.

I

The Setting and
the Nominating Process

1

The Continued Convergence
of Demographics and Issues

Scott E. Buchanan

Introduction

By any measure, the 2008 elections were unprecedented from a historic standpoint. After eight years of a Republican administration, voters were looking for a change. Since 1932, the Democrats and Republicans have succeeded in controlling the White House more than eight consecutive years on two occasions: the Franklin Delano Roosevelt and Harry Truman administrations (1933-1953) and the Ronald Reagan and George H. W. Bush administrations (1981-1993). Coupled with the unpopularity of President George W. Bush and a general malaise among the voters about the Republican label, 2008 shaped up to be a distinctly unfavorable year for Republicans.

Despite this, Republicans held high hopes that John McCain would have a better than even chance of winning the White House. GOP expectations in this regard revolved around a combination of McCain's notable public service to the country and his longtime appeal to political independents. Democrats countered with relative newcomer Barack Obama. Despite a short career in the U.S. Senate, Obama's message of hope and change resonated with many independents, young voters, and the Democratic base to overwhelm the Republicans on election day. Obama won an easy victory in the Electoral College, besting McCain by a vote of 364-174, the largest electoral vote total for a Democrat since Bill Clinton's reelection in 1996. Beyond the Electoral College, Obama was able to make inroads and erode Republican support in many southern states and was able to win outright the states of Florida, North Carolina, and Virginia. This chapter will examine the issues that played a factor in southern states in the 2008 presidential election.

The South and the 2008 General Election

For southern voters, this was the first presidential election since 1976 not to feature a southerner, either native or adopted, on the ticket of at least one of the major parties. This flew in the face of the experience of the previous two decades, where having a southerner was seen as a bonus, if not a necessity. Since the 2004 election, the eleven states of the former Confederacy have controlled 153 electoral votes, or nearly 57 percent of the 270 votes needed to win the presidency. As Earl and Merle Black discuss, the South has continued to grow in importance and has become a vital source of support for Republican candidates since the 1960s.[1] Having a southerner on the ticket, especially for the Republicans, had become commonplace.

While John McCain had southern ancestry, neither Barack Obama, Joe Biden, nor Sarah Palin had any ties to the South, although Palin certainly drew southern support based upon her social conservatism and personality.[2] Unlike President Bush in 2000 and 2004, McCain failed to sweep the South. In itself, this did not deny McCain the presidency, but he certainly needed the region to have any realistic chance of victory. In addition, Obama won Virginia, North Carolina, and Florida en route to victory. Most notable of these three states is Virginia, which had not been carried by a Democratic presidential candidate since Lyndon Johnson in 1964. Overall, McCain garnered an average of 54.5 percent of the popular vote across the eleven southern states and won only 98 electoral votes in comparison to Bush's 153 electoral votes and average of 57 percent of the popular vote across the region. On average, Obama ate into the Republican margins from 2004, picking up a number of independent voters, young voters, and winning the support of Hispanics as well (see Table 1.1). Pew Research states that Hispanics favored the Obama/Biden ticket by a two-to-one margin over McCain/Palin.[3] Exit poll data indicate that Hispanics favored Obama by a margin of 57 to 42 percent in Florida, 63 to 35 percent in Texas, and 65 to 34 percent in Virginia.[4] While the 2004 exit poll data do not include Old Dominion Hispanics, the Hispanic vote in Florida and Texas was almost the complete opposite, with Bush winning 56 percent of the Hispanic vote in Florida and 50 percent in Texas.[5]

Table 1.1 Demographic Support for John McCain (in percent)

Characteristics	AL	AR	FL	GA	LA	MS	NC	SC	TN	TX	VA	Average	Change from 2004
Race													
White	88	68	56	76	84	88	64	73	63	73	60	72.9	0.1
Black	2	5	4	2	4	2	5	4	6	2	8	3.9	-7.2
Hispanic	—	—	42	—	—	—	—	—	—	35	34	37	-16.0
Gender													
Male	62	58	47	58	64	62	56	58	60	59	47	57.7	-2.6
Female	58	58	47	46	56	53	44	51	52	52	46	51.3	-3.7
Age													
18-24	49	48	39	50	45	45	28	42	40	47	34	42.5	—
25-29	48	50	35	51	53	42	24	—	46	42	44	43.5	—
30-39	56	59	45	47	55	54	50	41	61	51	46	51.4	—
40-49	63	58	54	55	59	58	55	52	57	55	50	56	—
50-64	62	59	44	51	65	58	56	64	56	59	47	56.5	—
Over 65	78	65	53	54	69	—	56	66	59	66	53	61.9	—
Income													
$50,000 or less	51	47	37	42	45	41	42	41	47	42	37	42.9	-5.0
$50,000 or more	67	65	55	56	70	74	56	64	61	63	50	61.9	-4.7
White Party Identification													
Democrat	51	28	18	22	60	—	16	19	19	20	14	26.7	—
Independent	82	74	52	73	76	82	71	63	61	72	52	68.9	—
Republican	98	96	89	97	98	96	95	97	95	95	93	95.4	—
Evangelical													
Yes	92	77	77	89	93	94	74	85	75	83	79	84.1	-2.8
No	34	34	37	32	43	24	31	35	36	42	35	34.7	-8.1
Size of Place													
Urban	53	41	47	37	56	—	34	—	43	47	37	44.4	-0.5
Suburb	63	64	45	52	64	71	54	67	64	61	48	59.4	0.8
Rural	66	64	57	57	60	57	56	46	61	63	53	58.2	-2.8

Source: National Election Pool Exit Polls, November 4, 2008.

Note: Age categories were slightly different in the 2004 exit polls, rendering the percentage change impossible to compute. White party identification for the GOP was not asked of respondents in the 2004 exit polls.

Demographic Issues

Despite the importance of the South in any Republican coalition to win the presidency, the two reddest states were non-southern states (Oklahoma and Wyoming), with Alabama's 61 percent support for McCain/Palin rounding out the top three. Clearly, 2008 was not a typical election year in either the nation or within the South. As will be illustrated, a variety of issues combined to allow a Democrat to carry three southern states and significantly erode Republican support in other states in the region.

Turnout and Race

One of the biggest issues was the diverse nature of both parties' tickets in 2008. The Democrats became the first major party to nominate a member of a minority group, while the GOP ticket featured its first female running mate. Given the symbolism of the tickets, especially the Obama ticket and the region's long history of racial politics, race itself was a potential issue in 2008. The sensitive nature of racial feelings, however, makes them the hardest to gauge. Still, the exit polls from 2008 can give some indication of what may have been occurring among southern voters. Another expected outcome of the Obama candidacy was that black southerners would turn out in much larger numbers, along with newly registered and young voters. Across the region, though, turnout in general was unchanged and went down from 2004 levels in some states. Even black turnout was not substantially higher than in previous years. Table 1.1 illustrates the demographic support for the McCain ticket.

A quick perusal reveals no huge surprises when examining the demographic support for the GOP. Taking a closer look, though, illustrates some potentially disturbing trends developing for Republican support in various states. In the Rim South states of Arkansas, Florida, North Carolina, Tennessee, Texas, and Virginia, McCain lost ground to Obama in virtually all demographic categories save one: the elderly vote. In the five Deep South states, Obama won in most demographic groups except older voters, but his drop-off was more modest than in the Rim South.

Age. As expected, Senator Obama won among voters under the age of thirty, but Obama nearly won the thirty to thirty-nine age group as well. As age increased, though, so did support for McCain. In particular, McCain did very well among Rim South voters sixty-five and older, where he picked up an average of 4.7 percent points compared to George W. Bush's support in 2004. This finding would seem to indicate that race could have been a governing factor for older white voters in these states. Given that those who are over sixty-five grew up during a segregationist era, this is not entirely surprising. While McCain's advantage among older voters did not increase in the Deep South, this is largely explained by the fact that those 65 and older were already voting for Republicans at a higher rate than Rim South whites in 2004.

Income. Traditionally, Democrats have performed better among voters who earn smaller salaries, while Republicans generally win more votes from those in the upper income brackets. In 2004, Bush won nearly 48 percent of lower-income southerners, but Obama cut that edge by nearly 5 percentage points in 2008. Even more telling was that Obama also made inroads among upper-income southerners, especially among Virginia voters earning more than fifty thousand dollars a year.

Evangelical Whites. For a number of years, religious conservatives have played a large role in southern politics. As Earl and Merle Black pointed out, evangelical Protestant voters have become a core support group for Republicans.[6] Bush won large margins of victory in this group in his reelection bid in 2004. McCain, though, had never been the darling of religious conservatives. In the South, McCain lost some support among evangelical whites in 2008. In the region, McCain lost ground among religiously oriented voters by about 3 percent. In the Deep South, McCain performed better than Bush's numbers in 2004, but religious conservatives in the Rim South did not support McCain with as much fervor as they had Bush in 2004.

Size of Place. Although the 1950s saw the southern Republican Party begin to grow in urban areas, suburbia—and eventually rural areas of the South—became the growth engine for the GOP by the 1990s and early twenty-first century. Since 2000, the Republicans have increasingly been winning among rural whites concerned over a litany of social issues.[7] The Obama/Biden ticket expanded upon what has become the Democratic base in the South and into suburban areas to some degree. The Democrats made the most dramatic headway in rural counties, besting their performance from 2004 by nearly 3 percent. Again, though, one finds a difference in the Deep South versus the Rim South. Most of the increase for Obama came in the heavily black rural counties of the Deep South.

Race. As expected, an examination of the exit poll data by racial grouping yields the most telling story. Table 1.2 presents the exit poll data by race and gender. As expected, black southerners were almost unanimous in support of Obama. While Bush was able to win around 10 percent of the black vote in the region, according to the 2004 exit polls, McCain

Table 1.2 Support for John McCain by Race and Gender (in percent)

Characteristics	AL	AR	FL	GA	LA	MS	NC	SC	TN	TX	VA	Regional Average	National Average
White													
Male	88	67	55	78	83	90	67	76	64	75	61	73	57
Female	88	68	57	74	85	87	62	70	63	72	59	71	53
Black													
Male	0	—	5	2	7	3	13	3	—	—	11	5	5
Female	4	—	3	2	2	1	0	4	4	1	6	3	3
Hispanic													
Male	—	—	40	—	—	—	—	—	—	43	—	42	33
Female	—	—	45	—	—	—	—	—	—	28	—	37	30

Source: National Election Pool Exit Polls, November 4, 2008.

Note: On the 2004 exit polls, race and gender were divided into white and nonwhite, making it impossible to compute a percentage change.

lost significant ground among southern blacks in 2008. The largest decline in Republican support came among blacks in the Deep South. Interestingly enough, the exit polls suggest black females were a source of more strength for Obama compared to black males.

While the decline in black support for the GOP is not surprising, the average number of white males and females who voted Republican is roughly equal from 2004 across all eleven states. In comparison to the rest of the nation, white southerners were much more likely to vote for McCain than their counterparts in other regions of the nation. While the overall white vote in the region is not that different than in previous elections, the data from individual states reveal an interesting pattern. In the three southern states won by Obama, Republican support among white males dropped fairly significantly, while white female Republican support showed a slightly more muted decrease as well. Given that white male support has been the backbone of the Republican Party in the South since the 1980s, this is a troubling fact for the GOP.

Among the other eight states, McCain actually increased his support among white males and females. Most notably, white support for McCain reached the highest levels in Deep South states. Given the long history of racially motivated politics in the Deep South, this would seem to indicate that McCain was winning more votes based upon racial animosities. As a corollary to this possibility, the exit poll data on who white Democrats were supporting are revealing. Across the region, nearly 27 percent of self-identified white Democrats supported the McCain/Palin ticket. The highest numbers of white Democrats who voted Republican were among whites in the Deep South, with nearly 60 percent of Louisiana white Democratic respondents claiming a vote for McCain. If this is representative of the region, it appears that race was playing a large role in those states that V. O. Key discussed nearly sixty years ago as being the most influenced by race and racial politics.[8]

Hispanics. As Hispanics have become a larger component of the southern population, so has their influence upon the region's politics increased. Historically, most attention surrounding Hispanic political involvement has focused on Texas and Florida. However, the entire region has seen increases in Hispanic population, with Georgia, North Carolina, and Virginia having the highest numbers of Hispanics registered to vote after Texas and Florida.[9] In 2004, a majority of Hispanics in Texas and Florida supported Bush's reelection bid. In 2008, the Hispanic vote went in the opposite direction, with 63 percent of Texas Hispanics and 57 percent of Florida Hispanics supporting Obama. For the first time, the 2008 exit polls sampled Hispanic voters in Virginia and found 65 percent support of Obama there. This shift from 2004 underscores how the Hispanic vote is in more flux than any other southern racial group today. Hispanics can potentially play the role of kingmaker in a close contest.

Political Issues in 2008

Besides the roles of race, gender, and turnout, other issues were important in the 2008 presidential election. How often voters cast votes on the basis of issues has been the focus of a plethora of research in the last sixty years. In their seminal work, Angus Campbell and others argued that only a minority of voters cast a ballot on the basis of issues.[10] The research in *The American Voter* is not without its doubters. The first major critic to emerge was V. O. Key in his last book, *The Responsible Electorate,* in which he quipped, "the perverse and unorthodox argument of this little book is that voters are not fools."[11] Key argues that issues do, in fact, play a role with vote choice.

Others have argued that issues play a role but are a more complex phenomenon than first meets the eye. Edward Carmines and James Stimson argue that issues fit into two categories: easy and hard.[12] Easy issues are those that require little background information and are simple to understand. Often voters have an almost emotional instinct toward such issues.

Some examples are race, gay marriage, or abortion. In many cases, easy issues tend to involve social issues. Hard issues, such as federal environmental regulations or monetary policy, are more technically oriented, subtle, and require more "contextual knowledge."[13] These types of issues are more difficult for voters to grasp and do not lend themselves to influencing voters' behavior on election day.

With the culmination of the nation's economic woes and concerns about the high price of oil, the direction of the nation, and the nation's future place in the world, voters had many hard issues and relatively few easy issues with which to deal. The 2008 exit polls give some indication of this, as they focused on the voters' sense of the most important issues and how they affected their vote. The issues most important to voters are found in Table 1.3. By far, the economy was the most pressing concern for national voters, followed by the war in Iraq, terrorism, health care, and energy policy.

Within the South, voter concerns largely mirrored those of the national voter. Southerners were slightly less concerned about the economy when compared to the nationwide exit poll sample, while somewhat more concerned about the war in Iraq. While the southern subset is almost identical to the national sample on the importance of terrorism and health care, the issue of energy garnered a bit more attention than observed among the national electorate. One possible reason for this is that gas prices were higher in the South following the 2008 hurricane season than was the case in the rest of the nation.

Next, we examined which candidate benefitted from voters considering one of these five issues to be the most important. In the exit polls, voters were asked which candidate they supported and which issue they felt was most important. Regionally, McCain did better than the national average on each issue position. This is not surprising given the nature of

Table 1.3 Issue Positions by State (in percent)

Issue	AL	AR	FL	GA	LA	MS	NC	SC	TN	TX	VA	Regional Average	National Average
Energy Policy	10	10	7	9	11	7	9	8	10	10	10	9	7
Iraq	11	12	10	8	13	12	9	11	10	11	12	11	10
Economy	57	54	62	61	53	60	60	63	57	54	58	58	63
Terrorism	10	11	10	8	10	8	9	8	11	10	9	9	9
Health Care	8	10	8	11	10	9	11	6	10	12	7	9	9

Source: National Election Pool Exit Polls, November 4, 2008.

Table 1.4 Issue Positions and Support for John McCain (in percent)

Issue	AL	AR	FL	GA	LA	MS	NC	SC	TN	TX	VA	Regional Average	National Average
Energy Policy	—	61	61	70	66	—	40	—	69	67	46	60	46
Iraq	47	52	39	35	47	50	46	36	47	49	39	44	39
Economy	58	56	42	52	60	56	48	56	54	51	45	53	44
Terrorism	—	87	92	84	90	—	80	—	84	92	86	86	86
Health Care	—	51	25	23	39	—	40	—	40	42	23	35	26

Source: National Election Pool Exit Polls, November 4, 2008.

Republican strength in the South. An examination of the individual states, though, reveals that McCain's support varied among the eleven southern states, and a pattern emerges where GOP support differs between the Rim South and Deep South. Table 1.4 presents the results of the exit poll data on issue positions and support for McCain.

It's the Economy, Stupid!

This now famous exhortation from the 1992 election could well apply to 2008 as well. Unlike the 1991–92 recession, the nation was in the throes of a major financial meltdown by the autumn of 2008. The financial crisis that had begun in late 2007 erupted dramatically in mid-September, and this had an impact on the presidential contest. In fact, for the first two weeks of September, McCain held a marginal lead in opinion polls only to find his lead evaporate as the crisis rapidly deepened. With each passing day of the financial crisis, McCain's numbers slipped further before plateauing in early October, where they essentially remained unchanged through the election. Within the South, the old Deep South/Rim South dichotomy is evident. While no great variation on which issues were most important appears in the two subregions, voters differed on who they were voting for based upon those issues.

Deep South. Overall, Deep South voters were more likely to support John McCain when the economy was their biggest concern. Across the five Deep South states, 56 percent of respondents in the exit polls stated they voted for the McCain/Palin ticket when the economy was their biggest issue. Among these five states, Georgians concerned about the economy were the least favorable toward McCain at 52 percent. In large part this dovetails with the relatively close margin of victory for McCain in the Peach State. McCain's support in the economic category was the highest in Louisiana, at 60 percent of respondents, with the other three states averaging about 57 percent support for McCain.

Further analysis in the two outliers reveals that Georgians who were "very worried" about the economy were 51 percent of the sample, and those voters supported Obama by a 51 to 45 percent margin. In Louisiana, 58 percent of voters stated they were "very worried" about the economy. Pelican State respondents, though, supported McCain by a 58 to 40 percent margin.[14] These contrary results in two Deep South states give some indication about not only the relative concern of voters when it came to economic issues, but also that voters in these two states had different opinions on who was best able to deal with the nation's economic woes. In itself, this finding gives a glimmer of hope to Democrats seeking office in Georgia, as it raises questions about the state's "redness" on the most important political issue in 2008.

Rim South. The six states of the Rim South were less favorable to McCain than Obama. Here, the GOP ticket attracted only a margin of 49 to 46 percent of respondents who were the most concerned about the economy. Largely, this close margin was driven by the three states that Obama carried: Florida, North Carolina, and Virginia. Arkansas, Tennessee, and Texas voters did not differ substantially from their Deep South brethren on economics. As one might expect, Floridians were the most likely to support Obama when considering economic issues. Obama had the largest margin in the South on McCain in the Sunshine State, at 56 to 42 percent. Given the number of retirees who were hit hard by the stock market plunge, this is not a surprising finding, and it also goes a long way toward explaining Obama's victory in Florida. While Obama's support in Virginia (54 percent) and North Carolina (52 percent) were slightly more modest, voters concerned over the economy helped to propel Obama to victory given the tight margins in those two states.

Other Issues

Though the economy occupied center stage for voters in 2008, voters also rated other issues as most important to them. Still, the other four major issues—Iraq, terrorism, energy policy, and health care—clearly lagged well behind economic concerns. An examination of these relatively minor issues is instructive as it reveals the depths of McCain's disadvantage

War in Iraq. Despite being a significant issue from 2005 to 2007, the Iraq war took a backseat in early 2008. This was because of a combination of the war going much better after the troop surge in mid-2007 and the overriding concern about the economy after spring 2008. By the November election, voters were relatively unconcerned about Iraq, although those who were gave an overwhelming majority to McCain. This was consistent with polls throughout the year that showed voters had more confidence in McCain's abilities to deal effectively with the war in Iraq. While the national exit poll sample showed that 10 percent of respondents were the most concerned about Iraq, 11 percent of southern respondents rated Iraq as their primary concern. Support for Republicans among such voters greatly varied from an apex of 52 percent in Arkansas to a low of 35 percent in Georgia. Since the end of the Vietnam War, national defense has been a Republican issue.[15] Yet sentiment among some voters turned pro-Democratic in this area after the setbacks in the war in Iraq.

Terrorism. When it came to terrorism, McCain had a decisive advantage over Obama. Unfortunately for the GOP, only 9 percent of southerners rated terrorism as their primary concern. In large part, concerns over terrorism have faded since the September 11, 2001, attacks. Despite having overwhelming support among this group of voters, Republicans had a distinct disadvantage given the small size of this group. This is not a surprising finding given a litany of preelection polls that indicated that the nation's voters harbored concerns about Obama's ability to deal with terrorism. McCain's support was more substantial among voters who called terrorism their most important issue compared to those who pegged Iraq, and the pro-McCain pattern was consistently high among Ssuthern respondents.

Energy Policy and Health Care. Energy and health care were tied among respondents naming them as their top issue. Energy had come to the forefront after oil prices soared in early 2008 only to go higher after Hurricane Ike hit the Texas coast. No general pattern emerges from the exit poll data, although exit poll respondents in the Gulf Coast states of Alabama, Mississippi, Louisiana, and Texas showed slightly more concern over energy. Southern voters were not substantially different in their concerns when compared to national voters, with the average between the region and nation being virtually identical. Only among North Carolina and Virginia respondents did those primarily concerned about energy policy go for Obama. This is largely due to the perceived hostility of the Democratic Party toward offshore drilling.

Concerns over health care similarly were not discernibly different among southern respondents when compared to the national pool. Here, though, this had varying effects for the Obama and McCain campaigns. As one might expect health care would be a winning issue for Senator Obama. However, state differences were quite scattered among respondents most concerned about health care. The range in favor of Obama was from 75 percent in Georgia to 58 percent in Texas. In Arkansas, 51 percent of respondents most concerned about health care actually voted for McCain. In the end, concerns over health care lagged far behind the economy, Iraq, and terrorism concerns.

Gay Rights. Finally, two states, Arkansas and Florida, had proposals related to gay rights on their ballots. Unlike in 2004 and 2006, these were the only real social ballot issues that faced southern voters. In Arkansas, an initiative that, if passed, would ban gay couples (and other nonmarried couples) from adopting children passed by a margin of 57 percent to 43 percent. While rural and suburban white evangelical Christians strongly supported the ban, exit poll data indicate that black voters supported the ban by a 54 percent to 46 percent margin. Among Arkansas respondents, support for the ban was consistent among all age groups, with one exception: voters under the age of twenty-nine opposed the ban 55 to 45 percent.

By a vote of 62 percent to 39 percent, Florida voters approved a state constitutional amendment defining marriage as a union of a man and woman. Again, white evangelical Christians were very supportive of the amendment, but opposition to gay rights was not confined to white evangelicals. An overwhelming 71 percent of black respondents voted in favor of the amendment as well. Like Arkansas, the only age group that showed any opposition to the amendment were voters under twenty-nine, who split their vote 51 percent to 49 percent.

While bans on gay rights had been a very successful formula to arouse voters for the GOP in 2004, there was no clear advantage for the McCain campaign in 2008, giving an indication of how other issues were occupying the minds of voters. Delving deeper into the exit polls, one finds that 44 percent of respondents who supported the Arkansas initiative and 43 percent of respondents who voted for the Florida amendment also cast votes for Obama. What had been a Republican issue in 2004 ceased to be so in such overwhelming fashion in 2008. One possible explanation for this trend is that black voters are often opposed to gay marriage and are willing to part with the Democratic Party's stated policy goals on this issue.[16] In fact, blacks in Florida were even more supportive of the amendment than whites, according to exit polls.

Conclusions: Lessons for the Future

By any measure, the 2008 presidential election was historic both in symbolism and substance. Forty-four years after the passage of the Civil Rights Act of 1964, three southern states cast their votes in favor of Barack Obama. The prospect of such an event would have been unthinkable in the 1960s South, and one could argue that it was equally implausible as late as the 1980s. Still, a very definite pattern emerged from the exit poll data. The three states won by Obama were all Rim South states where electoral politics has in the past been decidedly less racially charged than in their Deep South counterparts. Also, much of the support for Obama that tipped the scales in his favor was from citizens who had migrated from other areas into the South.

It would be hyperbole though to state that Obama's win in three states reflected a fundamental shift in southern voting patterns. As illustrated in this chapter, exit poll data reflect that the voting patterns of both black and white southerners did not dramatically shift during the past four years. In fact, issue stances and candidate choice remained remarkably unchanged for many southern voters in 2008. The problem for the Republicans, though, lies in the absence of any controversial social issues. As the economy took center stage in 2008, voters' concerns over issues like gay marriage and abortion receded, which spelled doom for Republicans. As the GOP has seized upon social issues to cement its support among evangelical Christians, it has run the danger of making a Faustian bargain. When hot-button social issues are on the ballot, like prohibitions on gay marriage in 2004, the Republicans have the potential of riding such issues to victory. When economic issues rise to the forefront like 2008, the Democratic Party benefits.

The exit polls revealed the continuation of a pattern where the distinctiveness of southerners' voting behavior and issue positions was not substantially different than in the non-South. As early as the 1980s, scholars were arguing that the distinctiveness of the South was becoming less obvious than in previous decades.[17] In 2008, little difference existed between southerners and non-southerners on what issues were the most important to them. Additionally, the South as a region did not differ dramatically from other regions on which candidate could best deal with the most important issues of the day.

Just as V. O. Key once discussed southerners' "eye for distinction," so another pattern rears its head. Splitting the South into Deep South and

Rim South reveals that the Deep South remains the area where conservatism is most entrenched among white voters. While some white voters in the Rim South migrated toward Barack Obama, white voters in the Deep South remained much more supportive of the GOP ticket. This pattern is consistent across age groups, evangelical Christians, and genders. It should be noted that rural areas through the Deep South and Rim South remain the most conservative, while the fast-growing suburbs and urban areas are more moderate in their political tendencies.

One final note revolves around what lessons can be drawn from 2008. Based upon the exit poll data from 2008, the Republican Party faces a potential challenge in the region if the same pattern from 2008 holds. Obama was able to make headway in attracting voters under forty. As older voters are replaced by younger generations, this could possibly shift southern voting patterns in the future. In addition, economic issues are likely to dominate politics for the next four years, giving little opening to the GOP in the foreseeable future. With a lack of social issues, the Democrats might anticipate continued gains in Rim South states. While that opportunity certainly exists, a miscue could lead to other outcomes as dictated by political circumstances.

2

The 2008 Presidential
Nomination Process

John A. Clark

Introduction

Well before the first vote was cast, it was apparent that the 2008 presidential nominations would be historic. For only the third time since 1968, the sitting president was not up for reelection. Moreover, for the first time in the post-reform era (and the first time since 1952), neither the sitting president nor vice president was a candidate for his party's nomination. The wide open contests in both parties attracted large fields of high-quality candidates, including current and former governors, senators, and members of the U.S. House of Representatives. The mix of top-tier candidates included a woman, an African American, a Hispanic, a former Southern Baptist preacher, and a Mormon.

The race for the 2008 presidential nominations was longer and more complex than most observers anticipated. John McCain, the eventual Republican nominee, nearly dropped out of the race months before the first contest was held. On the Democratic side, Barack Obama emerged from relative obscurity to edge out Hillary Clinton for the party's nomination before beating McCain for the presidency itself. Unlike recent election cycles, neither party's nomination was decided until most (and on the Democratic side, all) states had the opportunity to weigh in.

The South's role in the nomination process was both similar to and different from the recent past.[1] As has been true for several election cycles, individual southern states had a disproportionate impact on the race because of the way candidates and the media perceived them as make-or-break contests. In contrast to the recent past, later primaries in southern states helped to prolong the Republican race and decide the Democratic nomination. The mix of candidates, the sequence of contests, and the rules of the game combined to increase the overall influence of the region in 2008 and helped to shape the outcome of the general election.

Sequence and Rules in 2008

The rules and procedures that govern presidential nominations are, for most citizens, a source of much confusion and little interest. For candidates, on the other hand, the structure of the nominating system can have a profound impact on the outcome of the race.[2] Each state (and often each party within a state) has its own rules for getting candidates on the ballot, determining which voters may participate in the nominating contest, and allocating delegates. Moreover, each state and/or state party determines when its contest will be held. Finally, all candidates must raise and spend their campaign funds under the framework set out by the national laws regulating campaign finance. These rules played an important—though not deterministic—role in the 2008 nomination races.

The Republican and Democratic national committees have the final say over who can be a delegate to their respective national conventions,[3] but they have little direct input into the decisions made in individual states. The Democrats traditionally focused more on delegate selection rules than did Republicans, creating a series of reform commissions following their tumultuous 1968 convention to formalize the procedures states must follow. The current rules include a requirement that states allocate delegates in proportion to vote outcomes in their nominating contests, and that delegates to the national convention share the race and gender characteristics of the state electorates they represent. Some state Republican parties also use proportional representation for delegate allocation, but some use a winner-take-all system with no reward for finishing in second place. The Democratic rules create a category of unpledged "superdelegates" made up of party and elected officials and representatives of key constituencies. Superdelegates are selected for the positions they hold rather than whom they support. They made up about 20 percent of the total number of delegates to the Democratic convention in 2008.[4] Republicans do not have superdelegates, but members of the Republican National Committee (three from each state) are similarly unpledged delegates to the national convention.

Decisions by state legislatures and parties to move their nominating contests to earlier dates have created what some have called the "frontloading problem."[5] Early contests, in particular the Iowa caucuses and New Hampshire primary, are considered more important than those that come later. Candidates who falter in these contests may see their nomination hopes dashed before most voters ever get the chance to cast ballots. Frontloading puts a greater emphasis on fundraising and media coverage during the "invisible primary" leading up to the actual primaries and caucuses.

Both national parties took steps to address the frontloading problem for the 2008 nomination cycle. The Democrats granted four states (one from each region of the country) permission to hold their contests prior to February 5. This move preserved the "first in the nation" status of Iowa and New Hampshire while incorporating the diverse electorates of Nevada and South Carolina. States that violated the February 5 date stood to lose their entire convention delegations. The Republicans took a slightly different tack, penalizing any state that allocated its delegates before February 5 by cutting its delegate allocation in half. The penalties may have deterred some states, but not all. The Michigan and Florida legislatures moved their primaries to January 15 and 29, respectively, incurring the wrath of both national parties. In addition, the Republicans penalized New Hampshire and Wyoming for their early contests. Democratic candidates pledged not to campaign in Michigan and Florida, and several asked that their names be removed from the Michigan ballot.[6]

The February 5 date was designed to keep states from exacerbating the frontloading problem. Instead, twenty-two states held a delegate-selection event for one or both parties on that date (see Table 2.1). Few candidates were able to obtain the resources to run a truly national campaign so early in the election year. Rather than reducing the influence of the early contests and the power of money in the nomination races, the 2008 calendar actually had the opposite effect in terms of winnowing the fields. Only two top-tier candidates in each party remained in the race after this truly "super" Tuesday. Contrary to expectations, however, the nominations were far from decided. It took John McCain another month to clinch the Republican nomination, while Barack Obama and Hillary Clinton battled until the final delegates were selected.

The system for financing presidential nomination races was established in the 1974 amendments to the Federal Election Campaign Act. Candidates who voluntarily accept limits on their campaign spending may be eligible for matching funds on contributions of $250 or less. Between 1976 and 1992, only one candidate bypassed the matching fund option.

Table 2.1. Schedule of 2008 Nomination Contests

January 3	Iowa caucuses
January 5	Wyoming Republican caucuses#
January 8	New Hampshire primaries#
January 15	Michigan primaries*#
January 19	Nevada caucuses; *South Carolina Republican primary*#
January 25	Hawaii Republican caucuses
January 26	*South Carolina Democratic primary*
January 29	*Florida primaries**#
February 1	Maine Republican caucuses
February 5	*Alabama primaries;* Alaska caucuses; Arizona primaries; *Arkansas primaries;* California primaries; Colorado caucuses; Connecticut primaries; Delaware primaries; *Georgia primaries;* Idaho Democratic caucuses; Illinois primaries; Kansas Democratic caucuses; Massachusetts primaries; Minnesota caucuses; Missouri primaries; Montana Republican caucuses; New Jersey primaries; New York primaries; Oklahoma primaries; *Tennessee primaries;* Utah primaries; and West Virginia Republican state convention
February 9	*Louisiana primaries;* Nebraska Democratic caucuses; Washington caucuses
February 10	Maine Democratic caucuses
February 12	District of Columbia primaries; Maryland primaries; *Virginia primaries*
February 19	Hawaii Democratic caucuses; Wisconsin primaries
March 4	Ohio primaries; Rhode Island primaries; *Texas primaries and Democratic caucuses;* Vermont primaries
March 8	Wyoming Democratic caucuses
March 11	*Mississippi primaries*
April 22	Pennsylvania primaries
May 6	Indiana primaries; *North Carolina primaries*
May 13	Nebraska Republican primary; West Virginia primaries
May 20	Kentucky primaries; Oregon primaries
May 27	Idaho Republican primary
June 3	Montana Democratic primary; South Dakota primaries

* penalized by Democratic National Committee for violating party scheduling rules
# penalized by Republican National Committee for violating party scheduling rules
Southern states are italicized
Source: CQPolitics.com.

The Bipartisan Campaign Reform Act (BCRA) of 2002 doubled the maximum contribution that an individual could make to a candidate but left the matching funds program unchanged. In 2004, President George W. Bush and two Democrats (John Kerry and Howard Dean) declined to accept matching funds and thus avoided the associated spending limits.[7]

The matching fund system essentially fell apart in 2008. Of the top-tier candidates, only John Edwards participated in the system. John McCain, one of the chief proponents of the BCRA reforms, was certified to receive matching funds but opted out in February 2008. By the end of 2007, the candidates had received nearly six hundred million dollars in total contributions. Democrats Hillary Clinton and Barack Obama each raised nearly one hundred million dollars for their nomination campaigns before the first ballot was cast. Among Republicans, Mitt Romney led the way with ninety million dollars in campaign funds, although more than a third of it was his own money.[8] Even with such large sums of money at their disposal, few candidates were able to raise enough to run a national campaign for their party's nomination.

The Republican Nomination Race

After eight years of the George W. Bush presidency, with a sluggish economy and stagnating wars in Iraq and Afghanistan, most observers saw 2008 as a golden opportunity for the Democrats to take over the White House. The gloomy forecast did little to deter contenders for the Republican nomination. A large and diverse field entered the race, and even more candidates considered a run before deciding not to get in. Several candidates had southern ties, and all of them claimed the conservative mantle of the Reagan revolution.

One early frontrunner in terms of name recognition was Arizona Senator John McCain. McCain had been Bush's top challenger in 2000, winning several primaries before his campaign stalled. Since then, he had worked to rehabilitate his image within the party while simultaneously preserving his "maverick" persona with the general public. McCain was an outspoken supporter of the war in Iraq and pushed his Senate colleagues to support Bush's troop surge in 2007. He also pushed the administration's immigration reform proposals, albeit with less success. Both issues nearly scuttled his campaign in 2007 when, saddled with a bloated campaign staff and meager fundraising, it appeared that he might have to withdraw from the race. He managed to stay in, however, but dramatically cut back the number of paid staff members and campaign offices, as well as other expenses.

The other frontrunner with strong name recognition was former New York City mayor Rudy Giuliani. Giuliani's popularity skyrocketed following the terrorist attacks of September 11, 2001, and he made national security and terrorism the basis of his campaign strategy. Many of Giuliani's positions on domestic issues seemed out of synch with the rest of the field, however, and his candidacy never really caught on with voters.

Former Massachusetts governor Mitt Romney lacked the name recognition of McCain or Giuliani. He was able to raise considerable sums of money for his nomination bid, however, and to tap into his personal wealth. In addition to Massachusetts, Romney had ties to Michigan (where his father had been governor) and the mountain west, where his Mormon religion was more an asset than a liability.

Two candidates hoped to parlay their southern roots into a presidential nomination. Mike Huckabee, the former governor of Arkansas, was a compelling speaker with an interesting personal story: he dropped more than one hundred pounds after he was diagnosed with type 2 diabetes. Huckabee's previous career as a Southern Baptist preacher gave him an important connection to religious conservatives, but his economic populism became something of an anathema to the business community. Former Tennessee senator Fred Thompson was a late entry into the field. Thompson resigned his role on the popular *Law and Order* television series to run for the presidency. He hoped to appeal to primary voters as the one "true" conservative in the field.

Several other candidates entered the race, but only Rep. Ron Paul of Texas garnered much attention from the electorate. A darling of the Internet community due to his libertarian positions on issues, Paul failed to break double digits in any of the primaries in the South, including his home state.

The Early Contests

The early contests did little to provide clarity in the crowded Republican field. Huckabee surprised many observers by winning the Iowa caucuses, but he finished third in New Hampshire and Michigan. McCain bounced back from a poor showing in Iowa to repeat his 2000 success in New Hampshire and finished second in Michigan. Romney finished second in Iowa and New Hampshire before winning his native state of Michigan and the caucuses in Wyoming. Thompson and Giuliani focused their campaign efforts on South Carolina and Florida, respectively, and largely ignored New Hampshire and Michigan.

The stage was set for a hotly contested primary in South Carolina. Nearly all of the candidates sought support from religious conservatives, a key constituency in the Palmetto State.[9] McCain, who alienated many conservative Christians in the 2000 campaign, gave the commencement address at Jerry Falwell's Liberty University in Virginia and was endorsed by pro-life elected officials in South Carolina and nationally. Romney won endorsements from Bob Jones III (president of fundamentalist Bob Jones University in Greenville) and Senator Jim DeMint. Giuliani was endorsed by televangelist and former presidential candidate Pat Robertson. Huckabee seemed to have the best chance of winning the votes of evangelicals, but Thompson, who won the endorsement of the National Right to Life Committee, specifically targeted him as they appealed to the same potential voters. Despite their overt appeals to Christians, the campaigns of all four candidates seemed less than charitable behind the scenes. South Carolinians complained about all types of dirty tricks aimed at one candidate or another as the primary date drew near.[10]

Preprimary polling indicated a close race and a volatile electorate in South Carolina. When the dust settled, McCain eked out a 33 percent to 30 percent victory over Huckabee. Thompson finished third with 16 percent of the vote, but it was not enough to keep him in the race. Romney finished fourth, although he did win the Nevada caucuses on the same day.

Exit polls in South Carolina showed that six out of ten Republican voters identified themselves as born again or evangelical.[11] Huckabee was the choice of 43 percent of those voters, while McCain was supported by 27 percent of that group. Among those not born again or evangelical, McCain won 43 percent while Huckabee took only 14 percent. The two candidates were even among the self-identified Republicans voting in the open primary, but McCain won among self-identified independents by a 42 percent to 25 percent margin.

The next contest was held in Florida ten days later. McCain was endorsed by Gov. Charlie Crist and Senator Mel Martinez on the weekend before the primary. Crist's nomination was especially significant, as most observers—including the candidates themselves—expected him to stay neutral.[12] This time McCain held off a strong challenge from Romney, winning 36 percent to 31 percent. Because Florida is a winner-take-all state for Republicans, McCain captured the state's fifty-seven delegates while Romney got none.[13] Giuliani had made Florida his make-or-break state, bypassing the earlier contests in the hope that a strong showing in

Table 2.2. Republican Primary Outcomes in the South (in percent)

	McCain	Huckabee	Romney	Giuliani	Thompson
SC	**33**	30	15	2	16
FL	**36**	13	31	15	—
AL	37	**41**	18	—	—
AR	20	**60**	13	—	—
GA	32	**34**	30	—	—
TN	31	**34**	24	—	—
LA	42	**44**	—	—	—
VA	**50**	41	4	—	—
TX	**51**	38	—	—	—
MS	**79**	12	—	—	—
NC	**74**	12	—	—	—

Note: Winning percentage is in bold.
Source: CQPolitics.com.

the Sunshine State would keep him in the race. He managed to win only 15 percent of the vote for a third place finish. The following day, he withdrew from the race and endorsed McCain. Huckabee finished fourth but remained an active candidate.

Super Tuesday and Beyond

Coming off wins in New Hampshire, South Carolina, and Florida, John McCain seemed to be in the driver's seat heading into the February 5 primaries. Still, Romney's win in the Maine caucuses kept him in contention, and Huckabee's low-budget campaigning showed little signs of tapering off. A virtual sweep by any of the three would have all but clinched the nomination. The results were far from conclusive, however. McCain won eleven states, Romney won seven, and Huckabee won six, all southern or border states. More importantly, however, McCain opened up a commanding lead in delegate support. With campaign funds running low, Romney suspended his campaign February 7. Aside from a Huckabee win in the Louisiana primary the following Saturday, McCain won the remaining contests and clinched a majority of delegates March 4.

The Democratic Nomination Race

The clear front-runner for the Democratic presidential nomination was New York senator and former First Lady Hillary Clinton. Clinton's name recognition was unmatched. Although she was a polarizing figure in American politics, she was highly regarded by most rank-and-file Democrats. In addition to her appeal to female voters, Clinton hoped to capitalize on former president Bill Clinton's southern roots and the connections the two had made with the African American community over the years. Many observers expected her to sweep to the nomination in record time, others expected an anti-Clinton alternative to emerge from the remaining Democratic candidates, but nearly everyone agreed the nomination was hers to win or lose.

Illinois Senator Barack Obama was another candidate expected to do well in the South. Obama was thrust into the national spotlight with a dynamic speech at the 2004 Democratic National Convention. Despite low visibility in the public at large, he proved to be a prodigious fund-raiser in the early stages of the nomination contest. The only African American in the field, Obama hoped to capitalize on the large proportion of blacks who voted in southern Democratic primaries. His campaign was designed to appeal across racial lines, however, and his strategy was predicated on winning votes from whites as well as blacks.

A third candidate with southern appeal was former North Carolina senator and 2004 vice presidential nominee John Edwards. Edwards won the South Carolina primary in 2004 and had campaigned effectively for the Kerry ticket in the general election campaign. Other notable candidates included New Mexico Governor Bill Richardson and Senators Chris Dodd of Connecticut and Joe Biden of Delaware.

The Early Contests

The road to the 2008 Democratic presidential nomination kicked off in Iowa on January 3. Obama pulled off an improbable win, capturing the support of 38 percent of caucus attendees. Edwards finished second, followed closely by Clinton. The win put Obama in the media spotlight and propelled him toward the New Hampshire primary. Clinton won narrowly in New Hampshire and overwhelmingly in Michigan, a state where neither Obama nor Edwards was listed on the ballot.

The Democratic primary in South Carolina was held January 26, a week after the Republicans. Each of the top candidates had reason to think they would do well. Edwards had won his native state in 2004, while Obama hoped to capitalize on the heavy concentration of African American voters likely to participate. Former president Bill Clinton campaigned in South Carolina in support of his wife, whose commanding lead in early polling tapered off once Obama emerged as a credible candidate.

What appeared likely to be a close race turned into a landslide. The South Carolina electorate gave a majority of its support to Obama, who won 55 percent of the vote in the primary. Clinton placed second with 27 percent, while Edwards finished third with only 18 percent. Exit polls revealed that 78 percent of African American voters supported Obama. Edwards was the choice of 40 percent of white voters, followed by Clinton at 36 percent and Obama with a respectable 24 percent. More than a quarter of those participating had not voted in a primary before; those new to the nomination process were especially likely to support Obama.[14]

Obama's success among black voters in South Carolina almost became a liability during the rest of the campaign. Up to that point, his success had resulted from the support of white voters in states where there were few racial or ethnic minorities. Now, he risked becoming pigeon-holed as "the black candidate" and thus marginalized among whites. This possibility was not lost on his main opponent's campaign. Former president Clinton compared Obama's South Carolina win to Jesse Jackson's success there in 1984 and 1988 in remarks that some perceived to be disparaging, and it was reported that the Clinton campaign was trying to make Obama's race an issue.[15]

The verbal jousting between Obama and Hillary Clinton continued as the campaign moved to Florida. Technically speaking, the candidates pledged not to campaign in Florida and Michigan because of those states' violations of Democratic National Committee scheduling rules. The Clinton campaign blasted Obama for airing commercials in Florida as part of a national advertising buy. Meanwhile, Clinton held three fundraisers in Florida the day before the election. The fundraisers themselves were permissible in light of the campaign boycott, but they did garner considerable coverage in local media.[16] Clinton won half of the vote in Florida to Obama's 33 percent. Edwards received only 14 percent and dropped out shortly after.

Super Tuesday and Beyond

The Florida primary had no bearing on the delegate race because the DNC had stripped the state of its delegates to the national convention, but it did provide much needed momentum for Clinton heading into Super Tuesday. She won ten of the contests that day, including delegate-rich California and New York, compared to fourteen for Obama. Her net gain of about twenty delegates did little to close the gap, however. The

Table 2.3. Democratic Primary Outcomes in the South (in percent)

	Obama	Clinton	Edwards
SC	**55**	27	18
FL	33	**50**	14
AL	**56**	42	—
AR	27	**69**	—
GA	**66**	31	—
TN	41	**54**	—
LA	**57**	36	—
VA	**64**	35	—
TX	47	**51**	—
MS	**61**	37	—
NC	**58**	42	—

Note: Winning percentage is in bold.
Source: CQPolitics.com.

two candidates split the four southern states holding primaries, with Clinton winning Arkansas and Tennessee while Obama won Alabama and Georgia.

Obama swept the remaining February primaries and caucuses, including wins in Louisiana and Virginia. The Democratic rules on proportional allocation kept Clinton in the race, however. She was able to pick up delegates even though she did not win the whole states. The media focus was on victories and defeats, but the underlying story was the delegate count. On March 4, Clinton won primaries in Ohio, Rhode Island, and Texas while Obama carried Vermont. The proportional allocation rules had helped Clinton while she lost nine straight contests. Her net take from the four March 4 primaries was only fifteen delegates, hardly enough to close the gap with Obama.

Clinton's March 4 delegate gains were mitigated even more by Texas Democrats' decision to hold precinct caucuses after the polling booths for the primary closed. Both events drew record numbers of participants: some 2.8 million voters cast ballots in the primary, and about a million attended the caucuses. The Texas situation is a good example of how rules can affect outcomes in nomination battles. Clinton narrowly won the primary, 51 percent to 49 percent, and with it sixty-five delegates to Obama's sixty-one. Obama fared better in the evening caucuses, which were open to any voter who had participated in the primary. He won thirty-seven of the sixty-eight delegates allocated in that stage, giving him a slight 98 to 95 victory in pledged delegates. Factoring in Texas' 35 super-delegates left the two in a 107 to 107 tie with 14 superdelegates unpledged at that time.[17]

Clinton and Obama traded victories over the next several months. Without the delegates from Michigan and Florida, neither candidate could claim the majority necessary to clinch the nomination. Delegates from those states were seated with half votes in May. On June 3, the day of the final two primaries in Montana and South Dakota, Obama crossed the majority threshold and could finally claim the nomination.

Analyzing the Nomination Races

Every election cycle, observers of campaign politics speculate on the conditions necessary to arrive at the party convention with the nomination still undecided. That parlor game nearly became reality in 2008. It seemed to many that a frontloaded system would not allow a sustained nomination battle. The 2008 Democratic race proved that a long nomination fight was still possible, and the Republican race lasted longer than many expected it to.

The Democrats

What accounts for Obama's nomination victory? Certainly some credit must go to the organization and execution of his campaign. With record campaign funds at his disposal, the Illinois senator could create organizational infrastructure and run advertisements in areas that were typically off limits to Democratic candidates. Accumulating small numbers of delegates in Wyoming or Utah or the United States territories of Guam or Puerto Rico mattered in this election cycle. Attention to detail made a difference, too. Rep. Jason Altmire, a first-term member of Congress from Pennsylvania and a superdelegate by virtue of his seat in the U.S. House of Representatives, told a National Public Radio interviewer that "Senator Obama first called me in June 2007 and asked for my support. At that time, no one thought Pennsylvania would be relevant. No one thought superdelegates would be relevant. He was already thinking to the long term." Clinton's campaign, in contrast, did not ask for Altmire's support until early March of 2008 after it became clear that every delegate mattered.[18]

While Obama was surging out of nowhere, most observers thought that the nomination was Clinton's to lose, and she did. Her campaign organization and strategy were focused as much on the general election as on the nomination phase of the campaign. When it became apparent that she would not be able to wrap up the nomination quickly, she was forced to loan her campaign five million dollars to stay competitive, an amount that grew to a total of thirteen million dollars over the course of the campaign.[19] Clinton rebounded in March and stayed close through the late contests, but she was not able to close the gap in delegates or in the perception that she still could win the nomination.

The southern states proved to be crucial to Obama's victory. He won seven of the states represented in this volume, compared to only four for Clinton. Obama ran especially well in the Deep South states of South Carolina, Georgia, Alabama, Mississippi, and Louisiana. African American voters made up roughly half of the primary electorate in each of these states, and Obama won between 78 percent and 92 percent of their votes (in South Carolina and Mississippi, respectively). Even with strong support from white voters, the margin was too large for Clinton to overcome. It is important to remember that black voters did not simply support Obama because of his race. Survey results suggest that African Americans flocked to the Obama candidacy only after he demonstrated he could win the support of white voters in places like Iowa and New Hampshire. This behavior is consistent with the theory that black voters—like other groups in primary elections—want to select the candidate who will best represent their interests *and* have the best chance of winning the general election.[20]

The importance of the South to the Obama campaign can be demonstrated by examining his delegate support in the region compared to the rest of the country. Omitting Florida because of the uncertain status of its delegates, Obama won 499 pledged delegates in the South, compared to 386 for Clinton, giving him a margin of 113. The rest of the country delivered a margin of only fifteen pledged delegates to the eventual nominee.

Conventional wisdom holds that a divisive primary battle weakens the likelihood that the eventual nominee can win the general election.[21] Fears that Clinton supporters would abandon the Democratic ticket proved to be unfounded, even after Obama selected Senator Joe Biden of Delaware to be his vice presidential running mate instead of Clinton. John McCain's selection of Alaska Governor Sarah Palin may have backfired with this group. Obama also used the nomination race as a springboard to the general election. By actively contesting a number of traditionally Republican states to win the nomination, he established campaign organizations that could be applied to the general election. His wins in places like North Carolina and Virginia in November can be traced in part to his active campaigning for those states' convention delegates.

The Republicans

If Barack Obama's nomination can be described as a marathon, John McCain's path to the 2008 Republican presidential nomination resembled a rollercoaster. The presumptive frontrunner, he nearly was forced from the race months before the first ballot was cast. In the end, he was the only Republican candidate to establish national appeal. Even when he did not win, he managed to outlast his rivals in all parts of the country.

The contrast with the other top candidates is telling. Mitt Romney was successful in many parts of the northeast and western states, but he was shut out of a victory in the South. Mike Huckabee, on the other hand, was unable to expand his base beyond the South. Both Rudy Giuliani and Fred Thompson were forced to put all their attention on single states, mostly because they were unable to connect with voters in the earliest contests and across the nation as a whole.

If Obama's southern success won him the nomination, Mike Huckabee's strength in the region kept him in the race. All five of Huckabee's primary victories came in southern states. His other wins (Iowa, Kansas, and the West Virginia state convention) came in states with caucus/convention systems that generally benefit candidates who appeal to smaller but highly motivated segments of the electorate. Despite his success in the South, Huckabee was not able to expand his base of support very far beyond his conservative religious base. The southern states with low proportions of born-again voters, like Florida and Virginia, went for McCain. In every southern state but Arkansas, a majority of those who did not claim to be born again voted for McCain, usually by large margins. Also, Huckabee's economic populism may have hurt his chances of winning over the larger Republican electorate.

Reforming the System for 2012?

Calls for reform to the presidential nominating system continue to mount. Despite the length of the 2008 campaigns, states continue to feel pressured to frontload their nomination contests. This situation, combined with the long "invisible primary" before the first votes are counted, has led many people to call for further reform of the system. Some have called for a national primary or a series of regional contests for the 2012 cycle.

More than any other region, the South has experience with a regional primary. The Super Tuesday experiment was not a total failure in 1988, but it seemed to work better for the Republicans than for the southern Democrats who created it.[22] The lesson for potential reformers is to proceed with caution, as a new system—whatever it entails—may not deliver as its proponents expect.

The enormous sums of money raised and spent in pursuit of the party nominations will make the system of campaign finance a potential target for reformers. In particular, the impotence of the system of matching funds as a way to level the playing field among candidates may need reconsideration. Changes seem unlikely in the short term, given the ability of the Obama campaign to raise funds for both the nomination and general election stages. Serious candidates seeking the presidency in 2012 may need to plan on raising one hundred million dollars or more prior to the first contest in order to be competitive.

Perhaps the most likely area for reform involves the Democratic Party's superdelegates. Superdelegates appeared especially controversial when it looked like they could have provided the decisive margin. The Democratic National Committee could decide to eliminate this category of unpledged delegates on its own, which increases the likelihood that this reform could happen. The evidence suggests that superdelegates may be less problematic than they appear, though, as they have little incentive to defy the wishes of voters.[23]

II

Elections in
the Deep South

3

Alabama

Electoral Continuity and Racial Voting

Patrick R. Cotter

Introduction

The partisan forces that led to Democrat Barack Obama's victory nationally had relatively little effect on the 2008 presidential election in Alabama. Neither the state's partisan balance nor its general pattern of voting was substantially altered by the contest. Instead, the results of the 2008 presidential election largely confirmed the Republican leaning national-level, but more evenly divided state-level, politics that have existed in Alabama for more than two decades. Indeed, some of the election's voting results show the continuation of some very traditional patterns in Alabama politics.

The continuity of the 2008 Alabama election does not mean that it was uninteresting or unimportant. Rather, the contest offers an opportunity to study, though not determine, the bases of the state's current electoral system. In particular, one of the central issues in the study of southern politics involves determining the role of race in the region's elections. The conjunction of Barack Obama being the first African American to gain a major party's nomination and then to win the presidency and the overwhelming support given to Republican John McCain by Alabama's white voters provides a new opportunity to consider this question.

The Political Context for the 2008 Election

During the last several decades, Republicans have generally dominated, though not totally controlled, Alabama's presidential and congressional elections. GOP candidates have carried Alabama in each of the last eight presidential elections. Currently, both of Alabama's U.S. senators are Republicans. Since 1997, the GOP has also controlled a majority of the state's U.S. House delegation.

State-level politics during the last two decades have been more evenly divided. The GOP has won five of Alabama's last six gubernatorial elections. Generally, however, these contests have been quite competitive.[1] State constitutional offices, such as lieutenant governor and secretary of state, have generally been about evenly divided between the two parties. Democrats continue to hold a substantial majority within both houses of the Alabama state legislature.

A serious division, potentially undermining the party's electoral strength, appeared to be developing among the state's Republicans earlier in this decade.[2] In 2003, Republican governor Bob Riley proposed an extensive tax reform program. Then, in 2004, he supported a referendum removing segregationist-era language from the state's 1901 constitution. Both of these proposals generated strong opposition from other prominent Republicans, and both were ultimately defeated in statewide votes.

Among Riley's chief GOP critics was Roy Moore, a former chief justice of the state Supreme Court. Moore had first come to statewide attention through a dispute arising from his displaying a copy of the Ten Commandments in his Etowah County courtroom. Moore used this issue in 2000 to win election as chief justice. Once elected, Moore had an almost three ton granite block displaying the Ten Commandments placed in the rotunda of the state judicial building. When he refused to obey a court order to move the block, Moore himself was removed from office.

In 2006, Moore entered the GOP gubernatorial primary against Riley, thus setting the stage for a potentially divisive intraparty conflict. The fight, however, never occurred. Rather, after the 2004 election, Riley moved to reestablish his credentials as an orthodox, socially and fiscally conservative, Alabama Republican. This strategy proved successful, and as a result he won a surprisingly easy (66.7 to 33.3 percent) victory over Moore.

On the Democratic side in 2006, lieutenant governor Lucy Baxley, whose ex-husband, Bill, had also served as lieutenant governor and himself been a Democratic gubernatorial candidate in 1978 and 1986, won the Democratic gubernatorial nomination over former governor Don Siegelman by a 59.8 to 36.4 percent margin. The most interesting part of this election was that Siegelman spent much of the primary campaign in federal court defending himself against a variety of corruption charges.[3]

In the general election Riley, aided by a large campaign fundraising advantage, the state's good economic conditions, and the apparent effectiveness of his administration in responding to the aftermath of Hurricane Katrina, won a lopsided (57.4 to 41.6 percent) victory over Baxley.[4] Republicans did not fare quite so well in other 2004 Alabama elections. Instead, Democrats won the contests for lieutenant governor (Jim Folsom Jr.) and Chief Justice of the state supreme court (Sue Bell Cobb), while also retaining their majority in the state legislature.[5]

The 2008 Presidential Primary

During the last several election cycles, Alabama held its presidential primary in June, at the very end of the nominating process. As a result, the state attracted little preconvention attention from any of the presidential hopefuls. To change this situation, Alabama moved its 2008 presidential primary to early February, much closer to the beginning of the nominating process. The shift in date achieved its intended effect as presidential candidates from both parties made repeated campaign stops within the state.[6] In response to this attention, and the general national interest in the two parties' nomination contests, a record number of Alabamians voted in the state's Democratic (536,626) and Republican (552,209) presidential primaries.

In the Democratic primary, Illinois senator Barack Obama defeated New York senator Hillary Clinton, 56.0 to 41.6 percent. In the state's GOP primary, former Arkansas governor Mike Huckabee won with 41.2 percent of the vote, while senator John McCain got 37.1 percent and former Massachusetts governor Mitt Romney received 17.8 percent.

As the divided primary votes indicate, neither of Alabama's parties began the election year united behind any of the competing presidential candidates. Most noticeably, some prominent African American Democrats, such as Congressman Artur Davis, backed Obama, while others, such as Alabama Democratic Conference chair Joe Reed, were early Clinton supporters. Reed and others said they supported Clinton in part because they doubted that Obama or any other African American candidate could win the Democratic party nomination, let alone the presidency. Similarly, before he secured the nomination, several Republican officeholders expressed both personal and policy-based reservations about John McCain. However, once it became certain that Barack Obama and John McCain would be the presidential nominees, both Alabama parties united behind their candidates. Still, some elements of both parties remained more enthused than others.[7]

General Election for President

In the general election campaign, Alabama, as had been the case in most other recent presidential elections, became more of a spectator than a participant. Alabama was never designated as a battleground state. Instead both campaigns saw it as a sure GOP winner. Thus, Alabama attracted very little attention during the election from either the Obama or McCain campaigns.[8]

Despite the state's spectator status, the 2008 election generated considerable interest among Alabamians. Throughout the fall campaign, newspapers reported a surge of voter registration in the state.[9] Also included in these reports were stories about a continuing issue in Alabama regarding the voting rights of convicted felons.[10] In November, 2,099,819 Alabama citizens participated in the election, an increase of more than 216,000 votes from 2004.[11]

The increase in turnout did not produce any surprises in the outcome of the election. Rather, as expected, Republican John McCain easily carried the state, winning by a 60.4 to 38.8 percent margin (see Table 3.1).

Congressional Elections

Alabama also only partially participated in the struggle over control of Congress. The state's 2008 U.S. Senate race was never competitive. Incumbent Republican Jeff Sessions started his third term reelection effort with more than three million dollars in his campaign account. Faced with this financial reality, several potential Democratic opponents decided not to enter the contest.[12] The Democratic candidate who finally stepped forward to face Sessions was Vivian Davis Figures, an African American state senator from Mobile. Figures was certainly a serious candidate, but her campaign remained sorely underfunded. In the end, after an almost invisible campaign, Sessions easily defeated Figures by 63.4 to 36.6 percent.[13]

A somewhat different situation occurred in the state's contests for U.S. House of Representatives. In 2006 all of the state's incumbent rep-

Table 3.1 Results of the 2008 Election in Alabama

Candidate (Party)	Vote Totals	Percent
President		
Barack Obama (D)	813,479	38.8
John McCain (R)	1,266,546	60.4
Chuck Baldwin (I)	4,310	0.2
Bob Barr (I)	4,991	0.2
Ralph Nader (I)	6,788	0.3
U.S. Senate		
Vivian Davis Figures (D)	752,391	36.6
Jeff Sessions (R)*	1,305,383	63.4
U.S. House**		
District 2		
Bobby Bright (D)	144,356	50.3
Jay Love (R)	142,578	49.7
District 3		
Joshua Segal (D)	121,080	45.9
Mike Rogers (R)*	142,708	54.1
District 4		
Nicholas B. Sparks (D)	66,077	25.1
Robert Aderholt (R)*	196,741	74.9
District 5		
Parker Griffith (D)	158,324	51.8
Wayne Parker (R)	147,314	48.2

Key: * = incumbent, D = Democratic Party, R = Republican Party, I = Listed as independent on Alabama ballot.

** Incumbent Reps. Jo Bonner (R), Spencer Bachus (R), and Artur Davis (D) were reelected without opposition.

Source: Alabama Secretary of State.

resentatives (five Republicans and two Democrats) were reelected. Thus, Alabama had no role in the upheaval that then lead to Democrats becoming the majority party in the House. However, the change in the majority party in the House was soon followed by retirement announcements from two members of Alabama's congressional delegation, the Fifth District's Democrat Bud Cramer and the Second District's Republican Terry Everett.[14]

Not surprisingly, these two congressional openings attracted considerable attention within the districts and nationally. Both parties had contested primaries (and for Republicans runoff primaries) in each district.[15] The heavy and expensive campaigning then continued through November, with the contests in both districts attracting visits from a number of national officeholders or party leaders.[16]

Democrats eventually narrowly won both open seats. These victories suggest the revival of a "Presidential Republicanism" pattern of voting in which Alabamians split their votes to support GOP candidates for president while backing Democratic candidates in more local races. Specifically, in the Second District, Democratic Montgomery Mayor Bobby Bright defeated Republican state representative Jay Love 50.3 to 49.7 percent. Like other of the party's recent successful congressional candidates in the South, Bright ran as a conservative Democrat, emphasizing his pro-life and pro-gun positions.[17] By winning, Bright not only shifted the state's House delegation from a five to two to a four to three Republican majority, he also became the first Democrat to hold the Second District seat since the 1964 Barry Goldwater election.

A similar contest and outcome occurred in the Fifth District. Here, Democratic Huntsville physician, businessman, and state senator Parker Griffith defeated Republican businessman Wayne Parker 51.8 to 48.2 percent. Like Bright, Griffith ran "as a pro-life, pro-gun, pro-traditional marriage candidate."[18]

Among Alabama's incumbent congressmen seeking reelection, only one, the Third District's Republican Mike Rogers, was seriously challenged in 2008. The composition of this district makes it politically competitive, and Rogers had faced serious Democratic opponents in his three previous elections. In 2008, however, he was initially expected to have an easier time against political newcomer and Montgomery lawyer Democrat Josh Segall.[19] However, Segall's effective and aggressive campaign and the infusion of money from the national Democratic Congressional Campaign Committee, resulted in a high-profile, negative, and close contest.[20] Once again, however, Rogers managed to gain a narrow, 54.1 to 45.9 percent, victory.[21]

State Elections

The result of the few other statewide races on the 2008 ballot displayed a familiar pattern for Alabama's state-level politics. In particular, the outcomes of these contests were generally close and in the end both parties could claim victory. The GOP won each of the four statewide judicial positions up for election. The most competitive, expensive, and nastiest of these was a contest for a position on the state supreme court between Democrat Deborah Bell Paseur and Republican Greg Shaw. Shaw eventually won this race, though its outcome was not determined for almost a week after election day, by a 50.3 to 49.7 percent margin.[22] Democrats, meanwhile, won the contest for president of the Public Service Commission. Here, Lucy Baxley, the party's losing 2006 gubernatorial candidate, defeated former state Republican chair and advisor to Governor Riley, Twinkle Andress Cavanaugh, by the same 50.3 to 49.7 percent margin.

Analysis

The results of Alabama's 2008 elections are quite similar to those of other recent presidential elections in the state. Specifically, the proportion of the vote received by Obama and McCain in 2008 roughly matches that gained by other recent Democratic and Republican presidential candidates. For example, Obama, by winning 38.8 percent of the total vote, received nearly the same level of support as John Kerry in 2004 (36.8 percent), Al Gore in 2000 (41.6 percent), and Bill Clinton in 2006 (43.2 percent).

Voting patterns found in Alabama's 2008 election are also very similar to that of other recent presidential contests in the state. For example, almost perfect correlations are found for the county level pattern of voting between Obama and both Kerry in 2004 (r=. 97) and Gore in 2000 (r=. 93).

Additionally, Table 3.2 shows that Obama, like other recent Democratic presidential candidates, received more support in less wealthy and more African American counties. Like Kerry in 2004, but not Gore in 2000 or Bill Clinton in 1996, Obama also received somewhat greater support in more urban counties. Moreover, Obama was relatively competitive in counties containing the largest cities in Alabama. Finally, as was also the case for Democrats in earlier elections, Obama received his greatest support in the Black Belt section of Alabama. Ironically, the current Democratic strength in the state's more heavily African American areas and urban centers roughly parallels the conservative, Big Mule-Black Belt, coalition found when Alabama was a solidly one-party Democratic state (with a virtually all-white electorate).[23]

One further pattern shown in Table 3.2 is that since 1996, Democratic support has declined in the state's more rural and mostly white counties. The declining Democratic strength in counties from the Tennessee

Table 3.2 Voting in Recent Alabama Presidential Elections by County Characteristics (in percent)

	PERCENT DEMOCRATIC OF MAJOR PARTY VOTE				
	2008 Obama	2004 Kerry	2000 Gore	1996 Clinton	N
Total	38.8	38.4	44.6	43.2	67
County characteristics					
Median family income, 1999					
Less than $34,000	50.9	48.3	53.7	56.7	26
$34–40,000	31.4	33.7	42.2	45.0	24
More than $40,000	40.3	36.7	40.8	40.8	17
Percent African-American 2000					
Less than percent	24.3	27.5	35.5	38.3	19
15–40 percent	42.1	38.5	43.0	43.1	32
More than 40 percent	59.0	53.2	55.9	56.0	16
Percent Urban					
Less than 20 percent	32.2	34.2	42.4	46.7	24
20–49 percent	30.1	31.2	38.7	41.3	24
5 0 percent or more	43.8	39.9	44.0	43.6	19
*Region of state**					
Tennessee Valley	31.8	36.9	44.1	44.0	6
Hill Country	26.8	27.7	35.6	38.7	27
Black Belt	60.9	56.7	60.5	61.5	15
Wiregrass	28.6	26.7	34.2	37.7	9
Coastal	29.1	27.5	31.4	34.6	4
Metropolitan	47.8	42.9	46.1	45.1	6

* The regions of the state are composed of the following counties: Tennessee Valley: Colbert, Jackson, Lauderdale, Lawrence, Limestone, Marshall, Morgan; Hill Country: Autauga, Bibb, Blount, Calhoun, Chambers, Cherokee, Chilton, Clay, Cleburne, Coosa, Cullman, DeKalb, Elmore, Fayette, Franklin, Lamar, Pickens, Randolph, St. Clair, Shelby, Talladega, Tallapoosa, Walker, Winston; Black Belt: Barbour, Bullock, Butler, Choctaw, Dallas, Greene, Hale, Lownes, Macon, Marengo, Perry, Pike, Russell, Sumter, Wilcox; Wiregrass: Coffee, Conecuh, Covington, Crenshaw, Dale, Escambia, Geneva, Henry, Houston; Coastal: Baldwin, Clarke, Monroe, Washington; Metropolitan: Etowah, Jefferson, Madison, Mobile, Montgomery, Tuscaloosa.

Source: Calculated by author from data supplied by Alabama Secretary of State and U.S. Census Bureau.

Valley and Hill Country sections of northern Alabama (which tend to have rural, largely white populations) reinforces this pattern.

Continuity is also found when exit poll results are used to examine the preferences of individual voters (see Table 3.3). As was the case in previous years, voting preferences in Alabama in 2008 were strongly related to race. A large majority of the state's white voters supported McCain while an even larger majority of the state's African American voters backed Obama. Indeed, the results of the 2008 exit poll show that only about one in ten of Alabama's white voters supported Obama. Further, Democratic support among the state's white voters has declined, according to exit poll results, in each presidential election since 1996.

Additionally, Obama, like other recent Democratic presidential candidates, received greater support from females and lower income voters and those who did not describe themselves as some type of conservative Protestant. Finally, in each of the 1996 through 2008 elections, party identification was strongly related to voting preferences in Alabama. In 2008, most (85 percent) Democrats, a minority (33 percent) of independents, and very few (3 percent) Republicans supported Obama.

Race and Alabama Politics

Barack Obama's general lack of support in Alabama, particularly from the state's white citizens, provides an opportunity to reconsider one of the central concerns in the study of Alabama, southern, and national politics. This concern involves determining the role of race in state, regional, or national electoral politics.[24]

There are two very general and competing explanations for Obama's lack of support among Alabama's white voters. First, it is largely the product of antiblack attitudes among the state's white voters. That is, white Alabamians did not vote for Obama because he is black. Second, Obama's lack of support in Alabama is mostly the product of other, nonracial, politically relevant forces, such as his party or his positions on different issues. Thus, according to the second explanation, white Alabamians did not vote for Obama because he is a Democrat, a liberal, or both.

The data needed to determine conclusively which of the two explanations best accounts for voting in the 2008 election are not yet available. Still, it is possible to identify evidence supporting each explanation.

Specifically, there are several pieces of evidence that indicate race did play a central role in Alabama's 2008 election. First, as noted previously, the 2008 exit poll found that only one in ten of white voters in Alabama

Table 3.3 Alabama Exit Poll Results for the 1996, 2000, 2004, and 2008 Presidential Elections (in percent)

	2008 (N=1,070)		2004 (N=736)		2000 (N=831)		1996 (N=1044)	
	Obama	McCain	Kerry	Bush	Gore	Bush	Clinton	Dole
All voters	39%	60	37%	62	42%	56	43%	50
Race								
White	10	88	19	80	25	73	29	62
African American	98	2	91	8	91	8	87	11
Gender								
Male	36	62	30	69	36	62	37	53
Female	42	58	43	57	47	52	46	48
Income								
Less than $15,000	na	na	58	42	72	27	57	35
$15–30,000	53	46	47	52	53	45	43	49
$30–50,000	40	58	46	52	50	50	42	51
$50–75,000	41	57	22	78	31	66	38	56
$75–100,000	29	70	22	78	23	74	na	na
Religion— Conservative Protestant*								
Yes	8	92	12	88	18	82	na	na
No	64	34	42	56	52	46	na	na
Party identification								
Democrat	85	14	92	7	85	14	85	10
Independent	33	64	29	66	30	66	29	57
Republican	3	97	1	99	2	98	3	90

Note: Vote percentage for third-party candidates not shown.

na = Data not available.

* The 2004 and 2008 surveys asked respondents if they identified themselves as "white/evangelical/born-again." The 2000 survey asked respondents if they considered themselves a member of the "White religious right."

Source: http://www.cnn.com/ELECTION/2008/results.

supported Obama. This polling estimate may yet prove to be too low.[25] Still it is certainly true that a large majority of white Alabama voters did not support the Democratic candidate. This racial unity suggests, in turn, that racial concerns played an important role in the 2008 voting decision.

Second, it is possible to compare the exit poll results for Alabama with those for the entire nation (Table 3.4). This comparison shows little difference in voting patterns between Alabama and the nation in terms of evaluations of President Bush, religious identification, or party identification. Also, African Americans in Alabama and the nation were both almost unanimous in their support for Obama.

White voters in Alabama, however, were substantially less likely to vote for Obama than were their counterparts elsewhere. Further, examining the influence of party identification among whites shows that Republicans and independents in Alabama voted in the presidential election in a manner similar to their counterparts nationwide. White Democrats in Alabama, however, were much less likely to support Obama than were their fellow party identifiers elsewhere. Given the history of the state, it is reasonable to conclude that the distinctive voting behavior in 2008 of white Alabamians generally, and white Alabama Democrats in particular, was strongly affected by racial concerns.

Other pieces of evidence, however, suggest that Obama's lack of success in Alabama may be the result of other considerations. Specifically, comparisons of exit poll findings for the last several presidential elections (Table 3.3) show that white support for Democratic candidates has declined since at least 1996. This long-term change makes it difficult to attribute the low level of white support in 2008 solely to Obama's race.

Similarly, county level results (Table 3.2) show declining support over several election cycles for Democrats in more "white" parts of the state. Again, since this decline did not begin with the Obama candidacy, it is difficult to conclude that the lack of Democratic support in 2008 is due primarily to race.

Finally, and perhaps most persuasively, in the state's congressional election, Democratic candidates running as social conservatives were successful. These results support a conclusion that issue positions, rather than the race of the candidate, were the critical factor in affecting the 2008 vote.

Luckily, perhaps, Alabama may soon provide another test case for determining which of the two proposed explanations best applies to the state's contemporary electoral politics. African American congressman Artur Davis has made it clear that he intends to run for a statewide office,

Table 3.4 Exit Poll Results for the 2008 Presidential Election—Alabama and the United States (in percent)

	ALABAMA (N=1067)		UNITED STATES (N=17,836)	
	Obama	McCain	Obama	McCain
Race				
White	10	88	43	55
Black	98	2	95	4
Race and gender				
White Male	9	88	41	57
White Female	12	88	46	53
Black Male	100	0	95	5
Black Female	96	4	96	3
Party Identification				
Democrat	85	14	89	10
Independent	33	64	52	44
Republican	3	97	9	45
Party Identification— Whites				
Democrat	47	51	85	9
Independent	13	82	47	49
Republican	1	98	8	91
Religion				
White Evangelical/ Born Again Christian	8	92	24	74
Other 64	34	62	36	
Evaluation of Bush				
Approve	7	93	10	89
Disapprove	61	38	67	31

Note: Support for third-party candidates not shown.
Source: http://www.cnn.com/ELECTION/2008/results.

probably the governorship, in 2010. In discussing a potential campaign, Davis has argued that a black candidate can win in Alabama. However, Davis has also recognized that any candidate needs to take positions consistent with the views of the state's voters. "Anybody coming out of the national Democratic Party probably can't win election in Alabama," he has said.[26] But, Davis argues, the situation is different in state elections where Democrats generally take more conservative positions. Further, state elections are also different because, "Voters put on a different lens when they are assessing presidential races in the South than they do when they are assessing races involving people they've gotten to know."[27] In response to these concerns Davis has worked hard both to become well known throughout the state and to develop an image of a centrist, pragmatic officeholder. How well he does in his statewide campaign running as a more conservative Alabama Democrat will help show if race or other factors play the central role in the state's electoral politics.

4.

Georgia

Where Competitiveness Came Late

Charles S. Bullock III

Introduction

The national media focuses on the choices made in states thought to be critical to determining the outcome of elections. In November these are referred to as the swing or battleground states. In the primary selection process, the decisive states tend to come early in the sequence or, if they vote later, they are believed to be make or break for a candidate.

In the closing days of the 2008 general election, Georgia found itself in the unaccustomed position of being a battleground state. Georgia achieved this competitive stature as a result of Barack Obama having sewn up what had earlier been designated as the swing states. By early October as Obama built a growing lead in states like Iowa, New Hampshire, New Mexico, and Virginia, previously red states like Georgia, Indiana, and North Carolina suddenly found themselves courted by both campaigns. In the primary season, Georgia tried to stake out a position to enhance its significance but, instead, found itself overshadowed by larger states. Georgia was more important in 2008 than in 2004 but could not match its role in 1992 when it was the most closely contested state in the nation in November and the "New Hampshire of the South" in the Democratic nomination process.

The Primary

Georgia's political leaders assumed, as did much of America, that Super Tuesday would determine the presidential nominees. Georgia has a history of being among the first states in the nation to vote, having participated in the initial Super Tuesday in 1988 when the South held its presidential primaries on a single day early in March. Four years later Georgia jumped one week ahead of the rest of the South, scheduling its primary right after that of New Hampshire. Georgia kept its presidential primary in early March until 2008 when, fearing that the nominations might be decided quickly, it advanced the date to February 5, that year's Super Tuesday. With the shift, Georgians voted on the same day as much larger states such as California and New York. The nation's ninth-most-populous state struggled to attract candidates, and other states drew far more media attention. In retrospect, had Georgia shifted its election *back* in time, it could easily have found a week when it would have been the largest state voting and, at least in the prolonged Democratic selection process, would have occupied center stage alone.

Voting on the same day as much larger states meant Georgia got few visits from candidates near the time of voting. Although the candidates and the media gave Georgia relatively little attention, the state experienced a record turnout for a presidential primary. The Democratic contest attracted more than one million voters while almost a million Republicans participated in their primary. To put those numbers in perspective, in 2000, the last time the presidency was an open seat, 284,431 Democrats and 643,188 Republicans turned out for Georgia's presidential primary. Interest in the 2008 presidential candidates was so great that although this was the only item on the ballot in most precincts, far more people voted than have ever participated in the regular primaries when ballots include candidates for many offices. Lest the participation in the February primary be interpreted as a newfound interest in politics among voters, the turnout for both parties in the July primary failed to equal the participation level in either party's presidential vote in February. In July, 552,651 Democrats, along with 458,548 Republicans, picked up primary ballots.

The candidates campaigned most of the week leading up to Super Tuesday in other states, but Barack Obama had spent the day after winning the South Carolina primary in Georgia visiting with black congregations. The resulting media coverage may explain why Obama did so well in Georgia. He defeated Hillary Clinton by a margin of 66 to 31 percent. Only in the District of Columbia did Obama manage a larger percentage of the vote.

The makeup of the Democratic electorate in the primary goes a long way toward explaining Obama's success but cannot fully account for it. African Americans cast 55 percent of the Democratic votes, according to exit polls that show Obama attracted 87 percent of the black vote along with 40 percent of the white vote. Obama also did exceptionally well among younger voters. Those who were eighteen to twenty-four and who constituted a tenth of the Democratic electorate, preferred Obama over Clinton by a margin of 79 to 19 percent. He also attracted 72 percent of the vote from each age group younger than fifty. Clinton managed a majority only among the voters over sixty-five, a group that she won by a margin of 57 to 43 percent. A gender gap existed among white voters, with women preferring Clinton by a margin of 60 to 37 percent while among men it was much closer, with Clinton edging out Obama 48 to 45 percent.

Many saw Obama as the candidate for change while Clinton stressed her experience. Among voters who evaluated candidates primarily on the basis of their ability to achieve change, Obama beat Clinton 83 to 16 percent. Clinton attracted 90 percent of the vote of those who stressed experience. The problem for Clinton was that only one-sixth of the voters considered experience to be the most important factor, while 61 percent gave top priority to achieving change.

While Obama won handily with all ideological groups, it is notable that 46 percent of Democratic voters considered themselves to be liberals. That is three times as large a proportion of liberals as in Georgia's November electorate and indicates that the base of his primary support differed dramatically from the general election participants.

Obama scored his success despite divisions within the African American leadership. The dean of Georgia's congressional delegation, civil rights icon John Lewis, was an early and staunch Hillary Clinton supporter. David Scott, another Atlanta member of congress, state labor commissioner Michael Thurmond, former Atlanta mayor Andrew Young, and home run king Hank Aaron joined Lewis in the Clinton camp. Two other black members of Georgia's congressional delegation, Sanford Bishop from Albany and freshman Hank Johnson from suburban DeKalb County, were leading lights in the Obama effort. Ultimately, Lewis did sign on with the Obama campaign but only after an agonizingly slow process chronicled by the *Atlanta Journal-Constitution* on a daily basis. Lewis's support for Clinton and his hesitancy in shifting to Obama stimulated two primary challenges, which Lewis handily disposed of.

In contrast to the blowout in the Democratic primary, Republicans had a nail biter. In the run up to the primary, conservatives had found none of the options particularly to their liking. Early in the fall of 2007, Georgia conservatives joined those urging former Tennessee senator Fred Thompson to become a candidate. The Tennessean had a natural constituency in the northwest corner of the state, which gets its television and print coverage out of Chattanooga. Once he became a candidate, however, Thompson resonated no more strongly in Georgia than elsewhere, thereby casting his conservative base adrift again.

In the weeks just before the vote, conservatives began to coalesce behind what had been one of the minor candidates. Former Arkansas governor Mike Huckabee's surprising victory in Iowa catapulted him to the attention of religious conservatives in Georgia. Huckabee finished a close second to McCain in South Carolina and then won Florida's primary, which intensified his momentum heading into Super Tuesday.

The Republican primary resulted in a three-way split with Huckabee narrowly ahead in the winner-take-all contest with 34 percent of the vote. John McCain placed second with 32 percent of the vote, slightly ahead of Mitt Romney's 30 percent. Polling conducted during the month prior to the vote had shown each of the three contenders ahead at some point.

Critical to Huckabee's plurality win in Georgia was the heavy turnout by evangelicals, who constituted 62 percent of participants in the Republican primary. Exit polls conducted at general elections have shown Georgia's November electorate to be approximately 35 percent evangelical. These Christian conservatives are disproportionately Republicans, so they constitute a larger share of the GOP primary electorate, nonetheless the 2008 Republican presidential primary mobilized an exceptionally large number of the born again. Huckabee attracted 43 percent of the evangelical vote with the remainder being split 27 percent for McCain and 28 percent for Romney. McCain took a plurality among those who did not consider themselves to be born-again or evangelical Christians, with 40 percent of the vote. Romney finished a close second with 35 percent of the vote, while Huckabee managed only 19 percent of the vote among this part of the constituency.

While no gender gap emerged among Republican voters, an age gap did appear. McCain ran best among older voters and only among those who were over sixty-five did he have a statistically significant lead, although he did have a small plurality among those fifty to sixty-four. Huckabee's support correlated inversely with age as he won pluralities among younger voters. Indicative of what may be a shift among younger voters toward the Democratic Party, only four percent of Republican voters were younger than 24 compared with 10 percent of the Democrats.

Huckabee and Romney took almost equal shares of the two-thirds of the Republican voters who considered themselves to be conservatives. The vote for these two candidates constitutes almost three-fourths of the conservative vote. McCain won a majority of the 9 percent of the Republicans who thought of themselves as liberals and easily defeated his competitors among the quarter of the electorate who described themselves as moderates. McCain's third-place finish among conservative voters helps explain his selection of Sarah Palin as his running mate.

On the litmus test issue of abortion, Huckabee took a majority among the quarter of the Republican voters who consider it illegal in all cases. McCain won pluralities among those who would allow abortions in most or all cases.

In the general election, Democrats attacked McCain's candidacy as nothing more than a bid for a third Bush term. That was not how Georgia Republicans saw things in February. McCain won a plurality among Republicans who viewed the Bush administration negatively but finished third among those who had positive evaluations of President Bush.

The General Election

During the summer, the Obama campaign identified Georgia as one of eighteen battleground states in which it would compete. Prior to the Democratic National Convention, Obama spent more than $1.2 million to run half a dozen different television ads.[1] One ad sought to link Ralph Reed, former head of the Georgia Republican Party and associate of convicted lobbyist Jack Abramoff, to John McCain.[2] However by the end of the summer, the Obama campaign had decided not to seriously challenge in the Peach State. Its ad purchase had been a ploy designed to force McCain to expend resources in Georgia. When McCain did not rise to the bait, the Democrats withdrew and shifted some of their seventy-five paid staffers to other states.[3] Despite a scaled-back effort, the Obama campaign established three dozen offices and had fifty-two paid staffers and four thousand, eight hundred trained volunteers.[4]

The decision to pull some Obama staff out of Georgia and redeploy them to North Carolina coincided with polls conducted right after the Republican convention that showed John McCain with a double-digit lead and placed support for him above 50 percent. Three polls from mid-September gave McCain an average lead of 12 percent. The choice of Sarah Palin as his running mate united Republicans behind McCain, who now had almost universal (94 percent) support from his fellow partisans.

An *Insider Advantage* poll of September 11 showed McCain leading Obama by more than two to one among independents. McCain was also drawing one-sixth of the Democratic identifiers, perhaps individuals not yet reconciled to Hillary Clinton's defeat. A gigantic gender gap persisted, with McCain beating Obama 70 to 22 percent among men but losing to the Democrat by a margin of 53 to 42 percent among women.[5]

But when the financial crisis hit, McCain's lead contracted into single digits. Polls at the end of September put his average lead at seven points, with the Republican standard-bearer hovering around 50 percent. Obama, whose support had dipped below 40 percent, had added approximately 5 percentage points by the end of September.

After mid-September, Obama's support stalled at approximately 44 percent. Polls conducted between September 17 and October 22 put his support between 43 and 46 percent. His support edged up during the last two weeks of the campaign, peaking in a couple of polls that showed him with 48 percent of the vote. One of these, an *Insider Advantage* poll on October 23, actually gave the Democrat a one-point lead. However, the average of the final polls calculated by Real Clear Politics put Obama at 45.8 percent, four points behind McCain.

McCain, who would have attracted as much as 57 percent of the vote in mid-September, hovered around 50 percent during the next month, dipping occasionally to 49 percent and never rising above 54 percent. In the last ten days of the campaign, McCain's support ranged from 47 to 52 percent.

In mid-October, with most commentators showing Obama having more than enough states in his column to become president, the Democrat turned his attention back on Georgia. With Georgia increasingly seen as a battleground state, Obama shipped in one hundred additional volunteers to help get out the vote and made another television buy.[6] The energized Obama effort still did not elicit a response from McCain whose Georgia campaign was being run out of Tallahassee, Florida, and had no paid staff in Georgia, although Republicans claimed to have had as many as forty thousand volunteers active in promoting their candidates.[7]

Even though Georgia took on heightened significance toward the end of the campaign and those who develop color-coded maps changed the state from scarlet to pink, it did not get on the agenda of the candidates or their chief lieutenants. Neither party's presidential or vice presidential candidates campaigned in Georgia. McCain did visit the state shortly before the Republican National Convention but limited his exposure to well-heeled contributors from whom he raised $1.7 million.[8] Obama had even less of a personal presence in the state.

To win Georgia's fifteen Electoral College votes, Obama had to overcome two challenges. First, he needed to maximize black participation, because he could expect to win the votes of almost that entire part of the electorate. The Obama campaign began registering voters in anticipation of the February 5 primary and continued these efforts until Georgia closed registration for the general election on October 6. By that time, more than 337,000 new African American voters had signed up. This had the effect of increasing the black proportion of all registrants from 27.2 percent at the time of the 2004 election to almost 30 percent in 2008.

The get-out-the-vote effort among black voters also succeeded. Early in-person voting and absentee voting began in Georgia on September 22. For the first time, Georgia allowed "no excuses" early voting. Previously, a voter had to have an excuse such as being out of the precinct on the day of the election to get an absentee ballot and vote early. But Georgia election officials, anticipating a massive turnout, encouraged voters to cast ballots before the election. Every county had at least one site, while more populous counties tended to have multiple sites at which one could vote in the six weeks leading up to the election.

African Americans flocked to the polls to take advantage of this option. In the first week and a half, blacks cast 39 percent of the early ballots, approximately one-third more than their share of the registrants. By the time the early voting wrapped up on October 31, African Americans had cast more than seven hundred thousand ballots, which constituted 35 percent of all votes cast before election day. In previous elections, Republicans had a far more extensive effort than Democrats directed at getting supporters to cast absentee ballots. But the Obama campaign, with its hundreds of volunteers and targeting techniques, had become so sophisticated that Eric Tanenblatt, who had been Republican governor Sonny Perdue's first chief of staff, acknowledged, "They've used technology better than any campaign I've ever seen. They have taken networking to that next level—to social mobilization."[9] The Obama operation sent out e-mails to tens of thousands of supporters telling where their nearest early voting location was. Some Republicans did not get mailings from McCain encouraging them to request absentee ballots until it was too late for them to be counted.

Mobilizing African Americans by itself would not suffice for Obama to carry Georgia. He also needed to do substantially better among white voters than had other Democrats in recent years. For example, John Kerry managed less than a quarter of the white vote in 2004 and lost the state by more than five hundred thousand votes. Two-term lieutenant governor Mark Taylor headed the Democratic ticket in 2006. He lost his bid to become governor by more than four hundred thousand votes when he took only 26 percent of the white vote. Two factors would determine exactly how much of the white vote Obama would need. First, the larger the share of all ballots cast by African Americans, the smaller the share of the white vote Obama would need. Second, to the extent that former Georgia member of Congress Bob Barr, the Libertarian presidential nominee, siphoned off votes, the share of the white vote Obama would need would decline.

Despite record turnout among African Americans, Obama lost Georgia by 204,000 votes. Although he received 98 percent of the African American vote, Table 4.1 shows he failed to improve on Kerry's showing among whites, getting only 23 percent support from this component of the electorate. The Obama campaign had hoped to attract 31 percent of the white vote, and had it done so, that would have sufficed to win the state's electoral votes by a narrow margin. Georgia was one of only two southern states in which Obama failed to improve on Kerry's performance among white voters. Obama ran slightly less well among the core Republican constituency, attracting only 10 percent of the white evangelical vote. Kerry had received the votes of 16 percent of these voters. This dramatic

Table 4.1 Comparison of the 2008 Georgia Vote with 2004

	2008	2004
Percent Black	30	25
Percent White	65	70
Percent Black for Democrat	98	88
Percent White for Democrat	23	23
Percent White Evangelical	37	35
Percent White Evangelical for Republican	89	84
Percent 18-29	14	19
Percent 18-29 for Democrat	48	47
Percent Democrat	38	34
Percent Republican	35	42
Percent Conservative	39	41
Percent Moderate	48	44
Percent Liberal	13	14
Number of Counties for Democrat	34	25
Number of Metro Atlanta Counties Voting Democratic	6	3

Source: http://www.cnn.com/ELECTION/2008/results/polls/com and the Georgia Secretary of State's office.

rejection from white evangelicals proved slightly more difficult for Obama since they cast 37 percent of all ballots in 2008, up two percentage points from their share of the 2004 electorate. Barr did not help Obama, managing to win only 28,000 votes.

Because Obama did not improve upon Kerry's performance among white voters, the narrowing of the margin by which Republicans carried Georgia is attributable to two interrelated factors. First, the share of the vote coming from African Americans rose from 25 percent in 2004 to 30 percent in exit polls four years later. Second, while Kerry did exceptionally well with black voters, Obama managed 10 percentage points more than Kerry.[10]

Despite not winning Georgia, Obama exceeded the Democratic performance in 2004 in most of the state's 159 counties.[11] This resulted in Democrats carrying six counties in the Atlanta metro area. In recent elections for state as well as federal offices, only three counties in metro Atlanta (Clayton, DeKalb, and Fulton) had supported Democratic candidates. To these three Obama added Douglas, Rockdale, and Newton. This demonstrated an expansion of Democratic support into the first tier of counties surrounding the traditional heart of the metro area. Although he did not win Cobb and Gwinnett counties, Obama held McCain to less than 55 percent of the vote there. This bodes well for future Democratic candidates since these two counties are the second and third most populous in the state and in the 1990s gave overwhelming majorities to Republicans. Obama ran ten percentage points ahead of Kerry in Gwinnett and almost eight points better than the 2004 Democratic nominee in Cobb. The Obama surge was so pervasive that only in counties north of a line from Rome to Gainesville did McCain consistently do better than President Bush had in 2004. The increased Democratic vote share resulted in their carrying thirty-four counties as opposed to only twenty-five in 2004. In each election Democrats won the core county in the seven traditional metropolitan areas. In 2008 Democrats added suburban counties in three metropolitan areas.

Each party's core constituency cast a larger share of the vote in 2008 than 2004 and became more cohesive. The share of the vote coming from African Americans increased from 25 to 30 percent in 2008 and the share of the vote going to the Democratic presidential nominee rose from 88 to 98 percent. On the Republican side, white evangelicals' share of the total vote cast rose from 35 to 37 percent. This group became cohesive, giving 89 percent of its votes to John McCain as opposed to 84 percent for the reelection of President Bush.

Despite efforts to register large numbers of young voters and get them to turn out, the exit polls show votes from those aged eighteen to twenty-nine decreased as a share of the total electorate falling from 19 percent of the vote cast in 2004 to 14 percent of the 2008 turnout. Despite the antic-ipated appeal that Obama would hold for younger voters, his share of the youth vote in Georgia remained unchanged from what Kerry received.

Probably as a result of the increase in black registration, Georgia's elec-torate became four percentage points more Democratic, while the Repub-lican share declined by seven percentage points. As a consequence, a plurality of Georgia votes in 2008 came from Democrats, while in 2004 Republicans outnumbered Democrats by a 42 to 34 percent margin. Despite these changes, we observe little difference in the ideological makeup of the elec-torate across the two years. The most substantial change was an increase in the proportion of moderates, from 44 to 48 percent.

Nationwide, Obama received 53 percent of the vote while in Georgia he polled 47 percent. A number of factors identified in Table 4.2 show ways in which voting in Georgia differed from the national vote. While Obama failed to win the bulk of the white vote nationwide, he came much closer, taking 43 percent of that portion of the electorate, a full 20 percentage points better than his Georgia performance. The 20-point dif-ference in whites is quite visible among males, more than three-fourths of whom in Georgia rallied to McCain compared with 57 percent nation-wide. Obama also ran much better among younger voters nationally, tak-ing two-thirds of their votes, while in Georgia he managed less than half, losing this group 51 percent to 48 percent.

White evangelicals, or born-again Christians, constitute the core con-stituency of the GOP in the South. In Georgia, white evangelicals made up 37 percent of the electorate and McCain defeated Obama among these voters by a margin of nine to one. Nationally, white evangelicals made up only 26 percent of the electorate and McCain's showing with these vot-ers, while very impressive, was less dramatic than in Georgia. Nationally, McCain defeated Obama among white evangelicals by a margin of three to one.

Obama did exceptionally well with first-time voters. Nationally, he defeated McCain among those new to the electoral system by a margin of 69 to 30 percent. While the Illinois senator also drew strong support from these voters in Georgia, his advantage over McCain was 25 percentage points rather than the 39 points nationwide. In both Georgia and national exit polls, first-time voters cast 11 percent of the votes.

Table 4.2 Comparisons of the 2008 Presidential Electorate in Georgia with the National Electorate

	Georgia	US
Percent White for Obama	23	43
Percent White Males for McCain	78	57
Percent of Youth Vote (18-29) for Obama	48	66
Percent of First-time voters for Obama	62	69
Percent White Evangelicals	37	26
Percent White Evangelicals for McCain	89	74
Percent for whom Candidate's Race was Important	13	19
Percent for whom Race was Important Voting for Obama	63	53
Economy Most Important Issue: Percent for Obama	47	53
Energy Most Important Issue: Percent for Obama	28	50
Percent Liberal	13	22
Percent Conservative	39	34

Source: Exit polls available at http://www.cnn.com/ELECTION/2008/results/polls/.

Surprisingly, a larger share of the national population than Georgia voters considered the race of the candidate important for their decision. Of those for whom race was an important consideration, 63 percent in Georgia supported Obama compared with 53 percent nationally.

The economy was the most important issue for more than 60 percent of voters both in Georgia and nationwide. Nationally a slight majority of those for whom the economy was the most important factor supported Obama, while in Georgia, by an equally narrow margin, most voters worried about the economy sided with McCain. Energy, which was a much less significant issue for voters, showed a substantial difference, with Obama getting half of the vote nationwide from those voters for whom energy was the most important issue, while in Georgia slightly over a quarter of the voters concerned about energy policy backed the Democrat.

The Georgia electorate is more conservative than the national electorate. With conservatives voting overwhelmingly for McCain, the five percentage point greater share of conservatives in Georgia worked to his advantage. Liberals, who constituted 22 percent of the national electorate compared with 13 percent in Georgia, gave overwhelming backing to the Democratic nominee.

Down-ticket Elections

With regard to other elections, Georgia elects its constitutional officers in the presidential midterm and therefore had few statewide, partisan contests in 2008. Below the presidential election came a contest for the U.S. Senate and a seat on the Public Service Commission. Obama's presence at the top of the ticket drew large numbers of African Americans to the polls and in so doing helped the Democratic nominees for these two positions.

Democrats had thought during the middle of 2007 that incumbent Republican Saxby Chambliss' Senate seat offered an opportunity for a pickup. But with Republican retirements in Colorado, New Mexico, and Virginia, along with the vulnerability of Republican incumbents in New Hampshire, Oregon, and North Carolina, national interest in contesting the Georgia seat declined.

While the Georgia seat dropped off the radar for the Democratic Senate Campaign Committee, it did attract five challengers. Many thought that Vernon Jones, the term-limited chair of the DeKalb County Commission, had the inside track. Jones was the only African American in the field, and blacks were expected to cast almost half of the votes in the Democratic primary. However, Jones had encountered problems while leading Georgia's second most populous county, including accusations of rape and questions about the budget for his bodyguards. His leading opponent, Jim Martin, had been the unsuccessful Democratic nominee for lieutenant governor in 2006 and had served in the state House for nine terms before being appointed to head the Department of Human Resources. Jones led the primary field with 40 percent of the vote, while Martin attracted just over a third. But in the runoff, Martin easily bested Jones, who failed to increase his vote share.

While Jones's personal baggage made Martin the more viable candidate, few thought he could unseat Chambliss. Real Clear Politics did not consider Georgia's Senate contest to be one of the twelve most competitive until October. A Rasmussen poll in March showed Chambliss ahead by 18 points. No other independent pollster bothered to conduct a survey in Georgia until Survey USA explored voter preferences in mid-September and found Chambliss still had a 17 percentage point lead. But a Rasmussen poll conducted just as the Survey USA effort was being wrapped up showed Chambliss ahead by only 7 points. Then at the end of September, Survey USA released a poll in which the incumbent had fallen below 50 percent and led his Democratic challenger by only two points. Polls conducted from the end of September until the election never showed Chambliss with more than a six percentage point advantage and one poll showed the race tied. All but one of the polls of this period had the Chambliss advantage within the margin of error.

Why did Chambliss's seemingly insurmountable lead only seven weeks before the election evaporate? His vote for the seven hundred billion dollar bailout of financial institutions alienated many conservatives. All Georgia Republican House members and four of the Democrats voted against the initial version. The increase in black registration discussed earlier also helped make the contest closer.

Chambliss's decision to hold off on television advertising created an opportunity that Martin exploited. Incumbents are usually much better funded than their challengers and can use their financial advantage to define the challenger negatively before the challenger can develop a positive image with the voters. Although Chambliss had $1.2 million cash on hand at the end of September compared to Martin's $100,000, the incumbent not only failed to define Martin negatively, he responded slowly when the challenger began running television advertising. Martin enjoyed several weeks when he had television advertising and Chambliss did not. Prior to launching his TV ads, a Survey USA poll found that 46 percent of likely voters had no opinion of Martin compared with 32 percent who had no opinion of Chambliss. In the wake of the ads, a Research 2000 poll showed only 7 percent of respondents with no opinion about Martin. Not only had Martin become known, voters viewed him far more favorably than a month earlier. In mid-September, 31 percent of respondents had a favorable impression of the Democrat compared to 23 percent who viewed him unfavorably. In mid-October, Martin's favorables had soared to 56 percent as opposed to 37 percent unfavorable. Chambliss had been viewed favorably by 46 of respondents in mid-September and negatively by 22 percent. A month later his favorables were up to 57 percent but his unfavorables had reached 40 percent. By going on television before the incumbent, Martin got to present himself in a favorable light.

With Martin having almost caught up with the incumbent in the polls and with Democrats running comfortably ahead in Senate contests previously thought to be competitive in Virginia, New Hampshire, New Mexico, and Colorado, the Democratic Senatorial Campaign Committee turned its attention to Georgia. The DSCC made a $500,000 television advertising buy in early October.

The closeness predicted by preelection polls proved accurate, as Chambliss led Martin by 110,000 votes, taking 49.8 percent of the vote. Chambliss came within 9,200 votes of winning a majority, which is required for general elections in the Peach State. Chambliss came up short as a result of 128,000 votes going to the Libertarian nominee. That the Libertarian nominee for the Senate polled 100,000 more votes than Bob Barr, the Libertarian nominee for president and a former member of Congress from Georgia, suggests that Chambliss's vote for the bailout package, early support for President Bush's immigration proposals, or some other policy stand alienated a number of conservative voters.

While some conservatives "parked" their Senate vote with the Libertarian, Martin failed to maximize his showing among Democrats. Exit polls showed blacks casting 30 percent of the votes in the presidential election but only 28 percent in the Senate contest. If those African Americans who failed to vote for senator had voted as blacks did who registered preferences in the Senate contests, then Martin might have actually finished ahead of Chambliss, although he would not have gotten a majority.

Martin's share of the vote generally exceeded Obama's in counties that Obama lost, but where the Democratic presidential nominee won, he ran ahead of the senatorial nominee. When the Martin vote share is regressed on the Obama vote, Martin received 8.4 votes for every 10 for Obama.

Martin swept the black vote, taking 91 percent of it, according to the exit polls. Chambliss dominated the white vote, defeating Martin by a margin of 75 to 25 percent. Despite spending far more money in the Senate race than he did two years earlier when he ran for lieutenant governor, Martin received a slightly smaller share of the white vote. The election revealed a gender gap, with 59 percent of men supporting Chambliss while 51 percent of the women cast ballots for Martin. Adherents of each political party provided near unanimous support for their party's nominee. Chambliss won the support of the 30 percent of the electorate who identified themselves as independents by a margin of 54 to 38 percent. White evangelicals, who made up 38 percent of the Senate voters, provided the core support for Chambliss, preferring him by a margin of 81 to 15 percent. Martin dominated the vote from Liberals and defeated Chambliss among moderates by 56 to 41 percent. Chambliss took more than three-fourths of the conservative vote.

During the course of the campaign, Martin, like Obama and other Democrats challenging sitting Republicans, sought to link the incumbents to the unpopular Bush administration. Martin's television ads criticized Chambliss for supporting the economic policies of the previous eight years that, Martin charged, created the conditions that led to the economic collapse. Martin also chastised Chambliss for backing the $700 billion economic rescue package but opposing relief for the middle class and not recognizing that the United States had plunged into a recession.

Much of the talk in Washington revolved around the television ad run by Chambliss in 2002 that juxtaposed pictures of Osama Bin Laden and Saddam Hussein with incumbent Democrat Max Cleland, a triple amputee from Vietnam. However, in Georgia the old television ad was not a factor.

Chambliss ads sounded a theme common to Republican campaigns by labeling Martin a liberal. Chambliss accused Martin of supporting past tax increases and padding his own expense account. Another ad claimed that governor Sonny Perdue relieved Martin of his responsibilities as the head of the Department of Human Resources following the death of two children in DHR care.

The only other statewide contest involved a position on the Public Service Commission. Here, as with the Senate contest, the work of the Obama campaign left its mark. Democrat Jim Powell, a political novice, led Bubba McDonald, a former PSC member trying to regain his position, by 23,000 votes. The Obama effort at energizing an enlarged black electorate was critical to Powell's success. However Powell, like Chambliss, failed to win a majority because of the presence of a Libertarian candidate that threw the election into a December runoff.

Obama's influence had no impact on the makeup of Georgia's congressional delegation, although it enabled two Democrats who narrowly escaped defeat in 2006 to win comfortably. Obama coattails helped Democrats pick up four suburban seats in the state House while McCain's strength in northeast Georgia contributed to the defeat of two Democrats.

General Election Runoff

With all other contests that could be resolved at the ballot box having been settled, political operatives turned their full attention to the Georgia Senate runoff. A galaxy of Republican luminaries that included John McCain, Mike Huckabee, Mitt Romney, and Rudy Giuliani campaigned for Chambliss. The current GOP superstar, Sarah Palin, visited four sites with Chambliss on the eve of the election. Martin tried to counter with visits by Bill Clinton and Al Gore. In an effort to mobilize black voters, he appeared with Ludacris and other rappers. Barack Obama declined Martin's invitation to campaign in the state although he cut a radio ad and he and his wife each recorded messages for use in robo calls.

Substantial amounts of money came in to buy television advertising during the runoffs. The Chambliss campaign acknowledged plans to spend $4.5 million during the four weeks and speculated that its opponent would spend at least as much.[12] Independent groups spent at least one million dollars on ads urging Chambliss's election, with Freedom Watch alone spending six hundred thousand dollars.[13] Final figures may show that the two campaigns and supporting groups, such as the Democratic Senatorial Campaign Committee and the National Republican Trust, spent more in the runoff than the estimated fifteen million dollars expended in the general election campaign.

With that kind of money, advertising breaks during news shows subjected the viewing public to as many as four campaign ads. Both campaigns linked Martin to Obama. Martin's ads promised that he would help the new president achieve change. Ads for Chambliss warned that Martin would support Obama's tax increases, threaten Second Amendment rights, and help labor unions expand. The most effective Chambliss ads warned that a Martin win would give Democrats a filibuster-proof Senate so that conservatives would have no means of stopping the liberal Democratic agenda. A poll found that 52 percent of voters would be less inclined to support Martin if his election would give Democrats sixty seats in the Senate.[14] Even one in ten respondents who had just indicated a preference for Martin said that should his be the 60th Democratic seat they would be less likely to support him.

Chambliss's warning that his defeat might remove the last check on Democratic liberalism brought some who had supported the Libertarian candidate in the general election back to the Republican fold.[15] As some who had voted for Allen Buckley got behind Chambliss, the Libertarian stated the terms for his endorsement: the candidate must sign a pledge to slash federal spending and embrace other Libertarian positions.[16] Neither candidate accepted these demands.

Martin turned to Obama's extensive network of supporters. About twenty-five of the thirty-three Obama campaign offices stayed open, and most of the paid staff remained on the payroll.[17] The Obama campaign sent in a hundred workers from other states to help Martin. Chambliss had no McCain organization on which to draw but did open ten campaign offices on his own.

The Democratic effort collapsed in the December runoff. Chambliss took 57 percent of the vote to beat Martin by a margin almost three times his November lead. Chambliss scored gains across the state. In November he had won 115 counties, in December he added 15 more. In November, Chambliss took more than 70 percent of the vote in 11 counties where he had his strongest showing. A month later, he got at least 80 percent of the vote in a dozen counties, and in 57 counties the Republican polled more than 70 percent. Even in heavily Democratic counties, Chambliss's vote share increased, growing from 21 to 25 percent in DeKalb, from 33 to 38 percent in Fulton, and from 35 to 38 percent in Clarke. A drop in black participation probably accounts for the stronger Republican showing. In the early voting for the runoff, blacks cast less than 23 percent of the vote, compared with 35 percent in early voting prior to the November vote.

The Republican turnout machine coupled with the failure of blacks to return for the runoff also resulted in a Republican victory in the Public Service Commission runoff. McDonald won by more than a quarter of a million votes, a swing of approximately 275,000 votes from the November election.

Conclusions

September saw Georgia transformed from a state thought to be solidly in the GOP camp to one in which Democrats believed they just might be able to steal victories. Polling showed both the presidential and the Senate contests tightening as Republican leads shrank to less than the margin of error. Once Obama had sewn up enough Electoral College votes to ensure his election, he began investing resources in Georgia. For the first time since 1992, a Democrat contested Georgia's electors. Although the candidate did not visit the state, he committed additional paid staff and volunteers and bought television time. The Democratic Senatorial Campaign Committee, which had long ignored Jim Martin, ran ads on his behalf shortly before the November election.

Ultimately, Democratic efforts came up short. Obama lost to McCain by 204,000 votes; and while Martin succeeded in denying Chambliss a majority in November, the Republican easily secured a second term in the December runoff. The Democrat who had a narrow lead in November in a bid for an open Public Service Commission seat also came up short in the December runoff.

Republicans proved far more adept at convincing their supporters to return to the polls just after Thanksgiving. To the dismay of Democrats, many African Americans were not sufficiently interested to come back to the polls. As Emory University political scientist Merle Black observed, "For a lot of African-American voters, the real election was last month. The importance of electing the first African-American president in history generated enormous enthusiasm. Everything else was anticlimactic."[18]

5.

Louisiana

From Political Bellwether to Republican Stronghold

Robert E. Hogan and Eunice H. McCarney

Introduction

For nearly four decades, voters in Louisiana have backed the winner of
the presidential election, but in 2008 the state deviated from this trend,
and the result was not even close. Republican John McCain led Democrat
Barack Obama by double digits in polls throughout the summer and fall,
and neither major party candidate invested significant amounts of time or
resources in the state. This is a departure from previous presidential races
where the state's electoral votes have often been up for grabs. While the
election results damaged Louisiana's reputation as a bellwether, it did
bring the state in line with other southern states that have generally supported Republican presidential nominees.

While Louisiana was not a battleground in 2008, the state did attract
some national attention in other ways. First, early in the election cycle
New Orleans served as a backdrop for candidates interested in highlighting the past missteps of the Bush Administration. And in the weeks leading up to the Republican convention, speculation swirled around the state's
popular governor, Bobby Jindal, as a possible vice presidential choice. In
terms of candidate attention to voters, however, Louisiana citizens received
far less than residents in other states. While the state's primaries were held

before either nomination was sewn up, these contests occurred just four days after Super Tuesday so much of the candidates' resources were directed elsewhere. However, Mike Huckabee's unexpected win caught the attention of both parties and demonstrated the continued importance of social conservatives within the Republican Party. The prevailing view by late spring was that Louisiana was firmly in the Republican column, and neither party's nominee expended much effort in the state. In the end, McCain won the election with 58.6 percent of the total vote—the largest victory by a presidential contender in Louisiana since Reagan's reelection in 1984.

Brief History

As in most southern states, the political landscape in Louisiana was dominated by the Democratic Party following Reconstruction and throughout most of the twentieth century. Republicans made early inroads at the presidential level in Louisiana when voters supported Dwight Eisenhower in 1956 and Barry Goldwater in 1964. However, it was not until the 1970s that competition between the parties in Louisiana really took root in presidential elections. State voters threw their support heavily behind Richard Nixon in 1972 with 65.3 percent of the vote, but then went with Jimmy Carter in 1976 with 51.7 percent of the vote. Ronald Reagan barely prevailed in 1980 with 51.2 percent, but then won resoundingly with 60.8 percent four years later. In 1988, George H. W. Bush received 54.3 percent of the vote, while the state swung for Bill Clinton in 1992 (45.6 percent) and again in 1996 (52 percent.). In 2000 George W. Bush won 52.6 percent of the vote and increased his percentage to 56.7 in 2004. While these elections were not always close, they do demonstrate that both parties have been competitive in the state's presidential contests over the past several decades.[1]

These changes in party fortunes within Louisiana's presidential contests make sense if one considers the electoral transformation that has occurred in the state over the past forty years. Party allegiances have certainly shifted over this time, as evidenced by changes in party registration. Whereas 95 percent of registered voters were Democrats as late as 1972,[2] today only about 52.5 percent of voters are Democrats while about 25.3 percent are Republicans. In recent years, an increasingly large number of registered voters have chosen to affiliate with neither party (22.2 percent).[3] These altered party allegiances are certainly reflected in how party nominees have fared in elections. Almost no Republicans were elected in the twentieth century prior to 1964, but by the 1970s the party was contesting and winning important offices, including the governor's mansion in 1979. Republican success has been steady throughout this period, but the result has not been a movement toward one-party Republican domination. It was not until the mid-1990s that Republicans held a sizeable minority in the state legislature (one third or more), and several statewide officials, including the governor, in recent years have been Democrats.[4] However, the recent demographic changes in the state brought about by Hurricane Katrina in 2005 have perhaps shifted the state even more toward the Republican Party as many African Americans left the region. The most recent statewide elections in 2007 were a boon for Republicans who won several statewide offices including the governorship. Democrats currently hold only two statewide offices (lieutenant governor and attorney general) although they continue to maintain a slight majority of seats in both houses of the legislature. Going into the 2008 elections, the state's congressional delegation was fairly evenly divided with Senator David Vitter, a Republican, and Mary Landrieu, a Democrat, as well as three Democrats and four Republicans in the state's U.S. House delegation.

Primary Election

Because of significant problems faced by New Orleans in the aftermath of Hurricane Katrina, presidential candidates from both major parties focused early attention in the state. As Louisianans struggled toward recovery, the failures of Katrina became a favorite stumping topic for candidates, especially Democrats who used the federal government's slow response to the disaster as a symbol for the perceived failures of the Bush administration. At the beginning of the election season Democrat John Edwards brought Louisiana into national prominence by announcing his candidacy in New Orleans' Ninth Ward, an area heavily devastated by the hurricane. Even Republican Senator John McCain made visits to Louisiana as early as August 2006 to tour and comment on recovery efforts. A "Hope and Recovery Summit" hosted by Louisiana Senator Mary Landrieu to mark the second anniversary of Hurricane Katrina garnered national media attention as four candidates for the parties' nominations (Hillary Clinton, John Edwards, Duncan Hunter, and Mike Huckabee) accepted invitations to outline their plans for the region.

In keeping with the national trend of frontloading primaries, Louisiana's legislature voted to move its primary up by one month from March to February in order to give the state's voters more influence in the nomination process. Louisiana was one of three states to hold primaries or caucuses on February 9, four days after the "Super Tuesday" primaries, when twenty-four states held their contests. For Democrats, the system of delegate selection was based on a closed primary system for allocating fifty-six of sixty-seven total delegates to the Democratic National Convention. Of these fifty-six delegates, thirty-seven were allocated based on the results in each of the seven congressional districts while the remaining nineteen were based on statewide results (a 15 percent threshold was required to receive delegates at either level). The remaining eleven delegates were "superdelegates" who attend the national convention unpledged.[5] The state's Republican Party used a more complicated system for allocating its forty-seven delegates to the National Republican Convention that included both a primary and caucuses. On January 22, registered Republican voters could participate at one of eleven caucus sites around the state to cast votes for delegates who would attend the state convention pledged to particular candidates. The results of this election, along with the decisions at the state convention on February 16, determined the allocation of twenty-four of the state party's delegates (an additional three state Republican leaders would go to the national convention unpledged). The remaining twenty were allotted based on the results of the February 9 primary in a winner-take-all contest. A candidate who won 50 percent of the vote would win all twenty delegates, or if no candidate met this threshold these delegates would remain uncommitted.[6]

While moving Louisiana's primary to an earlier date was intended to give the state a greater say in the nomination process, its particular place on the calendar just four days after Super Tuesday meant candidates had limited time and resources to spend in Louisiana. Among the Democrats, the Obama campaign had an upper hand in executing its plan for a protracted nomination struggle and Obama made appearances in Louisiana a few days prior to the primary. Bill Clinton campaigned in the state in an effort to shore up support for his wife, but Hillary never made an appearance. Among the Republicans, Mitt Romney's suspension of his campaign just two days prior to the primary appeared to seal the nomination for McCain, and none of the remaining candidates made a significant effort in the state.

The lack of attention by the candidates coupled with the closed primary system in place among both parties meant that turnout was quite low. In the end Obama won a substantial victory over Clinton—57.4 to 35.6 percent. Overall, he won forty-five of the state's sixty-four parishes including its major metropolitan areas. Clinton won nineteen parishes that were generally more rural and had lower percentages of African American voters than the state overall. Exit polls indicate that the coalition of support for each candidate in Louisiana was typical of what was observed in other parts of the county. For example, Obama drew heavy support from African Americans, younger voters, those with higher levels of education, and urban dwellers. Clinton, by contrast, drew support heavily from older voters, whites, citizens with low levels of education, and those living in rural areas. As in other parts of the country, Obama gained substantial support from African Americans (86 to 13 percent for Clinton), but in Louisiana he received substantially less support from whites, who voted for Clinton by a margin of 58 to 30 percent. If one examines differences in voting by both party identification and race, one finds that white independent voters gave Obama a slight edge over Clinton (45 to 42 percent). Among white Democrats, however, the disparity was quite large, with 66 percent supporting Clinton and only 25 percent going for Obama.[7]

On the Republican side, Romney's suspension of his campaign seemed to remove the last major roadblock to McCain's nomination. Given McCain's delegate count and the winner-take-all nature of the Republican contests, it seemed for many pundits that the contest was over. However, Mike Huckabee continued on, vowing to pursue a civil campaign on issues of importance to his base of social conservative supporters. While he had spent some time and resources in Louisiana, it came as a surprise to many that he won the plurality of votes cast in the state's Republican primary with 43.2 percent of the vote to McCain's 41.9 percent. National media accounts described the loss as "embarrassing" for McCain and said it "underlined the thinness of support for him among religious and social conservatives."[8]

A look at the results by parish indicates that Huckabee's support was centered in the central and northern parts of the state where Protestants are concentrated. The twenty-one parishes won by McCain were in southern, more Catholic areas. Exit polls confirm the importance of religion to voting in the Republican primary. Whereas McCain won 55 percent to Huckabee's 28 percent of Catholic voters, Huckabee won 52 percent of Protestant voters to McCain's 35 percent. Key to Huckabee's support were those who consider themselves evangelicals or "born again" (58 percent to McCain's 29 percent) and those who attend religious services more than weekly (Huckabee won 61 percent to McCain's 30 percent). However, other differences separated support for these two candidates. For example, McCain drew more votes from older voters, those in urban areas, and those with lower levels of education. Large differences also existed between voters with regard to what they considered to be the top candidate qualities. To voters who said experience and electability were of greatest importance, McCain led Huckabee by a whopping margin (85 to 7 percent on experience and 88 to 9 percent on electability). For voters who said the most important quality was a candidate who "shares my values," Huckabee outdistanced McCain 61 to 20 percent. Voters concerned about a candidate who shares their values proved to be quite helpful to Huckabee's success given that they constituted 51 percent of the Republican electorate in Louisiana.[9]

One of the more telling findings from the exit poll that sums up the differences between McCain voters and Huckabee voters involved the issue of ideology. Among self-described moderates McCain led Huckabee by a margin of 55 to 28 percent while among "very conservative" voters, Huckabee led McCain by a margin of 54 to 30 percent. Given that so many Louisiana Republicans consider themselves "very conservative" (44 percent in the exit poll), these voters clearly contributed to Huckabee's slim win over McCain.[10] Of course, because Huckabee failed to garner the needed 50 percent of the vote, he did not win any committed delegates. Under the state party's rules, all of Louisiana delegates attended the national convention officially uncommitted and ultimately all backed McCain for the nomination.

The results of the nomination struggle in Louisiana brought to light divisions within each party that the standard-bearers would have to address in order to be competitive in the general election. For Democrats the challenge would be to convince enough white voters as well as low-educated and rural voters to support Senator Obama. For Republicans, the key would be to unite a party divided on religious and ideological issues to back a candidate whose conservative credentials were questioned by many Republicans.

General Election Campaign

One could argue that a speech given by John McCain in Louisiana on June 3 marked the unofficial start of the general election campaign. This was the final day of the Democratic nomination battle, and McCain used the opportunity in Kenner, Louisiana, to directly criticize his presumptive opponent. In this prime-time speech covered by many of the national cable networks, McCain cast Obama as a candidate "who makes a great first impression" but does not have the experience and ability to bring about real change in Washington.[11] Many viewed this as McCain's most pointed attack on Obama to date and one that crystallized the major campaign theme that would be used by Republicans throughout the fall. The event was also memorable because of the lime green backdrop that was mocked by late-night comedians and commentators alike who referenced the speech throughout the course of the campaign as the "green screen speech."

While Louisiana may have been where the campaign started, the state's voters were rarely the target of either campaign's efforts. Throughout the spring and summer months, McCain led Obama in every statewide poll conducted. Surveys by Rasmussen and Zogby in June showed McCain with a 7- and 9-point lead respectively, but all other polls conducted for the remainder of the campaign showed McCain with at least a double-digit lead.[12] Obama made no further visits after events leading up to his February primary win and while McCain visited several times during the summer, most of these visits revolved around fundraising. Such visits provided McCain's campaign with needed cash, enabling him to raise approximately $2 million to Obama's $845,000 from state contributors.[13]

The groundwork for any national campaign effort centers on voter registration and mobilization; however, most of these efforts throughout the summer months were conducted not by the campaigns themselves but by political parties and outside groups. The Louisiana Democratic Party voter drive effort, "Voting in Power," submitted 74,000 registration applications, exceeding their June 2008 goal of registering 70,000 new voters.[14] They focused on registering new voters in areas of the state with large concentrations of African Americans. In mid July, Howard Dean, the Democratic National Committee chairman, traveled to Louisiana and other Southern states to drum up support for the national push to register new voters.[15] Republicans also directed efforts to voter registration in anticipation of a historically high turnout, but it was the outside groups that were probably more active than either party in the state. Groups like ACORN and Project Vote focused their efforts on increasing African American registrations, and by mid June these groups had submitted over sixty thousand voter registration applications.[16] Such efforts drew complaints from some local officials charged with verifying the registrations, who noted an abundance of duplicate, invalid, or incomplete registration cards. These complaints and other allegations of voter registration fraud prompted Secretary of State Jay Dardenne to begin an investigation into "Voting Is Power" to determine whether any state election laws had been violated. However, for all these efforts put in place by the parties and outside groups along with the concern it generated, it did not appear to make much difference for the total number of registered voters in the state. With purging of voter rolls by the Secretary of State's Office[17], there was a net gain of only about fifteen hundred new voters registered since July 2008.

As the summer came to a close and the national conventions approached, Louisiana came into the national spotlight again as speculation swirled around the popular Republican governor, Bobby Jindal, as a possible vice presidential choice. Earlier in the summer he and other leading contenders for the job (Governor Crist of Florida and former Governor Romney of Massachusetts) were invited to McCain's ranch in Arizona. Given his youth, popularity, and social conservative credentials, Jindal was viewed as a rising star who could bring balance to the Republican ticket. Much of the state's media attention focused on this possibility even after Jindal announced his lack of interest in late July.

As the fall campaign began, polls showed Senator McCain with a significant lead in Louisiana. The Rasmussen poll showed 55 percent of Louisianans supporting McCain while only 38 percent supported Senator Obama. Moreover the poll showed that McCain was doing a superior job compared to Obama in gaining the confidence of his fellow partisans. Whereas 92 percent of Republicans supported McCain, only 72 percent of Democrats supported Obama.[18] Such a large lead by McCain meant Louisiana would not be in play, and the candidates spent little on advertising in the state. According to data CNN received from TNS Media Intelligence and the Media Campaign Analysis Group, the Obama campaign spent only $367,736 in the state while the McCain campaign spent less than $1,000. The national parties and outside interest groups allocated very little money in the state as well.[19]

General Election Results

Early voting statistics suggested that turnout in 2008 was going to be quite high. A record number of voters, nine percent of total registrants, voted early.[20] However, the overall rate of turnout was not exceptionally high compared to previous presidential elections. A total of 67.2 percent of registered voters cast ballots in the presidential election, compared to 66.9 percent in 2004 and 63.5 percent in 2000. Turnout was greater, but not significantly greater, and not nearly as large as some had anticipated.[21]

Among subgroups of voters some interesting patterns emerge regarding turnout. As one might expect, African American turnout increased over 2004—64.6 percent compared to 61.1 percent. But for whites, the turnout actually decreased somewhat going from 70.4 percent in 2004 to 69.5 in 2008. Turnout among white Republicans was consistent across the elections, while turnout among white Democrats decreased from 71.2 to 70.4 percent. This suggests that the small increase in turnout overall was due mostly to higher turnout among African Americans.[22]

In terms of aggregate vote margin, McCain won the state handily with 58.6 percent to Obama's 39.3 percent. The size of the win was significant given that it was nearly as large here as in any southern state (only in Alabama and Arkansas did McCain have as large a win). McCain won fifty-four of the sixty-four parishes in the state, with his support coming mostly from rural and suburban parishes. Obama's wins were confined to parishes with large African American populations, especially in large urban centers such as Caddo, East Baton Rouge, and Orleans parishes. In Orleans Parish where approximately two-thirds of the residents are African American, Obama received more than 79 percent of the total vote.

Compared to the most recent presidential election in 2004, McCain's 58.6 percent was a slightly better performance than Bush's 57.6 percent, and he won the same number of parishes. However, McCain surpassed Bush's election margin in forty-six of the sixty-four parishes. In eighteen parishes, McCain's vote margin exceed that of Bush by over 10 percentage points, and in four parishes, McCain's margin exceeded Bush's by 20 points or more. For the most part, these parishes were rural or suburban areas with small concentrations of African Americans. However, one of the suburban parishes, Livingston, is the tenth-largest parish in population, and it also has the second-highest growth rate in the state (over 26 percent in the last seven years). This suggests that Republican strength in presidential elections is on an upward trajectory in the state.

If we look closely at various categories of voters, we find that McCain's level of support was quite strong across a wide assortment of demographic groups. Table 5.1 displays the percentage of voters supporting each major candidate as reported in exit polling in Louisiana and nationwide. McCain received a higher level of support in Louisiana from both men and women and across every category of age, education, and geography examined. McCain also did very well among Protestants and Catholics, evangelicals, and those with higher levels of income. His greatest level of support, however, was among white voters—84 percent supported McCain over Obama. Senator Obama drew heavy support in Louisiana, as he did nationally, from African Americans, who gave him a margin of 94 percent to 4 percent. Obama also did well among voters

Table 5.1 Support for Presidential Candidates in Louisiana and Nationally Among Various Categories of Voters (in percent)

	LOUISIANA			NATIONALLY		
	Obama	McCain	Total	Obama	McCain	Total
Gender						
Male	34	64	42	49	48	47
Female	42	56	58	56	43	53
Age						
18-29	48	49	23	66	32	18
30-44	44	55	27	52	46	29
45-64	33	65	38	50	49	37
65 and older	29	69	13	45	53	16
Race						
White	14	84	65	43	55	74
African American	94	4	29	95	4	13
Religion						
Protestant	38	60	56	45	54	54
Catholic	27	70	31	54	45	27
None	68	29	7	75	23	12
White Evangelical/Born Again						
Yes	6	93	32	24	74	26
No	54	43	68	62	36	74
College Graduate						
Yes	35	64	37	53	45	44
No	41	57	63	53	46	56
Income						
Less than $50,000	53	45	45	60	38	38
More than $50,000	28	70	55	49	49	62
Geography						
Urban	43	56	50	63	35	30
Suburban	34	64	31	50	48	49
Rural	37	60	19	45	53	21

Source: http://www.cnn.com/ELECTION/2008/results/polls.main/.

who did not express a religious experience, non-evangelical whites, and those who had lower incomes.

What is most striking about these findings is the high level of support McCain received across so many types of voters and how this contrasts with the relative levels of support the candidates received nationwide. For example, whereas men were closely divided nationally between McCain and Obama, in Louisiana McCain's level of support among men was nearly double that of Obama's. The contrast is particularly large if one considers the differences in the voting behavior of whites. Nationwide these voters went for McCain over Obama by a 55 to 43 percent margin, but among whites in Louisiana the margin was 84 to 14 percent in McCain's favor. Look as well at young voters, who supported Obama by a two-to-one margin nationally—in Louisiana McCain did slightly better than Obama among these voters (49 to 48 percent). Other notable differences in national voting trends and those in Louisiana can be seen with regard to Catholics, college graduates, urban, and suburban voters—while Obama did better among these groups nationally, in Louisiana McCain won these groups by fairly wide margins.

Additional insight into voting in Louisiana can be gained from Table 5.2, which displays the preferences of groups holding various political viewpoints. As with the demographic groupings, here too McCain drew votes from citizens who were not nearly as supportive of his candidacy at the national level. Looking first at party identification we find that Democrats in the state were more supportive of McCain than Democrats nationally (24 percent compared to 10 percent). Republican support for McCain in the state was also slightly higher—96 percent supported him in Louisiana but only 90 percent did nationwide. Among independents nationwide, Obama won 52 to 44 percent, but in Louisiana these voters supported McCain by nearly a two-to-one margin (62 to 32 percent). Given that conservative Democrats in the South so often split their tickets to vote for Republicans at the national level, such findings are not too surprising. However, when one looks at voting by ideological grouping one sees that even liberals and moderates in the state were less supportive of Obama than similar voters nationwide. Obama received 89 percent of the vote by liberals and 60 percent of moderates nationally, but in Louisiana only 77 percent of liberals and 45 percent of moderates backed him. The level of support among conservatives was consistent both nationally and in Louisiana (20 percent nationally and 18 percent in Louisiana). These results suggest that McCain's support ran deep while Obama's campaign had difficulty gaining traditional Democratic voters as well as moderate and independent voters.

Table 5.2 Support for Presidential Candidates in Louisiana and Nationally Among Voters with Differing Political Viewpoints (in percent)

	LOUISIANA			NATIONALLY		
	Obama	McCain	Total	Obama	McCain	Total
Party Identification						
Democrat	75	24	42	89	10	39
Republican	3	96	38	9	90	32
Independent	32	62	21	52	44	29
Ideology						
Liberal	77	19	16	89	10	22
Moderate	45	54	42	60	39	44
Conservative	18	80	42	20	78	34
Most Important Issue						
Energy Policy	30	66	11	50	46	7
Iraq	50	47	13	59	39	10
Economy	39	60	53	53	44	63
Terrorism	8	90	10	13	86	9
Health Care	58	39	10	73	26	9
Most Important Candidate Quality						
Shares My Values	15	83	31	32	65	30
Can Bring Change	83	15	29	89	9	34
Experience	5	95	23	7	93	20
Cares about People	59	37	11	74	24	12
Worried about Economic Conditions						
Yes	37	62	86	54	44	85
No	47	51	13	33	65	14
Approve of Bush's Handling of His Job						
Approve	5	94	43	10	89	27
Disapprove	63	34	56	67	31	71

Source: http://www.cnn.com/ELECTION/2008/results/polls.main/.

Table 5.2 lists other differences among voter attitudes and how these are associated with voting behavior. In Louisiana voters citing energy policy, the economy, and terrorism as their most important issue of concern were much more likely to vote for McCain, while voters choosing Iraq and health care were more likely to vote for Obama. Such levels of support are rather different than what we see in the nationwide sample where support for Obama is much higher in all groups except those believing that terrorism is the most important issue. Regardless of what issue voters viewed as most important, Obama's support was lower and McCain's was higher in Louisiana compared to voters nationwide. Similar differences are present if one examines voters based on the most important qualities they look for in a presidential candidate. Even among voters who say they look for a candidate who "can bring change," those in Louisiana supported McCain by a wider margin than voters nationwide. Whether these attitudes about issues and candidate qualities influence the support of particular candidates or whether they reflect underlying voter predispositions toward the candidates and parties, they indicate the deep levels of support McCain enjoyed in Louisiana.

A final perspective on voter attitudes that may help us understand voting behavior in the state involves the two major conditioning elements of the 2008 presidential elections—the unfolding economic crisis and the very low levels of support for the incumbent Republican president. Analyses of the exit poll data in Table 5.2 show that nationwide concern about economic conditions played into preferences for a particular candidate. Specifically, voters concerned over the crisis were more likely to vote for Obama. But in Louisiana, such concerns did not translate into support. In fact, those worried about economic conditions supported McCain 62 to 37 percent compared to nationwide support favoring Obama 54 to 44 percent. In terms of President Bush's job approval in the state, the relative levels of support for Obama and McCain did not vary dramatically between Louisiana and the nation. Louisiana voters approving of Bush's job performance were slightly more supportive of McCain than voters nationwide. However, Louisiana voters in general were much more supportive of Bush overall—43 percent of state approved of his handling of his job compared to only 27 percent nationwide. These contextual findings demonstrate that the economic conditions that helped Obama nationwide didn't help him very much in Louisiana. In addition, Bush's poor approval wasn't as low in Louisiana as in other parts of the country so this did less harm to McCain's support in the state.

The overall finding to emerge is that Obama's support was quite thin across various demographic groups and among voters holding a wide variety of political viewpoints. Even voting groups who strongly backed the Democratic nominee nationally such as young voters, moderates, and urban dwellers were more supportive of the Republican nominee in Louisiana. Worsening economic conditions and low popularity ratings for President Bush that conditioned the election and benefited Obama nationally did not have a similar effect in Louisiana.

Other Elections

The only other major election in Louisiana in 2008 was that for U.S. Senate, where incumbent Democrat Mary Landrieu faced Republican state treasurer John Kennedy.[23] Landrieu was viewed as the most vulnerable Democrat in the Senate and national Republicans were determined to defeat her. Karl Rove recruited Kennedy to challenge Landrieu, and Vice President Cheney came to aid in fundraising. Kennedy was a newcomer to the GOP, having won reelection as state treasurer in 2007 as a Democrat. His campaign focused on bringing "conservative change" to Washington and used the time-honored strategy of southern Republicans of associating their Democratic opponents with more liberal Democrats at the national level. He often emphasized his strong support for Senator McCain and pointed to Landrieu's backing of Senator Obama, whom he continually referred to as the most liberal U.S. Senator. Kennedy's attempt to capitalize on McCain's high popularity in the state prompted Senator Landrieu in one debate to tell Kennedy that "Senator McCain's coattails are not long enough for you."[24] For her part, Landrieu campaigned as a conservative Democrat, downplayed social issues, and emphasized her past efforts to bring federal funding to the state, especially for hurricane relief.

Large amounts of money flowed into the Senate race—Landrieu's campaign spent $8.6 million to Kennedy's $4.5 million and the national parties allocated significant amounts as well ($1.2 million by the Democrats and $3.2 million by the Republicans).[25] In the end Landrieu won with 52.1 percent of the vote to Kennedy's 45.7 percent. The race indicates the relative levels of support McCain enjoyed over Obama in Louisiana—so much so that the Republican candidate spent much effort to tie himself to the Republican presidential nominee. But the results of this race also demonstrate that while Republican strength may have increased in recent years, partisan effects on voting have their limits and conservative Democrats who downplay social issues and emphasize efforts to bring home federal dollars can succeed.

In addition to the statewide race for U.S. Senate, five of the seven U.S. House seats were also contested.[26] Two of the more interesting races involved the Second and Sixth district races, where incumbents were defeated. The Sixth Congressional District incumbent was Democrat Don Cazayoux, who had only been elected a few months earlier in a special election. The seat was vacated by longtime Republican congressman Richard Baker, and the district is one that favored Republicans. Cazayoux was able to win the special election, but the high-turnout election in November brought the district back to its natural Republican leanings and the Republican challenger, Bill Cassidy, won with 48.1 percent of the vote. The defeat of an incumbent Democrat provided Republicans with a small bright spot in an otherwise dismal election night nationwide. The other interesting House race involved indicted Democratic congressman William Jefferson representing the Second Congressional District. In 2008, as in 2006, the embattled lawmaker faced a variety of Democratic opponents who hoped to unseat him from this majority African American district. However, his luck ran out in 2008 due in part to Hurricane Gustav, which set back the election process in the fall by one month, meaning that the general election was not held until December. The odd timing of the election and the low turnout compared to the high turnout among African Americans that occurred on November 4 enabled a little-known Republican challenger to win. Joseph Cao was elected with 49.5 percent of the vote on December 6 to become the first Vietnamese American elected to Congress.[27] When the dust settled from the 2008 congressional elections, Republicans had picked up two seats, leaving only one Democrat representing Louisiana in the U.S. House.

Conclusion

Louisiana is no longer a bellwether state and appears to be moving in the direction of a stronghold for Republicans in presidential elections. Whether this is due to long-term changes or to circumstances of the present election it is hard to say, but it is clear that McCain did much better and Obama much worse than one would expect given the state's voting history. While Obama had little difficulty in gaining the votes of African Americans, he had a much harder time winning white voters, who constitute approximately two-thirds of the electorate. McCain outperformed Obama across most major demographic groups and among groups concerned about particular issues. The economic crisis did not appear to benefit Obama among the state's voters, and the fact that President Bush's popularity was not as low here as in other states also made it difficult for Democrats to gain traction. Democrats are still very competitive and often win elected office as evidenced by Democratic Senator Mary Landrieu's victory, however, at the presidential level voters appeared to be skeptical of going with the Democratic candidate favored nationally in 2008.

So what explains why Louisiana was not a bellwether state in 2008? Given the large role that race has played in the state's political history, one might wonder what effect this had on the outcome. In an election year when the Republican ticket did poorly nationwide, did long-standing racial prejudices of white voters in Louisiana contribute to a larger Republican win in Louisiana than President Bush saw in his reelection four years earlier? One could point to various pieces of evidence to support such a conclusion. For example, the primary exit polls showed that Clinton received nearly double the level of support from white voters that Obama received (58 percent to 30 percent). And in the general election, white support for Obama was much lower than white support for Democrat John Kerry in 2004. Whereas Kerry received 24 percent of the white vote in 2004, Obama received just 14 percent.[28] Clearly more detailed analysis at the precinct level will be needed before any definitive conclusions can be reached, but it does suggest that a nontrivial portion of white voters in the state had some hesitancy in casting a ballot for an African American.

While race may have played a role in the 2008 results, a more fundamental factor is probably the increasing levels of support for Republicans that have accrued over time. Republican fortunes are on the rise in the state and were probably accelerated by population shifts due to Hurricane Katrina in 2005. From this perspective, the 2008 presidential results are a manifestation of these underlying changes. Whatever the explanation, however, the result is that Louisiana looks increasingly like a stronghold for Republicans in presidential politics for some time to come.

6.

Mississippi

Democrats Fight for Relevance in an Increasingly Republican State

David A. Breaux and Stephen D. Shaffer

Political Context

Mississippi entered the 2008 federal elections with a political landscape that appeared more and more bleak for Democrats. Not since 1976 had a Democratic presidential candidate been able to carry the state, and even then only narrowly. Not since 1988 had Democrats been in control of one of the state's United States Senate seats. Republican gains were also evident in state elections, with the GOP winning four of the last five gubernatorial contests. Indeed, in the previous year's statewide races, which saw Haley Barbour reelected governor, Republicans swept all except one statewide office. Democrats were able to take some comfort in retaining control of both chambers of the state legislature, as well as in continuing to hold two of the state's four U.S. House seats, however.

The 2003 state and 2004 presidential elections suggested Democrats were not only being out-campaigned and out-spent, but also were sometimes too liberal for average Mississippians. Democratic governor Ronnie Musgrove was kicked out of office after starving much of state government during his term in order to deliver on a promise to the teachers' union to enact a multiyear teacher pay raise. Voters rejected his negative ads against Barbour that sometimes did not even mention the incumbent's name, and Republicans benefited from an aggressive GOP get-out-the-vote effort. Lieutenant governor Amy Tuck had switched to the GOP before the election after being pressured by Democratic activists to support a congressional redistricting scheme that would favor a Democrat over a Republican incumbent. Tuck promptly won reelection over a liberal African American woman who had insinuated that the pro-life and divorced Tuck had had an abortion. Republicans in 2003 also reelected as auditor Phil Bryant, who was known for his even-handed nonpartisanship, and outspent a well-qualified African American candidate, Gary Anderson, to elect Tate Reeves as treasurer, thereby giving Republicans half of the state offices elected statewide, a historic high for the party. The next year Democrats once again lost the presidential contest, with the only real memorable event being John Kerry's visit to the Magnolia State, where he equated discrimination against gays with the civil rights movement of the 1960s after an older African American woman expressed her distress at such comparisons.[1]

The 2007 state elections continued this theme of Democrats being out-organized as well as being ideologically divided among themselves. Democrats began the year by retaliating against their party's longtime insurance commissioner, George Dale, for publicly backing George Bush three years earlier. Dale was forced to go to state court to even get on the Democratic ballot after the state executive committee ousted him. After being defeated in the primary by Gary Anderson, Dale responded, "I'm going to be as kind to the Democrats as they have been to me."[2] State Republicans geared up for the statewide campaigns by contributing generously to their party's candidates—$450,000 to the insurance commissioner nominee, $287,500 for attorney general, $137,000 for auditor, $120,000 for secretary of state, $100,000 for the incumbent party-switching agriculture commissioner, and $65,000 for lieutenant governor. The only Democrat successful in attracting such a large sum was the incumbent attorney general Jim Hood, who received $850,000 over the year from the Democratic Attorney General Association.[3] Republicans also benefited by nominating solid candidates with impressive credentials. The major statewide newspaper, the *Clarion-Ledger*, endorsed governor Haley Barbour's reelection because of his leadership during Katrina and in attracting a new Toyota plant.[4] It also backed auditor Phil Bryant for lieutenant governor because of his nonpartisan approach and commitment to accountability, and endorsed attorney and businessman Delbert Hosemann for secretary of state by touting the Republican's businesslike approach that focused on openness in government and combating voter fraud.[5] Not only did Barbour win reelection, but Republicans also swept every other statewide office except for attorney general.

One hopeful note for Democrats was the success of their congressional, state legislative, and local candidates in avoiding the "liberal" label by adopting socially conservative positions on guns, abortion, and crime. Democrats retained control of the state legislature with a powerful biracial partnership.[6] Thirty-nine white Democrats joined thirty-six African American Democrats to outvote the forty-seven Republicans in the state house, while fourteen white Democrats and thirteen black Democrats more narrowly outpolled the twenty-five Republicans in the state senate. This biracial partnership even kept the Democrats competitive on the key political attitude of party identification. Indeed, an April 2008 Mississippi Poll even had Democrats regaining a slight 48 to 43 percent edge in partisanship among all eligible voters, a narrow edge that Republicans had enjoyed in the 2002 and 2004 biennial polls. One short-term factor helping Democrats was President Bush, whose popularity was the lowest for any Republican president in the twenty-eight-year history of the Mississippi Poll. Only 9 percent of residents rated his performance as excellent and only 24 percent as good, compared to 33 percent rating it as merely fair and a sizable 34 percent rating it as poor.[7]

The Presidential Primaries and Conventions

Absent any president or vice president seeking a major party presidential nomination for the first time since 1952, both parties conducted spirited campaigns that even reached the increasingly Republican stronghold of Mississippi. On the Republican side, Arizona senator John McCain amassed some impressive endorsements, with senator Trent Lott touting his electability and congressman Chip Pickering praising McCain's national security experience, his fiscal responsibility, and his "reliable leadership in promoting our conservative values."[8] Senator Thad Cochran initially backed former Tennessee Senator Fred Thompson, and then endorsed Mitt Romney after Thompson dropped out of the race, before finally settling on emerging nominee John McCain, who had once blasted the distinguished Mississippi senior senator as a king of pork.[9]

Democrats had a more spirited campaign, with the well-organized Illinois senator Barack Obama visiting in June 2007 and pointing out that "you win votes by showing up and people getting to know you and what your values are," followed the next month by John Edwards's ill-fated "poverty tour."[10] Obama quickly picked up some key endorsements, including that of Bennie Thompson, the state's sole African American congressman, who praised him for having had "the judgment to oppose the war in Iraq from the start."[11] Former Governor Ray Mabus also endorsed Obama, blasting New York Senator Hillary Clinton (who had made the off-handed comment while campaigning in Iowa that she couldn't understand how Iowa could be ranked with Mississippi in failing to elect women to important offices) for "writing off and criticizing . . . small states and Southern states."[12] As the Democratic contest became a two-person race, Clinton, her daughter Chelsea, and Bill Clinton all made campaign stops in the Magnolia State. But it was left to the "lean and long-limbed" Obama, while visiting Columbus and Jackson right before election day, to electrify the crowds with his eloquent voice that rang with "bell-like clarity" as he spoke comfortably "for more than an hour with no notes."[13] The soon-to-be Democratic nominee proceeded to blast the Bush administration for the host of domestic and foreign problems facing America, and promised a wide range of spending programs.[14]

The March 11 presidential primary provided big wins for Obama and McCain. Obama garnered 61.2 percent of the vote to 36.7 percent for Clinton and 2.1 percent for other candidates still on the ballot, while McCain swept 78.9 percent of the vote to only 12.5 percent for former Arkansas governor Mike Huckabee and 8.6 percent for other candidates.[15] One concern for the Democrats' hopes in November was Obama's association with more liberal elements, as exit polls showed him winning 92 percent of the African American vote but only 26 percent of the white vote, and winning 68 percent of self-described liberals and 61 percent of moderates but only 43 percent of conservatives.[16] Governor Barbour promptly lit into Obama, accusing him of having "the most liberal voting record in the United States Senate," and being "to the left of Hillary Clinton . . . Teddy Kennedy . . . Bernie Sanders, who runs for senator as Socialist."[17] Yet with Bush's great unpopularity, and with concerns over McCain's age, Republicans held only a 10-point edge over Democrats in the presidential contest, a margin nearly as narrow as 1992 when George H. W. Bush won Mississippi but lost the nation.[18]

Effectively wrapping up the nomination, McCain began his "Service to America" tour in Mississippi, where his family roots are so deep that two military facilities were named after his relatives. At his arrival, Congressman Wicker praised McCain's national security strength, pointing out that he understood what it was like "to lose freedom and be subject to harsh treatment by the enemy."[19] McCain himself sounded some conservative themes, advocating school choice and teacher accountability, as well as workfare rather than welfare.[20] State Democratic Party chairman Wayne Dowdy immediately shot back, accusing McCain of not understanding complicated economic issues, wanting to prolong the Iraq war for one hundred years, and being a continuation of the failed Bush administration.[21] Sensing a possible upset or at least a possible U.S. Senate seat pickup, Democratic National Committee Chairman Howard Dean's national bus tour came to Mississippi in July to stimulate voter registration.

With both candidates having wrapped up their parties' nominations before the conventions, the only remaining suspense was the vice presidential picks. Delaware Senator Joseph Biden's selection as Obama's running mate was praised by the new state Democratic chairman Jamie Franks for his foreign policy expertise and his middle class values.[22] Republican columnist Andy Taggart shot back that the Obama/Biden ticket was "the farthest-left ticket in recent history."[23] Alaska Governor Sarah Palin, the Republican candidate for vice president, was praised by state Republicans, particularly female state representatives, who described her as "an ordinary person," who was "very smart and very tough," while Democratic leader Franks ridiculed her as "a former part-time mayor of a town of 6,715 people" who had "absolutely no foreign policy and national security experience."[24]

The Invisible Presidential Campaign

Mississippi was viewed by the national campaigns as such a "safe" state for John McCain, because it had been thirty-two years since Democrats had last won the Magnolia State in a presidential contest, that both national campaigns largely wrote it off, concentrating their resources in more competitive states. The state Republican Party coordinated the McCain effort, and though Obama's camp did open its own headquarters, it was staffed with volunteers and relied on "neighbor-to-neighbor programs" with "local people talking to their own neighbors, family, and friends" rather than on paid ads and staff.[25] Third congressional district Democrats promptly held a regional rally, where long-time state representative Tyrone Ellis charged that the nation could not afford "four more years of Republicanism" and that we needed to "clean house" by electing Obama, who would bring about "real change."[26] State Democratic Party treasurer Paul Winfield then tried to tar McCain's reformist image by claiming that the lobbyists advising his campaign would "give the big corporations a big boost" while giving "Mississippians very little relief, if any at all," prompting the state GOP chairman, Brad White, to label the charge "so ridiculous that neither the Democrats' own chairman nor vice-chairman bothered to attend the press conference and make the claim themselves."[27] Obama did pick up some notable support from a prominent African American Republican, Columbus lawyer Wilbur Colom, who decried how "Republicans have busted the budget . . . just so they can stay in power," because they had become "big business barons who want to use the government as their own personal piggy bank."[28]

State GOP chairman White meanwhile touted McCain for sharing the views of most Mississippians and argued that Obama's numerous programs "would not do anything but raise taxes for all of us—except the people who don't pay taxes."[29] Some Mississippians were miffed after McCain responded to the financial crisis by threatening to boycott the first televised debate, held at the University of Mississippi, but after the debate neither candidate was viewed as a clear winner. McCain appeared to be benefited by his experience, while Obama was helped because he provided "'a broader vision' that departs from past mistakes."[30] Meanwhile, Senator Cochran found himself explaining how he could now back McCain as a man whose "roots run deep in Mississippi," after previously describing the Arizona Republican as "erratic," a "hothead," and a man who "worries me" because "he loses his temper."[31] In mid-October dozens of Obama supporters rallied at the Democrats' state headquarters along with U.S. House majority whip James Clyburn of South Carolina, prompting former state GOP chairman Jim Herring to respond that "Mississippi remains a conservative state and we are confident Obama's brand of socialism will not be successful in his effort to win Mississippi in November."[32]

Indeed, so confident were leaders of both parties in Mississippi that McCain would continue the streak of Republican presidential victories in the Magnolia State that both Republican governor Haley Barbour and former Democratic governor Ray Mabus spent the closing days of the campaign touting the strengths of their parties' presidential hopefuls in more competitive states such as Virginia.[33] One of the few signs that Mississippi might conceivably buck its presidential Republicanism was the *Clarion Ledger*'s endorsement of Obama for providing "charm, charisma, a positive vision for the future, a voice for empowerment, a role model for youth," and much-needed "change after eight years of corruption, division, war, greed, and economic failure."[34]

Congressional Campaigns: Incumbency Bucks the GOP Sweep

State Democrats offered more viable alternatives, who were generally more centrist than Obama, for the state's four congressional district races and U.S. Senate elections. Senator Trent Lott's midterm resignation prompted Governor Barbour to appoint First District congressman Roger Wicker as the interim senator in January. His Democratic opponent for the November special election was former governor Ronnie Musgrove. Though a conservative, Wicker also shared some progressive credentials, since as a state senator during the 1992 recession he had voted to raise taxes over Republican governor Kirk Fordice's veto in order to prevent cuts to public education. The state supreme court was twice forced to resolve procedural disputes between partisan officeholders, as the Democratic attorney general was first unsuccessful in forcing an early special election that would have denied Wicker an incumbency advantage, but then was successful in thwarting a Republican secretary of state's efforts to list the special election at the very bottom of the ballot. Musgrove held an early April lead because of his greater name recognition, as he had run three statewide campaigns while Wicker was less known outside of his north Mississippi district.

Wicker proceeded to skillfully identify himself with conservative issues and to blast Musgrove as being allied with national liberals, arguing that voters would prefer his "13 years of mainstream conservative Republican representation that reflects the values of Mississippi."[35]

Claiming Musgrove had accepted money from a national PAC that was "the largest gay rights group in the country" and promised to support the "liberal Democratic leadership" in Washington, Wicker's television ads also hammered the former governor for a failed beef plant project and an alleged budget deficit during his administration.[36] The state Republican Party piled on with a mail out reminding Republicans that as Governor Musgrove had "Tried to Change Our State Flag" to remove the symbol of the old Confederacy, as well as allegedly presided over a budget deficit and a loss of jobs. Republicans provided additional support to Wicker, as President Bush attended a closed-door fundraiser for him, and Governor Barbour appeared at many county Republican headquarters to stress the importance of turning out the vote.[37]

Political observers became increasingly distressed at the turn toward mudslinging on the part of both camps and their supporters who were running independent ads on their behalf. In debates and on television, Musgrove claimed Wicker had voted repeatedly to raise his own pay and that he had gone "to Washington promising change, but Washington politics changed him," while Wicker reminded voters that they had rejected Musgrove's gubernatorial reelection bid and had given "him his walking papers . . . We don't need that kind of record back in Washington, D.C."[38] As polls now showed Wicker with a 10-point lead late in the campaign, one glimmer of hope for Musgrove was his endorsement by the *Clarion Ledger*, which praised him as "an innovative and progressive leader" who as governor had provided "health care for children and basic education funding for schoolchildren."[39]

Wicker's resignation as First District congressman required a special election for the remaining year of his seat, in addition to the regular party primaries for the November general election for the same seat, thereby confusing voters. Democrats ended up nominating a longtime county chancery clerk, Travis Childers, who connected with voters by reminding them that his modest background required that he work "full-time jobs through high school and college to support my family," that he had "balanced 16 straight budgets" during his years in county government, and that he had worked across party lines in order to bring jobs to north Mississippi.[40] Backed by the "conservative" House Democratic Blue Dog coalition and calling himself a "Jamie Whitten Democrat," Childers stressed that he was "the rural candidate" in the race who understood "rural counties" and "small municipalities."[41] The Democrat promptly drew impressive campaign crowds that contained hundreds of city and county officials.

Meanwhile, Republicans got into a nasty primary runoff spat in a district that they fully expected to retain, since it had voted 62 percent for President Bush four years earlier. One ad by Southaven mayor Greg Davis even accused former Tupelo mayor Glenn McCullough of "fiscal irresponsibility as chairman of TVA [Tennessee Valley Authority]," with Davis aide Ted Prill blasting McCullough for allegedly "trying to hide the million dollars of taxpayer money he wasted at TVA flying on private planes and eating $75 dollar veal chops in Washington restaurants."[42] Though Davis won the GOP nomination, McCullough declined to endorse him, and some of his Republican supporters also refused to support Davis.[43] Democratic nominee Childers skillfully exploited the GOP rift in responding to Davis's attack ads against him by reminding voters that "It's very obvious that Davis and his special interest buddies in Washington want to smear my name just as he smeared his primary opponent's name."[44] Blasting Davis's "negative campaigning," the *Northeast Mississippi Daily Journal* endorsed Childers for the special election, praising his focus "on the needs of the 1st District," and his "ability to bring together people of divergent viewpoints to build consensus."[45]

After delighting Democrats by picking up a Republican House district in the special election and reducing Republicans to holding only one of the state's four congressional districts, Childers proceeded to institute aggressive mass e-mailings to his constituents and political observers, and to refrain from attending the national Democratic convention due to the need to serve his constituents, who needed help. As Davis sought to win the seat back for Republicans in the November general election by claiming that Childers would vote for liberal Nancy Pelosi for House Speaker, the Democratic incumbent skillfully turned the attack around by pointing out that his Republican challenger was "interested in working with only one party" while Childers had decided to "rise above that and work across the aisle."[46] A member of the conservative Blue Dog Democrats, Childers ran as a social conservative who was pro-life and pro-guns. The Democrat was even endorsed by the National Rifle Association after he convinced the House of Representatives to pass his pro–gun ownership amendment that sought to implement the Supreme Court's ruling striking down a gun ban in the District of Columbia.[47]

Rep. Chip Pickering's impending retirement as the Third District congressman elicited considerable interest in the Republican primary, since the district had voted 65 percent for Bush four years earlier. Former state senator and losing GOP lieutenant governor primary candidate Charlie Ross led in the first primary over Gregg Harper, longtime chairman of the Rankin County Republican Party. Harper proceeded to stress his conservative values, particularly on fighting illegal immigration and advocating smaller government, and gained support among evangelicals because of his vocal Southern Baptist faith.[48] Recounting to the GOP faithful how he had worked in the trenches since 1978 to build the party organization, Harper gained the backing of a major Republican financial backer, Billy Mounger, as well as of lieutenant governor Phil Bryant.[49] Harper's grassroots campaign stressed the personal touch, as his supporters "used their own stamps to mail out homemade letters and cards seeking support . . . sent personal e-mails," and "made personal phone calls."[50] With Harper pulling off an upset in the primary runoff, he then faced an easier target—Democrat Joel Gill, a cattle dealer who didn't even live in the district.

Longtime incumbents were widely expected to prevail in Mississippi's two other congressional district races, plus its regular U.S. Senate election. Republican Senator Thad Cochran, who had won every reelection beginning in 1984 by at least 61 percent of the vote, faced Democratic former state legislator Erik Fleming, who had won only 35 percent of the vote in his losing bid to unseat Senator Lott two years earlier. Rep. Bennie Thompson, an African American Democrat who had represented the Second District since 1993 and who in his last three reelections had beaten off spirited challenges from two conservative black Republicans by garnering at least 55 percent of the vote, faced white schoolteacher Richard Cook. Rep. Gene Taylor, a moderate Democrat and member of the House Blue Dogs, who had served in Congress since 1989 and had never won less than 58 percent of the vote, faced Republican John McCay, a local religious leader pursuing a Ph.D. from Trinity Theological Seminary in Indiana.

Election Results and Analysis

The 2008 presidential election results confirmed the wisdom of the national parties in virtually writing off the state as, despite an Obama victory nationally, McCain easily carried Mississippi by winning 56.2 percent of the vote to Obama's 43 percent. Indeed, the preliminary two-party results indicate that the Magnolia State voted 2.9 percent more Republican than did the South as a whole, marking the sixth presidential election in a row that Mississippi was even more Republican than a region that has become a bastion of Republicanism. An even bleaker comparison for Democrats is that McCain's percentage of the two-party vote in Mississippi was a sizable 10 percent greater than his vote in the rest of the nation, marking the seventh presidential election in a row that Mississippi was more Republican than the nation.[51] Republicans also easily reelected Senator Cochran with 61.4 percent of the vote, elected interim senator Roger Wicker with a respectable 55 percent of the vote, and kept Chip Pickering's Third District with Gregg Harper's landslide 62.5 percent popular-vote victory. Nevertheless, Democrats proved that they could remain competitive in Mississippi with appealing candidates, as they easily reelected incumbent congressmen Bennie Thompson and Gene Taylor with 69.1 percent and 74.5 percent of the vote, respectively. Most impressive was newly elected congressman Travis Childers' reelection with a comfortable 54.5 percent of the vote, thereby confirming that Democrats now controlled three of Mississippi's four U.S. House seats (see Table 6.1).

As early as April, the Mississippi Poll had demonstrated a major weakness of Barack Obama's—Mississippians' perceptions of his liberalism. In a state where 54 percent of likely voters labeled themselves as "somewhat" or "very conservative" and only 17 percent considered them-

Table 6.1 2008 Election Returns in Mississippi Federal Elections (in percent)

Candidate (Party)	Percent of Vote	Vote Totals
President		
John McCain/Sarah Palin (R)	56.2	724,597
Barack Obama/Joe Biden (D)	43.0	554,659
Chuck Baldwin/Darrell L. Castle (C)	0.2	2,551
Bob Barr/Wayne A. Root (L)	0.2	2,529
Cynthia A. McKinney/Rosa Clemente (G)	0.1	1,034
Ralph Nader/Matt Gonzalez (I)	0.3	4,011
Ted C. Weill/Frank McEnulty (Ref)	0	481
Total Presidential Vote	100.0	1,289,862
U.S. Senate		
Thad Cochran (R)*	61.4	766,109
Erik R. Fleming (D)	38.6	480,913
Total Senatorial Vote	100.0	1,247,022
U.S. Senate Special Election		
Ronnie Musgrove	45.0	560,062
Roger Wicker*	55.0	683,408
Total Senatorial Vote	100.0	1,243,470
U.S. House of Representatives		
First District		
Travis W. Childers (D)*	54.5	185,956
Greg Davis (R)	43.9	149,818
Wally Pang (I)	1.1	3,736
John M. Wages (G)	0.5	1,876
Total District Vote	100.0	341,386
Second District		
Richard Cook (R)	30.9	90,364
Bennie Thompson (D)*	69.1	201,606
Total District Vote	100.0	291,970
Third District		
Joel L. Gill (D)	37.5	127,698
Gregg Harper (R)	62.5	213,171
Total District Vote	100.0	340,869
Fourth District		
John McCay, III (R)	25.5	73,977
Gene Taylor (D) *	74.5	216,542
Total District Vote	100.0	290,519

Key: * = incumbent. R = Republican Party, D = Democratic Party, C = Constitution Party, L = Libertarian Party, G = Green Party, I = Independent, Ref = Reform Party.

Note: Results are complete but uncertified.

Source: Mississippi Secretary of State website: http://www.sos.state.ms.us/, accessed November 30, 2008.

selves "liberal," Obama was viewed by 65 percent of voters as "very" or "somewhat liberal." With the ideological self-identification scale in the poll ranging from a low of 1 for very liberal to a high of 5 for very conservative and 3 constituting the moderate category, Obama's mean score of 1.99 or "somewhat liberal" was far removed from the average Mississippian's ideological mean of 3.61 (slightly on the moderate side of "somewhat conservative"). On the other hand, voters perceived McCain to be their ideological soul mate, viewing his ideology on average as a 3.70 (see Table 6.2). Further illustrating the comparative disadvantage that Democrats held on the ideological perception issue was that not only was Obama generally viewed as a "liberal," but also he was viewed as even more liberal than previous Democratic presidential nominees. His ideological mean score of 1.99 was even further to the left of John Kerry's 2.12 and Michael Dukakis' 2.20 scores in previous polls.[52] On the other hand, John McCain's ideological consistency with Mississippians was shared by that of state Republican officials. Governor Barbour's 3.77 mean perceived ideology score and Lieutenant Governor Bryant's 3.42 mean score were both very close to the average voter's 3.61 ideological self-identification score, enhancing the credibility among voters of state GOP officials who were aggressively backing McCain.

Exit polls further illustrated the importance of ideology in shaping Mississippians' general election votes. Both candidates received overwhelming support from their party's ideological core supporters, with McCain winning 78 percent of conservatives and Obama carrying 77 percent of liberals. Since conservatives outnumbered liberals among exit voters by a three-to-one margin (49 percent to 16 percent), McCain was clearly advantaged by his ideological proximity to voters (see Table 6.3). McCain was also advantaged by the religious right factor, as an overwhelming 94 percent of white evangelicals who claimed to have had a born-again experience backed the Republican. These ideological and religious factors helped McCain counteract President's Bush unpopularity. Though 61 percent of voters expressed disapproval of Bush's performance as president, only 67 percent of them stuck with Obama, compared to a more impressive 90 percent of the smaller but more cohesive group of Bush approvers who stuck with McCain.

Another factor that appeared to help McCain was that of party identification and a likely partisan turnout advantage. Republicans slightly outnumbered Democrats among actual voters (45 to 40 percent), reversing the 5 percent advantage that Democrats in April had held among all adult Mississippians. Though identifiers of both parties were overwhelm-

Table 6.2 Voter Ideologies and Perceptions of Candidates' Ideologies (in percent)

Ideology	Voters' Own Ideology	Perceptions of Obama's Ideology	Perceptions of McCain's Ideology	Perceptions of Governor Barbour's	Perceptions of Lieut. Gov. Bryant's
Very Liberal	2	41	2	2	1
Somewhat Liberal	15	24	7	8	12
Moderate	24	9	27	19	15
Somewhat Conservative	32	10	34	37	27
Very Conservative	22	3	19	20	6
No Opinion	5	13	11	14	39
Mean Value of Opinionated	3.61	1.99	3.70	3.77	3.42

Note: Cell entries above Mean Value total 100 percent down each column. Ideology was a self-identification question asking respondents whether their political beliefs were "very liberal, somewhat liberal, moderate or middle of the road, somewhat conservative, or very conservative." Likely voters were those who "definitely" would vote in November.

Source: 2008 Mississippi Poll, telephone survey of 407 likely voters on April 2–22 by the Social Science Research Center at Mississippi State Univeristy.

ingly loyal to their parties' nominees, the 94 percent loyalty that Republicans gave to McCain trumped the 89 percent loyalty of Democrats for Obama. Furthermore, 63 percent of the small band of independents backed McCain, thereby helping to counteract the 55 percent of self-identified moderates who favored Obama.

Finally, in Mississippi Obama proved unable to move much beyond his African American and lower socioeconomic status bases. The Democrat won a staggering 98 percent of the African American vote but only 11 percent of the white vote. Though Mississippi boasts the highest percentage of African Americans in the nation, whites nevertheless outnumbered blacks among voters 62 percent to 33 percent. While Obama won a 59 percent vote share of those with incomes under fifty thousand dollars, McCain won an even greater 74 percent vote share of the 46 percent of voters with incomes above fifty thousand dollars. Furthermore, though a gender gap did emerge, McCain was able to win a majority of both

Table 6.3 Demographic and Attitudinal Sources of 2008 Presidential Vote (in percent)

	McCain	Obama	Others	Subgroup % of Sample
Ideology				
Liberal	22	77	1	16
Moderate	44	55	1	35
Conservative	78	22	0	49
Party Identification				
Democrat	11	89	0	40
Independent	63	35	2	15
Republican	94	6	0	45
Race				
White	88	11	1	62
African American	2	98	0	33
Income				
Under $50,000	41	59	0	54
Over $50,000	74	25	1	46
Sex				
Male	62	38	0	44
Female	53	47	0	56
Age				
18–29	43	56	1	19
30–44	54	46	0	31
45–64	59	40	1	38
Bush Job Rating				
Approve	90	9	1	38
Disapprove	32	67	1	61
Region of State				
Jackson Area/Delta	38	62	0	29
Southeast	67	33	0	39
Northeast	61	38	1	32
White Evangelical/ Born Again				
Yes	94	6	0	46
No	24	75	1	54

Note: The last column provides the demographic group's size of the sample. Groups that are too small to analyze, such as other races and those sixty-five and older, are omitted from the analysis.

Source: CNN exit poll of 1,053 respondents (http://www.cnn.com/ELECTION/2008/results/polls/#MSP00p1).

sexes with his 62 percent share of male voters, even more impressive than his bare majority of 53 percent of women. Obama's limited voter appeal translated into him carrying only one of the three geographic regions of the state (the majority black Delta and Jackson areas) with McCain carrying the majority white regions of the state. One positive note for national Democrats was that Obama was able to win a majority of 56 percent of voters under age thirty, but this group comprised only 19 percent of voters, and McCain won majorities among those over age thirty (see Table 6.3).

The Future of Party Politics in the Magnolia State

Mississippi Republicans continued to ride high in 2008. After winning every statewide office except attorney general the year before, Republicans continued their streak of presidential election victories begun in 1980 and maintained their control of both of the state's U.S. Senate seats that had begun in 1989. Democrats continued to be hampered with national tickets viewed as too liberal for Mississippians. Indeed, national Democrats did not even appear to make much of an effort, nominating two northern liberal candidates for president and vice president for the first time since 1984. Particularly disappointing for Democrats was their inability to pick up a virtually open U.S. Senate seat with a very capable candidate, Ronnie Musgrove, who had won two of three bids for statewide offices.

Lest political observers and national Democrats completely write off Mississippi, we should remind them of the party's success in continually maintaining control of the state legislature, as well as winning back majority control of the U.S. House delegation. The Democrats maintain a strong biracial partnership in the state legislature centered on strong support for such issues as education and racial fairness, coupled with tolerance for disagreement within the party on the emotional issues of crime and abortion. Unlike the uniformity of liberal Democratic presidential candidates, Mississippi Democrats are able to offer more ideologically diverse candidates for state and local offices who appeal to their local constituencies. Travis Childers's successful campaign for Congress provides a textbook example of how state Democrats can avoid becoming identified with unpopular liberal national causes, and instead stress their Mississippi roots and their connection with the concerns of Mississippians. And with the state's electorate being sufficiently racially and economically diverse to sustain a very competitive two-party system in terms of party identification, Democrats can continue to seek out electoral targets of opportunity from time to time.

7.

South Carolina

A Paler Shade of Red?

Cole Blease Graham

Introduction

Traditionally, South Carolina has been governed by a rural-oriented, culturally and socially conservative aristocracy.[1] The result is a difficult political context in which to have new ideas or find political support for them. The tendency since the post– Civil War strife has been for one party to dominate, beginning with the Democrats from the Civil War down through the civil rights revolution in the 1960s. The support of white South Carolinians for the Democratic Party began to erode when many supported the "Dixiecrat" ticket in 1948, headed by South Carolina's Strom Thurmond for president. For a while, national Democrats continued to win the state's Electoral College vote: Illinois Senator Adlai Stevenson in 1952 and 1956 and Massachusetts Senator John F. Kennedy in 1960. Only once since then, in 1976, has a Democrat, Georgia governor Jimmy Carter, won the state's Electoral College votes.

South Carolina Republicans found growing success after 1960 and gradually became the dominant party by the 1990s. Arizona Senator Barry Goldwater was victorious in 1964. South Carolina was the only Deep South state won in 1968 by Richard Nixon over Alabama Governor George Wallace.[2] Incumbent President Nixon won again in 1972.

Then, in 1980, Republicans really took off in South Carolina when governor Carroll Campbell and his political consultant, Lee Atwater, supported Ronald Reagan over Texas governor John Connelly. They led the effort to stop Connelly's bid for the Republican presidential nomination. He lost the South Carolina primary even with the support of legendary U.S. senator Strom Thurmond and former Republican governor James Edwards.

In recent decades, South Carolina has been among states with the highest rate of Republican support in the November election.[3] This electoral success is based on enduringly higher levels of citizen identification with the Republican Party than with Democrats or independents. Since 1989, the University of South Carolina's Institute for Public Service and

Table 7.1 Party Identification, by Selected Dates and Average for Thirty-eight Survey Periods, Fall 1989 through Spring 2006 (in percent)

Year	OVERALL (R)	(I)	(D)	WHITE (R)	(I)	(D)	BLACK (R)	(I)	(D)
Spring 1990	34.9	28.4	34.7	46.0	34.1	19.9	13.3	12.7	74.0
Spring 1995	35.5	37.9	26.6	45.3	39.8	15.0	9.0	34.0	57.1
Spring 2000	34.2	33.9	31.9	43.8	37.3	18.9	9.9	25.0	65.1
Spring 2006	41.0	29.4	29.7	54.2	30.5	15.3	4.7	25.8	69.5
Range									
Highest	42.6 Fall 2004	38.0 Fall 1990	33.9 Spring 1993	55.3 Fall 2004	42.2 Spring 1999	22.2 Fall 1993	13.3 Fall 1989	37.8 Fall 2002	74.0 Fall 1989
Lowest	30.1 Spring 1999	27.9 Fall 2004	26.4 Spring 2003	38.3 Spring 1999	29.9 Spring 2002	13.0 Spring 2003	4.0 Spring 2006	12.7 Fall 1989	56.3 Fall 1993
Average	35.8	33.3	30.8	43.4	35.6	18.1	8.3	26.8	65.0
Average N= (for thirty-eight surveys)	731			535			195		

Source: Abstracted by author from party identification table compiled by Dr. Robert Oldendick, Institute for Public Service and Policy Research, University of South Carolina.

Note: The original survey used a seven-point scale: strong Republican; not strong Republican; Independent to lean Republican; Independent; Independent to lean Democrat; not strong Democrat; strong Democrat. Republican and Democratic identifiers are calculated as strong and not strong; Independent identifiers are the three middle categories on the scale.

Policy Research has surveyed party identification in the state.[4] As shown in Table 7.1, identification with the Republican Party has averaged almost 36 percent, compared to about 33 percent for independents and 31 percent for Democrats. Republican support grew to its largest figure during the survey period at 42.6 percent in fall 2004 with the reelection of George W. Bush. In 2000, Bush had defeated Democrat Al Gore by 16 percent (57 percent to 41 percent) with 38.2 percent Republican identification. The full survey data show that surges in Republican identification are typically accompanied by decreases among independents. For example, independent identification decreased 5 percent from spring to fall of 2004, while the Republican identification increased 3.8 percent, suggesting that Republicans often convert Independents at a higher rate than Democrats.

The 2004 Election

Republicans did not hold a presidential primary in 2004, so Democrats had the stage to themselves. Native son and North Carolina senator John Edwards wound up battling Massachusetts senator John Kerry. Influential African American, Democratic congressman James Clyburn had supported Missouri congressman Dick Gephardt, but Gephardt dropped out early. The Democrats did not generate much enthusiasm for this primary. Fewer than three hundred thousand out of over two million registered voters participated. Edwards hoped for at least a majority, but eventually won 45 percent, a disappointment. Kerry garnered 30 percent. Al Sharpton managed 10 percent, primarily from African Americans, whose support Edwards had hoped to win. In the 2004 general election, incumbent Republican President George W. Bush defeated Democrat John Kerry by 276,275 out of almost 1.6 million votes (58 percent to 41 percent).

The 2008 Nominating Primaries

The Republicans. Republican senator John McCain and former Massachusetts governor Mitt Romney started campaigning early in 2007. McCain had run a hard-fought second place to George W. Bush in 2000, losing by 67,157 votes out of over 550,000 cast in the state. He was well known in the state, but questions lingered whether he could shake a loser's image.[5] Building on their friendship from the 2000 primary, McCain quickly won the endorsement of senior U.S. senator Lindsey Graham. The junior senator, Jim DeMint, elected in 2004, lined up behind Romney's appeal to business leaders. Former U.S. senator and actor Fred Thompson showed some early promise as a potential nominee, but then ran a lackluster campaign. Former Arkansas governor Mike Huckabee made a direct appeal to evangelicals and to "folksy" South Carolinians.

McCain was the consistent front-runner and went on to win with 33.2 percent. Huckabee gave McCain a scare with 29.9 percent, but Thompson and Romney only gained about 15 percent each. Ron Paul, Rudy W. Giuliani, Duncan Hunter, and Tom Tancredo saw their presidential hopes evaporate in South Carolina.

The Democrats. South Carolina hosted the first debate for Democratic Party candidates in April 2007.[6] John Edwards, a native of Seneca, South Carolina, and 2004 vice presidential candidate, returned, but did not do well compared to his earlier success. Senator Hillary Clinton had been third in Iowa, won in New Hampshire, and saw a South Carolina victory as a way to win the momentum to sweep subsequent primaries. She eventually lost South Carolina to Illinois senator Barack Obama.

The Clinton campaign was run poorly, despite spending seven million dollars in the state. In an early effort to head off opposition, Senator Clinton engaged consultants among ranking and established state leaders to win the state's Democratic power structure. It became an expenditure trap compared to Obama's "grassroots" effort. Obama's campaign was very controlled and relied more on a sophisticated voter mobilization effort. A longterm voter identification project, begun during summer 2007, had mobilized many younger voters and created widespread energy and interest in Obama long before the primary.

President Bill Clinton brought his reputation to South Carolina to help Hillary Clinton's campaign. He was very persuasive with black voters, who were expected to make up about 60 percent of Democratic primary voters. President Clinton squandered his influence with his constant criticism of Obama. He missed Obama's broader professional appeal compared to the usual, narrower representational interest in African American interests by black candidates. Bill Clinton was generally perceived as more divisive and less presidential in his visits to the state.

Obama came into South Carolina with a huge boost from his Iowa caucus win. It broke a huge psychological barrier and gave a clear signal it was acceptable for a Democrat, even a white Democrat in the South, to vote for a black man. White voters, both liberals and moderates, were increasingly able to cross the racial divide and vote with African Americans—a huge psychological change in South Carolina. The result was a surge in defections from Clinton to Obama. After the debate in Myrtle Beach, Senator Clinton left immediately by airplane to campaign in California. Senators Edwards and Obama stayed and her absence was seen as a negative even with President Clinton's constant campaigning in the state.

For state Democrats, the intensity of the primary campaign between Clinton and Obama and the national interest were new. Obama developed an enthusiastic following in a really short time. He was able to get huge crowds—without paying boosters—to hold up signs and cheer for him. At a large facility in Columbia, the Koger Center, on a winter Friday night at eleven, he was able to fill the five thousand seat auditorium and have several thousand outside wanting to get in. His presence was almost mystical. Eventually, on January 26, 2008, 532,468 voters showed up for the Democratic primary, about 88,000 more than participated in the Republican primary held a week earlier. Obama won 295,214 of them (55.4 percent). Clinton trailed at 26.5 percent, and Edwards received 17.6 percent.

South Carolina's primaries were significant milestones for each eventual presidential candidate.[7] Both South Carolina primary winners, McCain and Obama, went on to win the nomination at their national party conventions to campaign for president.

The 2008 Campaign

Were Yogi Berra a political analyst, he might say of South Carolina's expected Republican November victories, "It's over before it's over." That is not to say Democratic candidate Obama wrote off South Carolina; he just did not campaign here. To an experienced political tactician, McCain's challenge in South Carolina was to remind the voters occasionally that he was the Republican candidate so as not to lose any supporters. Obama's challenge was to remain positive and not waste political resources in a state he could not be expected to win.[8] In the end, McCain won South Carolina by 53.9 percent to 44.9 percent.

Results and Analysis

Voter Registration and Turnout. In 2008, South Carolina had 2.58 million registered voters out of an estimated 3.31 million voting-age population, a registration rate of approximately 78 percent of the voting-age population. State officials predicted a record turnout and in raw numbers almost two million, 1,927,153 to be exact, ballots were cast on November 4, a turnout rate of 74.7 percent of registered voters.[9] Of the registered voters,

Table 7.2 Results of 2000 South Carolina Presidential and Congressional Elections (in percent)

Candidate (Party)	Percent of Vote	Vote Total
President		
John McCain/Sarah Palin (R)	53.87	1,034,896
Barack Obama/Joe Biden (D)	44.90	862,449
Bob Barr/Wayne A. Root (L)	0.38	7,283
Chuck Baldwin/Darrell Castle (C)	0.36	6,827
Ralph Nader/Matt Gonzalez (P)	0.26	5,053
Cynthia McKinney/Rosa Clemente (G)	0.23	4,461
Total Presidential Vote		1,920,969
United States Senate		
Lindsey Graham (R)*	57.52	1,076,534
Bob Conley (D)	42.25	790,621
Write-in	0.23	4,276
Total Senate Vote		1,871,431
United States House of Representatives		
First District		
Henry Brown (R)*	51.93	177,540
Linda Ketner (D)	47.89	163,724
Write-in	0.18	615
Total District Vote		341,879
Second District		
Joe Wilson (R)*	53.74	184,583
Rob Miller (D)	46.18	158,627
Write-in	0.08	276
Total District Vote		343,486
Third District		
J. Gresham Barrett (R)*	64.69	186,799
Jane Ballard Dyer (D)	35.23	101,724
Write-in	0.08	218
Total District Vote		288,741
Fourth District		
C. Faye Walters (G)	2.39	7,332
Bob Inglis (R)*	60.09	184,440
Paul Corden (D)	36.91	113,291
Write-in	0.61	1,865
Total District Vote		306,928
Fifth District		
Albert F. Spencer (R)	36.99	113,282
John Spratt (D)*	61.64	188,785
Frank Waggoner (C)	1.34	4,093
Write-in	0.04	125
Total District Vote		306,285
Sixth District		
Nancy Harrelson (R)	32.47	93,059
James E. Clyburn (D)*	67.48	193,378
Write-in	0.05	134
Total District Vote		286,571

Key: * = incumbent; R=Republican Party; D=Democratic Party; L=Libertarian Party; G=Green Party; C=Constitution Party. Column percentages for each contest may not add to 100 percent due to rounding.

Source: Abstracted by author from South Carolina Election Commission website: http://www.scvotes.org

44.3 percent were male and 69.7 percent were white. The state election commission registration report indicates that non-white registration now approaches 30 percent for the first time in a decade. By age, two-thirds (69.7 percent) of voters are between the ages of twenty-five and sixty-four. Younger voters, eighteen to twenty-four years of age, make up 11.2 percent of registered voters; voters over sixty-five comprise 19.1 percent.

Analysis: The Presidential Race

The 2008 presidential race was an open competition with neither party running an incumbent. An open seat strips away any advantage for either candidate. South Carolinians watched the first national presidential debate with some anticipation that the state's vote might be a bit closer than usual. Yet, polls showed McCain with a steady lead over Obama by more than 10 percentage points; in September, it was 54 percent to 41 percent.[10] Given the national low approval rating of sitting President Bush, Senator John McCain may have avoided some negative spillover in South Carolina by running as an independent or "maverick." Even so, exit polls showed that about one- third of respondents approved of Bush's job performance, and 92 percent of them voted for McCain. This suggests a core of support for McCain regardless of Bush's image.

Another way to think of McCain's margin of victory is to define any result approaching 60 percent of the vote as a landslide. A vote between 55 percent and 45 percent may be called marginal or competitive[11]; an outcome approaching 40 percent or less as noncompetitive. By these standards, McCain's 54 percent victory places him in a competitive category. George W. Bush won the state in 2004 with 58 percent, a 1 percent improvement over his 2004 margin—both comfortable margins, even landslides. The potentially competitive nature of McCain's victory colors South Carolina "a paler shade of red," but red nonetheless for the foreseeable future.

The Political Landscape. There are at least three distinct political regions for South Carolina Republicans that overlay prevailing political ideologies.[12] There is an Upstate region where Republicans tend to emphasize social issues such as social services reform, freedom of religion, and independence in local decisions regarding schools or morals legislation more than other parts of the state. The Upstate contains about 28 percent of the total voters in 2008. National defense is the dominant concern among Midlands Republicans. There are major military facilities—Fort Jackson and Shaw Air Force Base—in the area, as well as the Savannah River Project near Aiken and the headquarters of the National Guard and many state law enforcement agencies around Columbia. Democrats compete more strongly with Republicans among the Midlands' 24 percent of South Carolina voters. Another fourth of voters are in the Pee Dee and Low-country where Republicans are more libertarian than in other regions. They see lower taxes and smaller government as the primary attractions of the Republican Party.

Another 25 percent of voters are in rural counties where Democrats are strongest. There are two crescent-shaped slices across the state, originating in Marlboro County on the northeastern border with North Carolina, that spread above and below Columbia to the Savannah River. About half of the state's counties are included in these slices, and many of them contain large proportions of minority voters. Obama won the rural part of South Carolina by a plurality of 49.2 percent to McCain's 48.6 percent. With black voters representing about 30 percent of the state's population overall, Democrats need to win about 30 percent of the 70 percent white population to get to a winning majority of 50 percent. Obama's final tally of 46 percent suggests that he won about 23 percent of the total white vote.

As suggested by the Winthrop University/South Carolina Education Television pre election polls,[13] McCain's appeal on social issues in the primary and general election campaign aligned him solidly with white voters in the Upstate. In six Upstate counties with low percentages of nonwhite voters, he won a landslide 61.1 percent on average, with even greater shares in Pickens County (71.4 percent) and Anderson (65.1 percent). Even in the more competitive counties in the region, Obama only topped 40 percent in Upstate suburban counties York (40.2 percent) and Laurens (40.0 percent). There is little to confirm extensive speculation that the suburbs might become more Democratic—the "blueburbs" in regularly conservative Republican areas.[14] Suburban Lexington County was the most Republican Midlands county, with McCain tallying 67.9 percent of the vote, followed by suburban Aiken County at 60.8 percent. Richland County lags at 34.9 percent for McCain along with Fairfield County at 33.2 percent. Richland has 49.7 percent registered nonwhite voters and Fairfield has 58.2 percent, in each case providing a formidable Democratic base. In the Pee Dee, Horry County, with only 14 percent registered nonwhite voters, voted 61.7 percent for McCain. In the Lowcountry, Dorchester County gave McCain the highest proportion with 56.3 percent.

Race, Gender, Age, and Income. White South Carolinians make up an overwhelming majority of the state's Republicans. It is this strong white Republican segment that is mainly responsible for Republican victories. Black

Table 7.3 2008 Urban/ Rural Regions in South Carolina by County and County Proportion of Total State Vote (in percent)

Region	McCain	Obama	Others	Percent of State Vote*
Upstate (Greenville to Spartanburg)				
Anderson	65.1	32.3	2.6	3.9
Greenville	60.5	36.8	2.7	10.0
Laurens	58.0	40.0	2.0	1.4
Pickens	71.4	25.6	3.0	2.4
Spartanburg	59.0	37.8	3.3	5.7
York	57.7	40.2	2.1	4.9
Totals for Upstate	61.1	36.2	2.7	28.0
Midlands (Columbia)				
Aiken	60.8	37.0	2.2	3.7
Calhoun	47.2	50.7	2.1	0.4
Edgefield	54.5	43.7	1.9	0.6
Fairfield	33.2	64.5	2.3	0.6
Kershaw	58.5	39.9	1.6	1.5
Lexington	67.9	30.2	2.0	5.7
Richland	34.9	63.6	1.5	8.6
Saluda	59.6	38.1	2.3	0.5
Sumter	42.1	57.1	0.8	2.3
Totals for Midlands	50.0	48.2	1.7	23.7
Pee Dee (Florence) and Lowcountry (Charleston)				
Berkeley	54.9	42.1	3.0	3.4
Charleston	44.9	53.1	2.0	8.1
Darlington	49.1	49.0	1.9	1.5
Dorchester	56.3	41.0	2.6	2.8
Florence	50.6	47.5	1.9	3.1
Horry	61.7	37.1	1.3	4.9
Totals for Lowcountry	52.3	45.6	2.0	24.1
Totals for Urban Regions	54.9	43.0	2.2	75.9
Totals for Rural Region (Remaining twenty-five counties)	48.6	49.2	2.1	24.1

*Each percentage in this column represents the percentage of the total number of votes cast in the county or region as a proportion of all votes cast in the state. Totals have been rounded and may not always add up to 100 percent.

Source: Calculated by the author from data on the South Carolina State Election Commission website: http://www.scvotes.org.

Republican membership remains very low and stable. These facts are consistent with the overall Republican approach of winning white conservatives away from the Democrats while competing for moderates at the same time.[15] Occasionally, some defections from the Republican segment by white identifiers have boosted the proportions of independent and Democratic identifiers, but without apparent lasting effects. Democrats have experienced some small, short-term gains among moderate or independent whites.

As indicated by the National Election Pool exit poll, McCain won 73 percent of white voters and Obama received 96 percent support among black voters. White men supported McCain at a higher rate than white women (76 percent to 70 percent), and white women supported Obama more than white men (29 percent to 23 percent). Obama had overwhelming support from black men (97 percent) and black women (96 percent) who responded to the exit poll.

Republicans have recently experienced long-term losses in the eighteen to twenty-nine age group and longterm gains in the sixty-five and over age group. There have been declines in Republican identification among the largest age groups, thirty to forty-four and forty-four to sixty-four. Democrats have made some long term gains among the eighteen to twenty-nine group. A greater percentage of younger voters are registered as Democrats than before, no doubt a reflection of the Obama voter mobilization effort for the primary and the general election. Democrats have some longterm losses in the sixty-five and over group, but their proportion of the thirty to sixty-four group has remained stable. Democrats are not winning Republican defectors in the thirty to sixty-four age group, they tend to identify as independents.

McCain had his highest level of support among the sixty-five and over group (66 percent) and his lowest among the forty-five to sixty-four group (39 percent). Obama did his best among the forty-five to sixty-four group (61 percent) and his worst among the sixty-five and older responding voters (33 percent). Perhaps the unsteady economy weighed more heavily on those forty-five-years old and older as they approach retirement. The respondents in South Carolina already of retirement age (sixty-five and older) did not seem to see much promise in Obama's economic relief proposals. Obama made an intensive effort to register and woo younger voters. He did win the majority of the eighteen to twenty-nine group, with 55 percent compared to 44 percent for McCain. Perhaps Obama's greatest success was with the younger segment in this category, so that poll respondents over twenty-five years of age balanced their

Table 7.4 Exit Poll Results Reporting Demographic Factors in the 2008 Presidential Vote (in percent)

Voter Characteristics or Attitude	McCain	Obama	Percent of Category
Race			
White	73	26	71
African American	4	96	25
Other	—	—	4
Gender			
Male	58	41	46
Female	51	48	54
Gender by Race			
White Males	76	23	34
White Females	70	29	37
Black Males	3	97	11
Black Females	4	96	14
Age			
18 to 29	44	55	18
30 to 44	46	54	29
45 to 64	39	61	39
65+	66	33	13
Education			
No High School	—	—	5
High School Graduate	53	47	22
Some College	55	44	31
College Graduate	63	37	24
Post to Graduate Study	50	50	18
Income			
Under $30,000	40	60	20
$30- 50,000	48	51	19
$50- 75,000	66	33	23
$75- 100,000	60	40	15
Over $100,000	63	37	22
Ideology			
Liberal	15	84	17
Moderate	42	58	42
Conservative	86	14	40
Party Identification			
Democratic	8	92	38
Republican	96	4	41
Independent/Other	57	40	20

continued >

Table 7.4 (continued)

Voter Characteristics or Attitude	McCain	Obama	Percent of Category
Christian Right (Whites Only)			
Yes	85	15	40
No	35	64	60
Direction of Economy Next Year			
Worried	58	41	87
Not Worried	51	49	12
Bush Job Rating			
Approve	92	8	36
Disapprove	39	60	64
Which Issue Mattered Most?			
Energy Policy	—	—	8
War in Iraq	36	64	11
Economy	56	44	63
Terrorism	—	—	8
Health Care	—	—	6
Race as a Factor in Deciding for Whom to Vote			
A Factor	59	41	31
Not a Factor	56	43	68
First Year Ever Voted?			
Yes	40	59	14
No	60	40	86

Source: MSNBC Exit Poll for South Carolina, November 4, 2008:
http://www.msnbc.msn.com/id/25384430/

enthusiasm with support for McCain. Only 14 percent of respondents said this was the first year they had voted, but among them Obama won 59 percent of the vote.

Turning to the effect of voter income levels on vote choice, Senator McCain had over 60 percent support in exit poll respondents making over fifty thousand dollars annually, 66 percent in the fifty thousand dollar to seventy-five thousand dollar group, 60 percent in the seventy-five thousand dollar to one hundred thousand dollar group, and 63 percent in the more than one hundred thousand dollar group. This yields an average support level of 63 percent for middle- to upper-income voters. Obama's greatest share was 60 percent support from the 20 percent of respondents who made less than thirty thousand dollars per year. There was about an even split, 48 percent for McCain and 51 percent for Obama, for the voters in the thirty thousand dollar to fifty thousand dollar category. Generally, African Americans have low incomes in South Carolina and various estimates of a black middle class range up to 10 percent of total population. The income shares are reasonable indicators of the correlation between race and income in South Carolina. Higher income categories, mostly white, supported McCain. Obama's support is the inverse: lower income categories, mostly black. There is also the paradox of low income whites voting against their apparent economic interests by supporting Republican policies that generally put them in a marketplace where it is difficult for them to compete. A South Carolina saying goes, "There is nothing like the voter who rails against high taxes, while paying no taxes." That tradition was established when many poor South Carolinians, white and black alike, paid no income taxes until paycheck withholding became an accepted practice.

Ideology and Party Identification. The National Exit Pool data in Table 7.4 confirm the ideological split in South Carolina. It appears as fundamental as the racial divide. Self-identified liberals, making up 17 percent of respondents, supported Obama at 84 percent, while self-identified conservatives, 40 percent of respondents, supported McCain at a rate of 86 percent. Moderates, 42 percent of respondents, gave Obama a solid advantage over McCain (58 percent to 42 percent). By this measure, South Carolina Republicans did not do their usually successful job of neutralizing moderates. By party identification, there were fewer independents than usual as tracked in the Institute of Public Service and Policy Research poll, which indicated only 20 percent of voters putting themselves in that category. These independents gave McCain 57 percent of their support. Democrats were 38 percent of exit poll respondents, which approached parity with Republicans at 41 percent. These Democrats supported Obama by a margin of nine to one.

Other Political Factors. Throughout the primaries and the campaign, much was made of the influence of evangelicals and the Christian right in South Carolina politics. Forty percent of whites identified with the Christian right and supported McCain at a rate of 85 percent. Obama won two-thirds (64 percent) of white respondents who answered "no" when asked whether they identified with the Christian right.

The state of the economy was by far the central issue surrounding the November vote. Eighty-seven percent of respondents reported being "worried about the direction of the economy next year." Fifty-eight percent of them endorsed McCain. Among all significant issues, 63 percent of voters mentioned the economy, and 56 percent of this category supported McCain. Obama was more convincing while discussing the war in Iraq as an issue, but only 11 percent of voters thought it mattered most, and Obama split their support with McCain (64 percent to 36 percent).

The disapproval rating for sitting president George W. Bush was high at 64 percent, but even the disapproving voters supported McCain 39 percent of the time. Among the 36 percent approving of President Bush's job performance, 92 percent supported McCain. Although there is no convincing evidence of positive or negative Bush "coattails," it does appear that the Republican core is consistently over one-third of voters in South Carolina and that moderates, while disapproving, are still loyal to the Republican candidate to a large degree, in this case almost 40 percent.

Lightning did not strike for the Democrats in the 2008 presidential campaign in South Carolina. The early enthusiasm for Democratic success faded to the expected Republican success. Maybe Palmetto State Democrats will hold out hope for 2012 on two grounds. They will have an incumbent president with a potentially successful first term to advertise. And the 2008 Republican margin in South Carolina was not as bright a red as usual. Should the 58 percent for Bush in 2000 followed by the 54 percent for McCain in 2008 fall another four percent, the 2012 November presidential contest may actually be competitive.

Analysis: South Carolina in the United States Senate

Lindsey Graham won reelection by a typical Republican margin in South Carolina, 57.5 percent to 42.3 percent over his Democratic rival, Bob Conley.[16] Some expected the race to be close. However, the Democrat was entirely unknown, not a party regular, and did not campaign actively. Graham had a 3.5 percent increase over his result in 2002 when he was elected to succeed Strom Thurmond. He received over 70 percent of the vote in Lexington County (73 percent) and hometown counties Oconee (73 percent), and Pickens (72 percent). In thirteen other counties his margin was over 60 percent, and it was over 50 percent in fifteen additional counties. The Democrat won fifteen counties, primarily in rural, less-populated areas. Conley carried small, largely African American Allendale County 73 percent to only 27 percent for Graham, for example.

Graham had generated some criticism among conservatives for being too "moderate" because he worked with Senate Democrats on expanding health care, limiting Chinese imports, and not filibustering judicial appointments. He also differed with the Bush administration on medical issues, payment of fees by litigants, and treatment of unlawful combatants. Graham also challenged the status quo as a steady advocate of national Republican Party reform. He consistently supported Senator John McCain's presidential campaign, to the chagrin of many Republicans. Yet, if the South Carolina tradition of endlessly reelecting U.S. senators continues, Graham should be around for a long time.

Analysis: South Carolina in the United States House of Representatives

South Carolina's congressional delegation has four Republicans and two Democrats, all of whom were reelected in 2008.

In the First District, incumbent Republican Henry Brown defeated a strong Democratic challenger, Linda Ketner, by a surprisingly close margin (51.9 percent to 47.9 percent). Ketner is the daughter of a founder of the Food Lion grocery chain and was able to finance most of her campaign. Brown had acquired a reputation as something of a "bumbler" who let a fire get off his property onto federal forest lands and who then threatened retaliation against the forest service if they fined him. He eventually paid a small fine. With an ultraconservative voting record since elected to Congress in 2000, he won in 2006 with 60 percent of the vote. This election was a wake- up call for an otherwise comfortable incumbent.

In the Second District, Republican incumbent Joe Wilson had a 7.56 percent margin over Democratic competitor Rob Miller. Miller is an Iraq war veteran and former U.S. Marine Corps officer who ran an active, well-financed campaign. The old story is that a challenger to an incumbent from Lexington County needs to win all the other parts of the district by at least twenty-five thousand votes before Lexington is counted. This time, Wilson carried Lexington by thirty-three thousand votes to a 54.7 percent to 46 percent victory, perhaps closer than he would have liked. In 2004 and 2006, Wilson had defeated the Democratic challenger, Michael Ellisor, by 65 percent and 63 percent, respectively.

In the Third District, Republican incumbent Gresham Barrett gained 64.7 percent versus 35.2 percent for female Democratic opponent, Jane Ballard Dyer. Dyer won small McCormick County, but did not do well elsewhere. Barrett was first elected in 2002 and won the district with 63 percent of the vote in 2006, about the same margin as President Bush polled in the district each time. Barrett is a popular campaigner who advocates the conservative cultural issues so important in the Upstate. He frequently says the government should be run like a business, Barrett's furniture store, for example. He is widely rumored to become a gubernatorial candidate in 2010.

In the Fourth District, returning Republican Bob Inglis won 60.1 percent against two rivals, C. Faye Walters of the Green Party and Paul Corden, a Democrat. Inglis is a second-round representative. He was first elected to Congress in 1992 and limited himself to three terms. He lost the U.S. Senate race to Ernest Hollings in 1998. In 2004, he won election to Congress again with 70 percent of the vote, taking the place of Jim DeMint. DeMint won the U.S. Senate seat in 2004 when Hollings did not run. Inglis carried 60 percent of the district in 2008 compared to 64 percent in 2006. He initially cultivated the reputation of an aloof intellectual, but now emphasizes practical politics and local district interests.

The Fifth District saw incumbent Democrat John Spratt win with 61.6 percent to 37 percent for Republican Albert F. Spencer and 1.3 percent for Constitution Party candidate Frank Waggoner. Spratt is a Democrat whom the Republicans oppose frequently, but can never seem to defeat. Spratt was first elected in 1982 and is a leading Democrat on armed services and budget matters. In 2008, Spratt carried every county in his district with almost 62 percent of the vote. He won 57 percent in 2006 when he had a tougher challenge from a high-spending Republican real estate developer whose employment practices proved controversial. The Republican base in the district is formidable. It is 64 percent white and supported George W. Bush by 55 percent in 2000 and 57 percent in 2004. Spratt's family roots in the area, his cosmopolitan education, and his broadly recognized congressional record help make him a successful Democrat in what might otherwise be a Republican district.

The Sixth District was not competitive again in 2008. Incumbent Democrat and U.S. House majority whip, James Clyburn, had 67.5 percent of the vote against Republican Nancy Harrelson's 32.5 percent. The district was created in 1992 as a black-majority district under the Voting Rights Act. Clyburn is a popular incumbent who has not faced significant opposition since his 1992 election. His 2004 and 2006 margins were over 60 percent (67 percent and 64 percent). He is a strong advocate of local projects and a favorite among congressional peers. In 2002 he became chair of the House Democratic Caucus and was named House majority whip in 2006.

Analysis: The General Assembly Races

Republicans first gained control of the state House in 1994 and of the Senate in 2001. Their dominance continues, as most House and Senate seats in the South Carolina General Assembly were not contested in 2008. Approximately two-thirds of the 124 House members and 46 Senators were incumbents with no opponents. Another quarter of the members in each body were new candidates from the same party as the outgoing occupant. As "shadow incumbents," all of them were challenged by the opposing party (twenty-eight in the House, and eleven Senators). Only about 10 percent (thirteen House races and five Senate races) were open, contested elections. With little opportunity for electoral challenges or upsets, the Republican domination continues in the General Assembly. There are seventy-six House Republicans to forty-eight Democrats and twenty-six Senate Republicans to twenty Democrats.

Uniquely, South Carolina has the lowest rate of women legislators across the nation. There are seventeen women in the House (13.7 percent) and no women in the state Senate. This equates to 10 percent of 170 legislative seats after the 2008 elections. Among House members there are twenty-nine African Americans (23.3 percent) and nine (or 19.6 percent) black senators. Three black Republicans ran in November for House seats. Two had opposition and lost; one had no opposition and became the state's first African American House Republican in over a century.

Conclusion

South Carolina has often been a key player in national politics, particularly in relation to the state's presidential primaries.[17] The 2008 election was no different, since both McCain and Obama solidified their campaigns and shed significant rivals in the South Carolina primaries. In the aftermath of the general election, both parties claimed success.[18] Republican state party chair Katon Dawson soon launched what was ultimately to be an unsuccessful campaign to become Republican National Committee chair, in an apparent effort to highlight South Carolina's key role in Republican nominating primaries and to give the state continued prominence in Republican affairs headed toward the 2012 election.[19]

The future of South Carolina politics turns on the question of whether South Carolina Republicans are the normal majority party or whether a more competitive political environment will emerge. Holding the first national debate among the contenders for the nomination and the

"First in the South" Democratic primary was a concession by the Democratic National Committee to give more prominence to South Carolina. Democratic gubernatorial candidate Jim Hodges had restored some hope for the Democrats after defeating an incumbent Republican governor, David Beasley, in 1998 by over 87,000 votes, a 53 percent to 45 percent victory. The Democrats' hope was short-lived as Republican Mark Sanford recaptured the governorship by 64,000 votes in 2002. In the face of continued Republican control of the General Assembly, the governorship, all statewide elected officers except the state superintendent of education, both United States senators, and the House congressional delegation (four to two), Republicans seem to be in control and elections are not very competitive, unless some special circumstances help the Democrats on occasion. The only exception is James Clyburn's safe majority-minority Sixth Congressional District seat.

Democrats were helped in January 2008 before the primaries when senators Hillary Clinton and Barack Obama were prominent participants in Dr. Martin Luther King Day. But, by the end of 2008, local leaders seemed less concerned with politics than with putting renewed interest in 2009 on King and his work.[20] South Carolina Republicans have often advertised the "Big Tent" concept, in which African Americans are welcomed. Like skeptics when the traveling preacher is in town and seeking converts under the revival tent, African Americans have depended more on direct connections with national Democratic leaders than South Carolina Republicans. As president, Obama has promised to emphasize performance and effective governance over issues of gender, ethnicity, race, or special needs. Consequently, Obama may not always appear to promote the specific interests of African Americans. Thus, Republicans hope to attract South Carolina blacks who are less dependent on a spoils system, but that prospect seems remote given the overwhelming support the state's African Americans have given to the Democrats in general and to Obama in particular. More interesting, perhaps, is whether Obama's performance and governance will succeed in attracting more whites to Democratic candidates. If so, Republican domination of the state's politics may be less clearly predictable.

III

*Elections in
the Rim South*

8

Arkansas

He's Not One of (Most of) Us

Jay Barth, Janine A. Parry,
and Todd G. Shields

Introduction

Purplish-red Arkansas received a fair amount of attention compared to its southern neighbors in both 2000 and 2004. While George W. Bush ultimately carried Bill Clinton's home state in both elections, he did so by only single digits. The 2008 presidential election once again found Arkansas in the spotlight, but only *after* the votes were counted. In sharp contrast with speculation in late 2007 that the state would be perhaps the only southern state with a chance at battleground status if Hillary Clinton were the Democratic nominee, the party's ultimate banner-carrier was crushed by Republican John McCain in the general election, with Barack Obama carrying only nine of the state's seventy-five counties. The margin, predicted by most polling organizations to be similar to the Bush margins, more than doubled from 2004 and quadrupled that of 2000. What explains the 20-point gap in favor of the Republican nominee in a state dominated by Democrats in state politics and so recently a regular battleground in other national-level contests?

Based on a detailed narrative of the campaigns, polling data, and county-level election returns, we conclude that the state's white, rural voters —despite being as disenchanted with the Republican brand as Americans as a whole—swung hard for McCain or, more accurately, against Obama. Once again, as has been the case in modern presidential elections, it is the behavior of Arkansas voters residing in the state's "rural swing counties" that shaped the large pro-GOP margin in 2008.[1] Especially in light of strong support in the state for his chief Democratic rival—former Arkansas First Lady Hillary Clinton—we conclude that Arkansans' emphatic rejection of Obama was the consequence of a persistent and distinctive provincialism which continues to drive the behavior of the Natural State's voters, especially the white voters from these rural swing counties.

The Primary Season

While the voters of Arkansas again found themselves irrelevant to the nominating process, two particular Arkansans played a vital role in shaping the dynamics on both the GOP and Democratic sides during the primary season. Hillary Clinton, First Lady of Arkansas for a dozen years, did an effective job of reconnecting herself with her adopted state of Arkansas during the lead-up to her presidential bid. She made, for example, two high-profile visits to the state during 2007. For her appearance at the state Democratic Party's large annual fundraiser, the Jefferson-Jackson Dinner in late June, about 4,000 were on hand to hear her headline speech. The day before that appearance, most of the state's elected Democrats had endorsed her candidacy.[2] As south Arkansas congressman Mike Ross put it, "I'm surprised that people would even ask who we're supporting."[3] During a visit back to the state for a series of events that raised her campaign $650,000 two months later, Clinton collected the endorsement of Arkansas's popular governor, Mike Beebe.[4] During her August appearance, Clinton said, "I not only know the difference between Mountain Home and Mountain View and not only have been to Magnolia and a lot of other places throughout the state, but I intend to campaign throughout Arkansas."[5] Bill Clinton and daughter Chelsea also made appearances in the state on behalf of the senator, while Hillary herself made one last appearance in central Arkansas the week before the primary.[6]

The fact that the Democratic establishment was so firmly in Clinton's camp from the beginning discouraged any of her Democratic rivals from investing precious time in the state. While he had made a late October 2006 visit to stump for then gubernatorial candidate Mike Beebe, eventual nominee Barack Obama made no appearances in the state of Arkansas during the primary period. Obama did send a handful of staff to establish a small Little Rock office just before the February primary, but it was dwarfed by the Clinton operation manned by large numbers of longtime Clinton activists.[7] Many of those Clinton activists also participated in a rebirth of the Arkansas Travelers program that sent Arkansans to other key states to tout their friend's attributes, as had been the case in 1992 for her husband.[8] Talking about her work in the state, Arkansas friends of Clinton also played prominent roles in a web-based advertising campaign "The Hillary We Know."

While it was no surprise that Clinton was a dominant force in the battle for her party's presidential nomination, an Arkansan was also one of the last two men standing in the messy battle for the GOP nomination. Former Arkansas governor Mike Huckabee began visiting Iowa to test the waters for a presidential run in the fall of 2005.[9] His investigation for a run continued after he left the governorship in early 2007 after a decade in office, and he was fully in the race by March. Huckabee lagged dramatically in fundraising throughout 2007 and, at times, his place in the Republican field appeared tenuous. The state's longtime governor, who had developed some enemies within the state's Republican establishment, was able to announce the support of barely a third of the state's GOP legislators when his "Arkansas GOP Leadership Team" was rolled out, even after Huckabee's surprise second-place finish in the Iowa straw poll in August had begun to gain him attention in that first caucus state.[10] In fact, two of Huckabee's most strident critics traveled to Iowa to campaign for rival Ron Paul during the caucus campaign there.[11] However, most Arkansas Republican activists came around to Huckabee, and the former governor reaped over a tenth of his total contributions in the race from Arkansans.[12]

While Huckabee raised considerably less than his rivals overall, his raw political talent and his success at earning free media from tactics like the so-called "floating cross" Christmas message maximized his resources, leading to his solid victory over Mitt Romney in the January Iowa caucuses. Further, Huckabee's success in Iowa meant that the former governor's Arkansas years received a great deal of analysis in the national press in the days just before and after that victory.[13] It also ensured he would remain in the race through the Arkansas primary and guaranteed that, as on the Democratic side, Arkansas would receive limited attention during that primary campaign, with no visits to the state by Huckabee's rivals.

State Democratic Party officials made a bid in 2006 that Arkansas should be one of the states to hold a contest before Super Tuesday.[14] They were unsuccessful, and South Carolina took the spot. Instead, Arkansas held its primary on Super Tuesday, February 5, having shifted from its traditional late May date. Because of Clinton's and Huckabee's dominance, the real drama on the primary election night in Arkansas came not from the election results but from a series of tornadoes that killed seven and shut down vote counting in several counties.[15] Still, Clinton won what was to be her largest percentage in a contest during the nomination period, gaining just over 70 percent of the state's Democratic vote, compared to just over 25 percent for Obama. Huckabee, who was in Little Rock to celebrate the victory, won the votes of six in ten GOP voters, tripling the primary vote of second-place finisher McCain. The victories of Clinton and Huckabee were comprehensive ones geographically (Huckabee won all seventy-five of the state's counties and Clinton won all but three) and across demographic groups, except that exit polls indicated that three in four African American voters in the Democratic primary supported Obama.[16]

With competition so effectively curbed by not one but two "inside" candidates, perhaps the most important story to emerge from the Arkansas primary election vote was the dramatic increase in the share of voters who cast votes in the Republican primary. Over 42 percent of Arkansans participating in the February 5 semiopen primary voted in the GOP contest, the highest percentage in modern history (see Table 8.1).[17] In previous cycles, except 1988, the Arkansas primary had been held after competition for the nominations had ended and had also been held in conjunction with local elections often determined in the Democratic primary. In a foreshadowing of Republican success in the fall, the state's traditional minority party showed evidence of significant strength in the state electorate.

The General Election Campaign

Hillary Clinton, had she been the nominee, clearly would have devoted substantial energy and resources to winning Arkansas's electoral votes in the fall. In her absence from the Democratic ticket, however, neither party's nominee aggressively competed for the Natural State's electoral votes. This was a significant deviation from the previous two election cycles, when voters were actively courted by candidates and party organizations of all stripes.

Both Clinton and Huckabee, as their parties' runners-up for the presidential nomination, of course were mentioned as running mates for Obama and McCain, respectively, but it soon became clear that neither was a serious option. Arkansan Wesley Clark also received some mention

Table 8.1 Primary Voter Turnout in Arkansas in Presidential Election Years, 1976–2008

Year	Democratic Primary	Republican Primary
1976	525,968	22,797
1980	415,406	8,177
1984	492,321	19,040
1988	497,506	68,305
1992	502,130	52,297
1996	300,389	42,814
2000	246,900	44,573
2004	256,848	38,363
2008	315,322	229,665

Source: Arkansas Secretary of State.

as an Obama running mate until his controversial June comments questioning whether McCain "getting shot down" in a "fighter plane" made him inherently qualified to be commander in chief.[18]

Consequently, aside from brief fundraising trips to the state by McCain in April and August, none of the four principals or their spouses made a stop in Arkansas in the lead-up to the general election.[19] The McCain campaign did not open an Arkansas office, and, reeling from its losses in 2006, the state's own Republican party was equally inactive. The Obama campaign finally did open a Little Rock headquarters in the late summer, but volunteers were used primarily to activate voters in other battleground states, especially neighboring Missouri.[20] To be sure, Democratic party operatives were stunned by the midday shooting of the state party chair, Bill Gwatney, inside state party headquarters in August. The tragedy contributed little, however, to the state's low political profile in 2008. All evidence suggests that state Democrats—many stung by Clinton's loss—were simply unmotivated to invest significant energy in the race. Tellingly, just before his murder, Gwatney observed, "Senator Obama can't expect that healing to begin unless he comes to Arkansas and campaigns at some point."[21]

But the Obama camp likely had concluded that Arkansas was a poor investment of time or resources. A win there was unlikely, and not solely because of so many Democrats' bitter disappointment that Hillary Clinton was not the nominee. The reality is that most white Arkansans remain racially conservative and the African American population is too small to counter the white majority's political preferences. For example, in the Arkansas Poll conducted in October, half of respondents were asked how many (of five) statements "troubled" them about Barak Obama; the other half heard a list that differed in only one respect: the item "he has two children" was replaced with "if elected, he will be the first black president." The result of this simple list experiment was telling: the average number of troubling statements was higher for the latter group (1.55 versus 1.49). For whites only, it was 1.74 and 1.63, respectively. (All differences were statistically significant at the .001 level.)[22]

Indeed, even when it came to light in late July that Obama had genealogical links to Arkansans through his mother's family, Arkansans remained unimpressed.[23] And the sense that the candidate was not "one of them," seemed to spread beyond race to other cultural attributes, with many Arkansans coming to believe that Obama differed from them in other fundamental ways. For example, one distant relative of Obama, an elderly Democrat, was emphatic in her belief that the presidential candidate was a Muslim. "He'd have to come to my home and eat some of my purple-hull peas before I'd believe him," the woman said of Obama. "And my fried okra. Anyone that breaks bread with me, I'd have more confidence in him."[24] Clearly, many white, rural Arkansans had difficulty seeing the urbane Obama eating fried okra in their homes.

Still, both Clintons stumped vigorously for their party's nominee as election day neared. Hillary Clinton appeared at a State Capitol rally and Obama fundraiser in Little Rock about three weeks before election day.[25] Two weeks later, Bill Clinton was joined by Beebe and other Democratic officials for three stops in the state. "Unless the wheels come off, [Obama]'s going to win and win big," the former president said at a Pine Bluff rally. "Those of us on this stage, who love this state, do not want to see Arkansas left off that train."[26] Such exhortations came to naught.

In the end, the relative absence of a presidential campaign in the state allowed superficial impressions about the presidential candidates—together with the residual disappointment over Hillary Clinton's failed bid for the nomination—to drive voters' attitudes. President Bush's low approval ratings in the state (27 percent in the fall Arkansas Poll) would suggest that Arkansans would be hesitant to give their votes to his party's standard-bearer. However, it was the deep impression that Barack Obama was not "one of them"—hardened by no contact with the candidate himself—that led independents, and even Democrats, to vote for McCain or, in the latter case, to simply stay home. The result was an Arkansas electorate skewed, in nearly every respect, more heavily Republican than in 2004.

The Outcome

The fact that Arkansas cast its six electoral college votes for Republican John McCain surprised no one. Every poll conducted in the state between February and late October of 2008 placed the state squarely in the red column (see Table 8.2); in fact, the average projected margin of victory among these polls was 15 points. Still, few anticipated the actual gap would be 20 points, more than double that of the 2004 election. Fully 58.8 percent of Arkansas voters cast ballots for McCain as compared to 38.8 percent for Obama (see Table 8.3).

Indeed, by every measure, the Arkansas contest was a rout of unexpected magnitude.[27] Although Massachusetts Democrat John Kerry managed in 2004 to pocket victories in twenty-one of the state's seventy-five counties (and Gore claimed thirty-three in 2000), Obama hung on to only nine of these, actually losing Democratic vote share in seven of them (see Table 8.4). In sharp contrast to nationwide patterns, Democratic vote share increased in only six Arkansas counties. Four of the six were among the most urban counties in the state, including the state's largest county—Pulaski—which provided Obama a healthy majority. As shown in Table 8.7, turnout also increased sharply from 2004 in Pulaski County, highlighting the gulf that developed between urban and rural Arkansas around

Table 8.2 Selected Polls in Arkansas, Presidential Race 2008

Poll and Polling Dates	McCain	Obama	Spread
Survey USA, February 26–28	53	33	20 points
UCA, March 6–11	43	27	16 points
Rasmussen, March 18	59	30	29 points
Rasmussen, May 12	57	33	24 points
Rasmussen, June 6	48	39	9 points
Rasmussen, July 17	52	39	13 points
ARG, September 20–22	53	41	12 points
Rasmussen, September 22	51	42	9 points
Arkansas Poll, October 1–21	51	36	15 points
Research 2000, October 21–22	52	41	11 points
Rasmussen, October 27	54	44	10 points
ARG, October 28–31	51	44	7 points

Source: Polling results compiled by RealClearPolitics.com throughout the election cycle; accessed at http://www.realclearpolitics.com/epolls/2008/president/ar/arkansas_mccain_vs_obama-592.html#polls, accessed November 29 2008.

Table 8.3 Results of the 2008 Arkansas Presidential and Congressional Elections (in percent)

Candidate (Party)	Vote Percentage (2004 party vote)	Vote Total (2004 party vote)
President		
John McCain/Sarah Palin (R)	58.8 (54.3)	628,711 (572,898)
Barack Obama/Joe Biden (D)	38.8 (44.6)	414,828 (469,953)
Ralph Nader/Matt Gonzales (I)	1.2 (0.6)	12,443 (6,171)
Bob Barr/Wayne Allyn Root (L)	0.4 (0.2)	4,633 (2,352)
Chuck Baldwin/Darrell L. Castle (C)	0.4 (0.2)	3,914 (2,083)
Cynthia McKinney/Rosa Clemente (G)	0.3 (0.1)	3,359 (1,488)
Gloria La Riva/Eugene Puryear (SL)	0.1 (na)	1,075 (na)
U.S. Senate		
Mark Pryor (D)*	79.4	784,934
Rebekah Kennedy (G)	20.6	203,447
U.S. House of Representatives		
First District		
Marion Berry (D)*	unopposed	
Second District		
Vic Snyder (D)*	76.6	212,366
Deb McFarland (G)	23.3	64,633
Daniel Suits (write-in)	0.0	105
Third District		
John Boozman (R)*	78.5	214,097
Abel Noah Tomlinson (G)	21.5	58,572
Fourth District		
Mike Ross (D)	86.2	200,469
Joshua Drake (G)	13.8	32,043

Key: * denotes incumbent, R = Republican Party, D = Democrat Party, P = Populist Party, L = Libertarian Party, C = Constitutional Party, G = Green Party, SL = Socialism and Liberation Party, I = Independent.

Source: Data compiled from the website of the Arkansas Secretary of State, http://www.arelections.org, accessed November 27, 2008.

Table 8.4 Republican Vote in Arkansas 2000, 2004, and 2008 by County
(in percent)

County	2000	2004	2008	Gain 00–04 % pts	Gain 04–08 % pts	Gain 00–08 % pts	% black
Arkansas	52.6	54.6	60.0	2	5.4	7.4	24.5
Ashley	46.9	53.7	62.3	6.8	8.6	15.4	27.8
Baxter	57.1	60.1	64.3	3	4.2	7.2	0.3
Benton	64.9	68.4	67.2	3.5	-1.2	2.3	1.1
Boone	62.8	66.3	68.3	3.5	2	5.5	0.3
Bradley	45.1	47.3	56.1	2.2	8.8	11	28.2
Calhoun	**51.6**	**58.2**	**65.9**	**6.6**	**7.7**	**14.3**	**23.2**
Carroll	57.9	59.0	57.5	1.1	-1.5	-0.4	0.3
Chicot	35.1	36.3	40.3	1.2	4	5.2	53.9
Clark	43.8	44.9	50.7	1.1	5.8	6.9	22.3
Clay	**38.2**	**45.3**	**55.0**	**7.1**	**9.7**	**16.8**	**0.3**
Cleburne	56.1	59.2	70.2	3.1	11	14.1	0.5
Cleveland	**52.8**	**57.5**	**69.9**	**4.7**	**12.4**	**17.1**	**13.5**
Columbia	53.9	57.8	61.1	3.9	3.3	7.2	36.6
Conway	**49.0**	**49.6**	**57.6**	**0.6**	**8**	**8.6**	**12.5**
Craighead	48.3	53.1	61.0	4.8	7.9	12.7	9.7
Crawford	61.3	65.6	71.5	4.3	5.9	10.2	1.1
Crittenden	44.3	45.3	41.9	1	-3.4	-2.4	49.4
Cross	48.8	54.6	61.6	5.8	7	12.8	23.4
Dallas	**47.2**	**50.2**	**53.0**	**3**	**2.8**	**5.8**	**40.7**
Desha	35.7	37.2	43.3	1.5	6.1	7.6	46.8
Drew	46.5	52.2	58.4	5.7	6.2	11.9	27.5
Faulkner	55.0	58.6	62.9	3.6	4.3	7.9	9.3
Franklin	53.4	57.4	68.1	4	10.7	14.7	0.7
Fulton	49.6	50.9	57.8	1.3	6.9	8.2	0.3
Garland	53.1	54.1	61.2	1	7.1	8.1	7.9
Grant	**54.6**	**62.1**	**73.9**	**7.5**	**11.8**	**19.3**	**3.1**
Greene	**46.7**	**51.9**	**63.0**	**5.2**	**11.1**	**16.3**	**0.3**
Hempstead	44.7	48.0	58.1	3.3	10.1	13.4	29.1
Hot Spring	**45.9**	**49.4**	**60.3**	**3.5**	**10.9**	**14.4**	**10.2**
Howard	**52.2**	**55.4**	**61.1**	**3.2**	**5.7**	**8.9**	**20.7**
Independence	**53.0**	**57.1**	**67.1**	**4.1**	**10**	**14.1**	**2.1**
Izard	**45.7**	**51.8**	**61.2**	**6.1**	**9.4**	**15.5**	**1.5**
Jackson	**37.5**	**42.3**	**55.9**	**4.8**	**13.6**	**18.4**	**19.4**
Jefferson	32.2	33.5	36.0	1.3	2.5	3.8	51.9
Johnson	**51.1**	**53.6**	**60.1**	**2.5**	**6.5**	**9**	**1.8**
Lafayette	**45.5**	**50.3**	**58.1**	**4.8**	**7.8**	**12.6**	**36.1**
Lawrence	**43.5**	**44.6**	**57.6**	**1.1**	**13**	**14.1**	**0.7**
Lee	32.8	36.6	38.7	3.8	2.1	5.9	57.2
Lincoln	43.0	46.8	57.1	3.8	10.3	14.1	32.9
Little River	43.4	48.6	63.0	5.2	14.4	19.6	21.2

continued >

Table 8.4 (continued)

County	2000	2004	2008	Gain 00–04 % pts	Gain 04–08 % pts	Gain 00–08 % pts	% black
Logan	55.4	59.4	67.7	4	8.3	12.3	1.3
Lonoke	59.1	65.4	72.7	6.3	7.3	13.6	6.5
Madison	60.2	60.7	62.8	0.5	2.1	2.6	0.2
Marion	56.6	60.1	63.2	3.5	3.1	6.6	0.3
Miller	52.9	57.6	65.8	4.7	8.2	12.9	23.4
Mississippi	41.3	43.3	49.9	2	6.6	8.6	34.1
Monroe	40.4	43.3	50.9	2.9	7.6	10.5	39.3
Montgomery	**56.9**	**59.8**	**65.3**	**2.9**	**5.5**	**8.4**	**0.6**
Nevada	48.0	50.4	56.7	2.4	6.3	8.7	32.7
Newton	64.4	63.5	67.0	-0.9	3.5	2.6	0.2
Ouachita	**45.6**	**50.2**	**53.9**	**4.6**	**3.7**	**8.3**	**40.2**
Perry	**52.8**	**55.0**	**64.2**	**2.2**	**9.2**	**11.4**	**2.0**
Phillips	33.9	35.6	34.5	1.7	-1.1	0.6	61.4
Pike	**57.3**	**59.8**	**68.8**	**2.5**	**9**	**11.5**	**3.9**
Poinsett	**41.3**	**46.0**	**61.8**	**4.7**	**15.8**	**20.5**	**7.4**
Polk	64.0	66.6	71.3	2.6	4.7	7.3	0.3
Pope	61.0	65.1	70.9	4.1	5.8	9.9	3.0
Prairie	**53.1**	**56.0**	**65.8**	**2.9**	**9.8**	**12.7**	**14.5**
Pulaski	43.9	44.6	43.5	0.7	-1.1	-0.4	34.0
Randolph	**45.5**	**47.4**	**57.2**	**1.9**	**9.8**	**11.7**	**1.2**
Saline	57.5	63.2	69.4	5.7	6.2	11.9	50.5
Scott	**60.3**	**62.3**	**69.9**	**2**	**7.6**	**9.6**	**3.2**
Searcy	64.3	64.3	70.9	0	6.6	6.6	0.5
Sebastian	58.5	61.8	66.3	3.3	4.5	7.8	0.2
Sevier	49.2	54.7	68.3	5.5	13.6	19.1	6.3
Sharp	51.9	54.9	62.5	3	7.6	10.6	4.4
St. Francis	40.2	39.8	41.7	-0.4	1.9	1.5	0.9
Stone	**54.0**	**57.5**	**66.4**	**3.5**	**8.9**	**12.4**	**0.3**
Union	55.4	58.9	62.2	3.5	3.3	6.8	33.0
Van Buren	49.9	54.1	63.8	4.2	9.7	13.9	0.5
Washington	54.9	55.7	55.5	0.8	-0.2	0.6	2.7
White	**59.5**	**64.3**	**72.2**	**4.8**	**7.9**	**12.7**	**4.0**
Woodruff	33.9	33.7	43.7	-0.2	10	9.8	28.7
Yell	**49.7**	**55.2**	**63.1**	**5.5**	**7.9**	**13.4**	**1.5**
Average (All Counties)	50.1	53.3	60.1	3.3	6.8	10.0	na
Average (RSC)	49.6	53.6	62.6	3.9	9.1	13.0	na
Statewide Vote	51.3	54.3	58.7	3.0	4.4	7.4	na

Key: Bolded counties denote Diane Blair's "rural swing counties." RSC = Rural Swing Counties. na=not available.

Source: Data compiled by the authors from the website of the Arkansas Secretary of State, http://www.arelections.org, accessed November 28, 2008.

the Obama candidacy. Also among the counties that shifted Democratic was Benton County, home to global retail giant Wal-Mart. On the surface, such a development is surprising, but the 2004 vote share there was so strong—68.4 percent—it could hardly be expected to grow. Instead, Benton County's Republican vote share dipped, barely, from 68.4 percent to 67.2 percent. The other two counties that shifted pro-Democratic from 2004 to 2008 were among the most heavily African American counties in the state.

Republican vote share, by contrast, increased in sixty-nine Arkansas counties. In many cases the rise was dramatic. For example, the percentage of ballots cast for McCain in Poinsett County jumped nearly 16 points over Bush's 2004 performance there, making it one of eleven Arkansas counties to switch from the Democratic to Republican column in 2008. Poinsett, notably, is one of twenty-six rural swing counties identified by Diane Blair in the 1980s.[28] Arkansas elections often turn on the behavior of voters in these counties, voters who are—generally speaking—disproportionately white and rural. Indeed, while the Republican vote share increase averaged four points among all Arkansas counties, it averaged more than nine points in the swing counties. Tellingly, not a single one of the state's rural swing counties awarded a majority of its votes to Obama. The ethnic dynamic in these counties becomes even clearer in looking at the relationship between Republican vote share and the final column of Table 8.4. Although African Americans comprise 15.7 percent of the statewide population, the twenty Arkansas counties with the highest Republican vote shares were, on average, only 5.1 percent black.

Social/Demographic Factors

To understand better the causes of the Arkansas blowout in 2008, we begin with the examination of pre- and post-election polling in the state presented in Table 8.5. Clearly, the GOP picked up substantial support from nearly every demographic group. We highlight several of these below.

Gender. In terms of the gender gap, the differences between the preferences of male and female Arkansas voters witnessed in previous elections disappeared in 2008. Specifically, the 2004 Arkansas gender gap in support of Bush was 9 percentage points; in 2008, McCain garnered 58 percent of both men's and women's votes. Looking at the vote percentages among women only, we see that in 2004 Arkansas women split their votes nearly evenly, with 50 percent voting for Bush and 49 percent voting for Kerry. In 2008 only 39 percent of women voted for Obama while

Table 8.5 Poll Results of Arkansas Voters, 2008 (in percent)

Characteristic	All	Obama	McCain	GOP '04	Would have voted for Clinton
Party Identification					
Democrat	36	77	21	18	87
Republican	32	7	93	97	16
Independent	31	30	67	60	51
Ideology					
Liberal	14	76	20	19	76
Moderate	41	52	46	40	66
Conservative	45	16	82	82	35
White Evangelical/ Born Again?					
Yes	56	20	77	71	47
No	44	64	34	35	59
Sex					
Male	45	40	58	59	53
Female	55	39	58	50	56
White Males	37	31	67	67	48
White Females	45	30	68	60	52
Racial/Ethnic Identity					
White	83	30	68	63	50
Black	12	95	5	6	81
Latino	3	—	—	—	82
Asian	1	—	—	—	75
Other	2	—	—	—	60
Age					
18–29	17	49	49	47	
30–44	27	39	60	60	
45–64	37	40	57	—	
65 or older	19	32	65	46	
Income					
Under $15,000	9	59	39	23	
$15–30,000	13	54	44	44	
$30–50,000	24	46	53	59	
$50–75,000	23	29	68	63	
$75–100,000	13	38	61	64	
$100–150,000	10	35	62	79	
$150–200,000	4	—	—	—	
$200,000 or more	4	—	—	—	

Table 8.5 (continued)

Characteristic	All	Obama	McCain	GOP '04	Would have voted for Clinton
Size of Community					
Urban	27	56	41	47	
Suburban	29	34	64	61	
Rural	44	33	64	55	
Vote on Initiative 1					
Yes	57	29	69	—	49
No	43	50	47	—	58
Most Important Issue					
Energy Policy	10	37	61	—	
Iraq	12	47	52	26	
Terrorism	11	11	87	83	
Economy	54	42	56	13	
Health Care	10	51	48	17	
Iraq War					
Strongly Approve	18	4	95	95	
Somewhat Approve	28	8	90	82	
Somewhat Disapprove	19	51	46	21	
Strongly Disapprove	34	77	21	6	
Race of Candidates Was					
Most Important Factor	6	—	—	—	
Important Factor	13	43	54	3	
Minor Factor	11	38	59	3	
Not a Factor	69	39	59	2	

Source: CNN 2004 and 2008 Arkansas State Exit Polls and the 2008 Arkansas Poll.

58 percent voted for McCain. The increased GOP support among women is significant given that women comprise a slightly larger portion of the Arkansas electorate than they do nationally (55 as compared to 53 percent). Further, if we narrow the focus to Caucasian women only, the gap grows even larger: white women cast a substantial 68 percent of their votes for McCain, compared with only 30 percent for Obama. Among white males the percentages were similar, with 67 percent voting for McCain and 31 percent voting for Obama, figures nearly identical to their 2004 behavior.

Ethnicity, Income, and Age. In contrast to gender, a large ethnic gap, as well as modest income and age gaps, are evident in the 2008 exit polls. Arkansas's relatively small black population (16 percent) again lent overwhelming support to the Democratic nominee, casting 95 percent of its ballots for Obama. The state's white voters, however, more than made up the difference by giving 68 percent of their substantial weight to McCain and only 30 percent to Obama. In terms of relative wealth, voters in the lowest and highest income categories strongly preferred Obama and McCain, respectively. With respect to age, we see that the GOP won by substantial margins across every category except for voters eighteen to twenty-nine years old. Among these voters, the division was evenly split, with 49 percent voting for Obama and 49 percent voting for McCain; only the very youngest Arkansans, those just eighteen to twenty-four years old (8 percent of the electorate), favored the Democratic candidate, and they did so just barely: 50 to 48 percent.

Other Social/Demographic Factors. Although the results are not shown here in the interest of space, there was little change between 2004 and 2008 in the role of education, religion, and marital status on the presidential preference of Arkansas voters. As with income, higher levels of educational attainment correlated both years with stronger GOP support. Identification with Christian evangelism and being married likewise increased the odds of casting a vote for the Republican ticket.

Political Factors

Issues. Perhaps strangely in light of their stark departure from the nation's vote choice, Arkansans ran nearly even with other Americans in identifying the most important problem. Fifty-four percent chose the economy while 12 percent saw Iraq as the most pressing concern. Still, among both groups of voters, a clear majority supported McCain. In fact, across nearly every issue included in the survey (for example, the economy, Iraq, terrorism, and energy policy) McCain received greater percentages of support. The only issue where Obama cleaved out a slight lead was among voters who chose health care as the most important problem. Among these voters, Obama received 51 percent while 48 percent voted for McCain.

Partisanship and Ideology. It was Arkansas's unaffiliated voters, long comparable to Democratic identifiers in size, who once again played a decisive role in the state's election outcome. In the 2004 election, Democrats and liberals, not surprisingly, gave their support to the Democratic nominee (82 and 79 percent, respectively). In the 2008 election, this support dropped—if only slightly. Conversely, Democratic support for the GOP candidate increased from 18 percent in the 2004 election to 21 percent in 2008. And although Republican support for that party's nominee fell from 97 percent in 2004 to 93 percent in 2008, the seven-point increase among independents more than compensated for that gap. Overall, then, despite the small drop in Republican Party loyalty, Arkansas Republicans cast their ballots in greater percentages for their party's nominee than did Democrats by an even wider margin than in 2004. This effect was boosted by McCain's advantage with independents. Further, although Obama won among ideologically liberal voters, his lead among moderates was only 6 percentage points. This was a substantial loss for Obama compared to Kerry's showing in 2004, when the Democrats picked up 58 percent of moderate voters (compared to 40 percent for Bush).

The Clinton Factor. Not only did the wounds of the failed Clinton candidacy demobilize Arkansas's Democratic Party activists, but evidence also suggests that the Clinton factor rippled into the Arkansas mass public. According to the October Arkansas Poll, for example, 54 percent of the electorate would have voted for the former First Lady had she been a nominee. Just 57 percent of these would-have-been Democrats in 2008 were prepared to cast ballots for Obama, compared with 26 percent for McCain. Exit poll findings on a similar question were nearly identical. Indeed, while we cannot know how a Clinton-McCain matchup actually would have been received in Arkansas or nationwide, Table 8.5 shows Clinton outperforming Obama—often by large margins—in every category, including in particular the white independents who often determine Arkansas elections.

Turnout. Despite the usual media hullabaloo about projected turnout in the days before November 4, Arkansas voters participated in 2008 at virtually the same rate as in 2004 (see Table 8.6). The absence of other high-profile competitive contests elsewhere on the ballot (see below) together with very little activity by either presidential campaign meant there was no direct mobilization effort in most communities. Even the state's black voters, expected by many to be particularly enthusiastic about the country's first major-party African American nominee, failed to show much life. Exit polls revealed just 12 percent of the Arkansas electorate was black in 2008, compared with 15 percent four years earlier.

Votes were concentrated, as in years past, in the state's ten largest counties, which together constitute about half of the state's total population (see Table 8.7). Again, however, turnout and vote preference varied widely in these counties. The relatively affluent suburban communities of

Table 8.6 General Election Voter Turnout in Arkansas, 1972–2008

Year	Percent Turnout (registered voters)
1972	69 (g)
1976	71 (g)
1980	77 (g)
1984	76 (g)
1988	69 (p)
1992	72 (p)
1996	65 (p)
2000	59 (p)
2004	64 (p)
2008	65 (p)

Key: Voter turnout figures are based on gubernatorial voting (g) or presidential voting (p), depending on the highest turnout race of the year. After shifting from two- to four-year terms in 1986, Arkansas gubernatorial elections are no longer held in presidential years.

Source: Data compiled from the website of the Arkansas Secretary of State, http://www.arelections.org, accessed November 29, 2008, and from various volumes of America Votes (Washington, D.C.: Congressional Quarterly Press).

Benton and Saline counties, for example, not only beat the statewide turnout average by five percentage points, but produced lopsided margins for the Republican nominee. Long-suffering Jefferson County, in contrast, diligently threw its support to the Democrat but managed only a 59 percent turnout rate, facilitating its dwindling influence against the Republican tide in Arkansas's presidential contests.

The statewide vote was further influenced by a notable shift in the partisan preferences of the active electorate. Specifically, the proportion of exit poll respondents identifying themselves as Democrats dropped from 41 percent in 2004 to 36 percent in 2008. While it is impossible to know whether some Democrats stayed home rather than voting for a nominee not of their choosing, or actually changed their partisan preference for this election, the consequence is clear: an expanded Republican advantage in Arkansas.

Other Elections

Just as consequential for turnout patterns in the state was the absence of major party opponents for any of the congressional candidates. This meant GOP congressman John Boozman was without a Democratic opponent,

Table 8.7 Registered Voter Turnout and Presidential Vote in the 10 Most Populous Arkansas Counties, 2008

County and Population 2007 estimate (2000 estimate)	Percent Pop. Change 2000–7 (1990–2000)	2008 Turnout % (2004)	Vote % Republican (2004)	Vote % Democrat (2004)
Pulaski 373,911	3.4	67.7	43.4	55.1
(361,474)	(3.4)	(59.6)	(44.2)	(55.0)
Benton 203,107	50.0	71.5	67.2	30.7
(153,406)	(57.3)	(70.5)	(68.4)	(30.5)
Washington 191,292	21.3	68.3	55.5	42.4
(157,715)	(39.1)	(72.5)	(55.7)	(43.1)
Sebastian 121,766	5.8	66.3	66.3	31.6
(115,071)	(15.5)	(69.0)	(61.7)	(37.3)
Faulkner 104,865	21.9	65.2	62.9	35.0
(86,014)	(43.3)	(62.3)	(58.6)	(39.6)
Garland 96,371	9.4	60.0	61.2	36.6
(88,068)	(20.0)	(57.0)	(54.1)	(44.9)
Saline 96,212	15.5	70.4	69.4	28.4
(83,529)	(30.1)	(66.1)	(63.2)	(35.9)
Craighead 91,552	11.4	57.9	61.0	36.5
(82,148)	(19.1)	(58.2)	(53.1)	(45.9)
Jefferson 78,986	-6.3	58.8	36.0	62.1
(84,278)	(-1.4)	(53.1)	(33.5)	(64.5)
White 73,441	8.9	60.2	72.2	25.0
(67,410)	(22.6)	(62.5)	(64.3)	(34.6)

Source: Data compiled from the U.S. Bureau of the Census and the website of the Arkansas Secretary of State, http://www.arelections.org, accessed November 28, 2008.

but, more importantly, none of the state's three Democratic congressmen nor the Democratic U.S. senator, Mark Pryor, was forced to campaign for reelection. (Pryor and three of the congressmen did face Green Party opposition. See Table 8.3.) Pryor had developed a war chest exceeding five million dollars, but the absence of a GOP opponent meant that he ran only a token campaign and developed no get-out-the-vote operation that might have promoted Democratic base turnout for the presidential election.

With the absence of legitimate congressional races, two initiatives—a proposed state constitutional amendment to allow the legislature to create a state lottery to fund higher education scholarships and a proposed

act to bar adoption or foster parenting by individuals in cohabitating relationships—received the most attention in the state. While the lottery had popularity across the political spectrum, the successful campaign by religious organizations for the adoption/foster parenting ban that passed with 57 percent of the vote may have promoted GOP turnout slightly.

Conclusion

It is puzzling that although Arkansans were just as troubled by a continuation of the policies of the Bush administration as other Americans, the participating electorate in the state did not shift Democratic as did voters elsewhere. Instead, Arkansans charged more emphatically toward Republicanism, compared with 2004, than any other state in the country. Although only time will tell for certain, the 2008 election had many attributes of a realigning election—an election that reveals dramatic, lasting shifts in the electorate. But in realigning elections of the past, while the vast majority of the country shifted toward the new majority party, other portions of the country rejected the change and shifted in the opposite direction. In rebuffing Barack Obama's Democratic Party, with its emphasis on social diversity so clearly exemplified in the candidate himself, many Arkansas voters—particularly those residing in homogenous, rural areas—demonstrated their emphatic discomfort with the "change" that inspired so many others nationwide.

This rejection of outsiders and their ideas is a central part of the Arkansas political experience. Generalized suspicion of meddlesome and intrusive outsiders was summed up in a traditional boast that Arkansas was the only state—because of its varied natural resources—that could survive even if a fence were built around it to prevent anything from coming in or going out. This proverbial bit of "wisdom" illustrates the imagined virtues and viability of an autonomous, culturally homogenous Arkansas. While all Arkansans are increasingly aware of a complicated and dynamic outside world, many are persistent in their belief that such change is undesirable. The 20-point gap in 2008 for Republican John McCain—or, rather, against Democrat Barak Obama—in a state that likely would have voted for Democrat (and honorary Arkansan) Hillary Clinton, is a telling example of the state's abiding provincialism.

9.

Florida

Obama Gives GOP the Blues

Jonathan Knuckey

Introduction

In 2008, Florida continued a record of having picked—with just the two exceptions of 1960 and 1992—the winner of the presidential election in every contest in the post–World War II era. Barack Obama's victory underscored how competitive Florida has become in presidential elections since 1992, and that is a state that now seems a perennial "battleground."[1] Gone are the days when Florida could be considered a reliably Republican state in presidential elections. In 1992, George H. W. Bush eked out a narrow win over Bill Clinton. Four years later Clinton devoted time and resources to the state and became the first Democrat to win the Sunshine State in twenty years. The 2000 presidential election, of course, essentially produced a tie between Al Gore and George W. Bush, and in doing so decided the outcome of the election. Bush increased his margin against John Kerry four years later, but Florida still remained the most competitive southern state.

Consequently, the fact that Florida was a fiercely contested state in the 2008 presidential election—with unprecedented resources being devoted to it—was not remarkable. On the other hand, the victory by a perceived liberal African American senator from Illinois was historic.

Prior Democratic victories in the post–World War II period were all achieved by southern Democrats (in 1948, 1964, 1976, and 1996)[2] and in the cases of Harry Truman, Lyndon Johnson, and Bill Clinton each had the advantage of being an incumbent president. Obama's victory against John McCain, in many ways a Republican candidate who was tailor-made for Florida, may indicate that the Sunshine State is evolving into a state that will increasingly lean Democratic in presidential elections.[3]

The 2006 Midterm Elections: A Mixed Partisan Outcome

The 2006 midterm elections featured two high-profile statewide races, for governor and U.S. Senate, the first time since 1998 that both offices had been contested in the same election cycle. The gubernatorial election was viewed as being the real battle, given that governor John Ellis "Jeb" Bush was term limited after two terms. In the end, the Republican candidate, attorney general Charlie Crist, comfortably defeated U.S. representative Jim Davis, 52 to 45 percent. In what was otherwise a poor year for the Republican party, Crist's name recognition and fundraising advantage, coupled with Jeb Bush's popularity, was enough to earn the GOP its third-straight gubernatorial victory in the Sunshine State.[4] Crist could also look forward to working with a state legislature that had solid Republican majorities in each chamber, with the GOP holding 64 percent of state House seats and 65 percent of state Senate seats.

Despite its status as a clear minority party in state politics, elections for the U.S. Senate seat and for the U.S. House of Representatives offered some solace for Democrats in Florida. Incumbent U.S. senator Bill Nelson cruised to victory over U.S. representative Katherine Harris, 60 to 38 percent. Harris, whose role as secretary of state in the denouement of the 2000 presidential election had garnered her considerable notoriety, was not even the overwhelming choice of many Republicans, having won less than 50 percent of the vote in the GOP primary. Any thought that the Republicans might take Nelson's seat disappeared with the emergence of Harris as the GOP nominee.

In addition to holding the U.S. Senate seat, the Democrats picked up two U.S. House seats. One of the gains, in the Sixteenth District, was the seat held by disgraced U.S. representative Mark Foley, who resigned his seat on September 29, 2006, just one day after allegations surfaced that he had sent suggestive e-mails and sexually explicit instant messages to teenage males who had served or were serving as congressional pages. Foley's name, however, would remain on the ballot for the congressional race even though the Republican Party of Florida chose State representative Joe Negron to run as the GOP's replacement candidate. Negron asked voters to "Punch Foley for Joe," in the hopes of holding the seat. Negron's strategy almost worked, as he narrowly lost 49 to 48 percent to Democratic candidate Tim Mahoney.[5]

The second Democratic gain saw E. Clay Shaw defeated in the Twenty-second District, in parts of Palm Beach. Shaw had handily won reelection in the prior two elections after a favorable redistricting plan in 2000. Still, the district was increasingly leaning toward the Democrats, with Al Gore and John Kerry carrying the district in the 2000 and 2004 presidential elections. Indeed, the district was the only Democratic presidential district in Florida with a Republican member of Congress.[6] It was a seat targeted by the Democrats in the 2006 midterm elections and one that was always likely to swing to the Democrats in a favorable political environment. The fact that the district was adjacent to the Sixteenth District probably also fueled an anti-GOP backlash. Thus, it was no surprise that Ron Klein, the former minority leader in the state Senate, won the seat, 51 to 48 percent.

Overall, the 2006 midterm elections suggested the 2008 presidential election would be intensely competitive. Given that the Republicans had a popular governor in Charlie Crist, and given the organizational strength of the state Republican Party, the GOP possessed a slight advantage heading into the election year. However, given that Florida was the closest southern state in 2004, with Bush defeating John Kerry 51 to 47 percent, and given some Democratic advances in the 2006 midterm elections, Florida could look forward to another intensely fought contest, irrespective of the identity of the two major party nominees.

The Presidential Nominations

Frontloading Florida

In an effort to garner the Sunshine State more attention and relevance in the 2008 presidential nomination cycle, the Republican-controlled state legislature decided to move the date of the presidential primaries to January 29, one week before "Super Tuesday."[7] On the Republican side, any state—other than Iowa and New Hampshire—holding a contest prior to February 1 would lose half its delegates at the Republican National Convention. This was clearly a price Republicans in Florida (along with Michigan, Nevada, South Carolina, and Wyoming) were willing to pay.

On the other hand, the penalty for an early Democratic primary was far more consequential. The Democratic National Committee adopted a proposal by its Rules and Bylaws Committee that only four states—Iowa, New Hampshire, Nevada, and South Carolina—could hold primaries or caucuses before February 5, 2008. Any state holding "unsanctioned" contests would be stripped of all delegates to the Democratic National Convention.[8] As Florida did not relent in its plan, it was duly stripped of delegates. Moreover, to ensure Florida would not take away attention from them, party officials from the four approved early-voting states asked all the candidates to sign a pledge not to campaign in Florida, with all the major candidates agreeing to do so. However, the names of the candidates remained on the ballot, as Florida election rules do not allow candidates to remove their names without withdrawing completely from the general election. Eight years after the 2000 election, Florida was once again playing a starring role in a disputed election, this time regarding whether to count primary votes at all.

Democratic Primary: A Primary without a Campaign

Having agreed not to campaign in Florida, there was no primary election-eering to speak of on the Democratic side, with only fringe candidate former Alaska senator Mike Gravel openly campaigning. However, the spotlight did turn to Florida when Hillary Clinton, sensing that she may need the delegates from both Florida and Michigan, began to advocate that the delegates from both states be seated at the Democratic National Convention.[9] Furthermore, just two days prior to the primary, Clinton visited Florida to hold fundraisers, which her opponents argued were campaign events in all but name. Barack Obama also sailed close to violating the "no campaigning pledge" when he ran a nationwide television advertising campaign that was shown in Florida. Although Obama's campaign asked for the ads not to be shown in Florida, cable networks suggested this was not possible. Despite an absence of candidates and open campaigning, interest in the primary among Florida Democrats was high, with 350,000 voters having cast early ballots. On primary election day more than 1.7 million votes were cast in the primary, a record number of votes for a seriously contested Democratic primary, beating the previous high of 1.2 million in 1988. Hillary Clinton won with 50 percent of the vote; Barack Obama was second with 33 percent; and John Edwards was third with 14 percent. Clinton's support was widespread across the state, perhaps reflecting a vote based on name recognition given the absence of a genuine campaign. Only in the Panhandle and Northern counties was the race competitive.[10] In the Panhandle, Obama led with 38 percent, followed by Clinton with 34 percent and Edwards with 24 percent. In the North, Clinton led with 39 percent, followed by Obama with 37 percent and Edwards with 20 percent. Clinton immediately held a post-victory "celebration" intending to give her campaign momentum going into Super Tuesday. Still, the fact remained that despite the vote, no delegates had been awarded to any candidate. The situation would not be rectified until the end of May when the DNC's Rules and Bylaws Committee voted to seat all of Florida's delegates, with each delegate having only half a vote.[11]

Republican Primary: Winnowing the Field

Unlike the Democrats, the Republicans waged a full–fledged, multimillion dollar campaign for the party's primary. Not only would a victory provide the winner with momentum going into Super Tuesday a week later, but it would also garner a haul of fifty-seven delegates given that a winner-take-all allocation was used. By the time of the Florida primary, four Republicans remained who had a realistic chance of being the party's nominee: John McCain, Mitt Romney, Mike Huckabee, and Rudy Giuliani. Of all the candidates Giuliani had staked everything on Florida, having stopped campaigning in New Hampshire and South Carolina, believing that the Republican primary electorate would not be quite as conservative in Florida as in the other early voting states. Indeed, Giuliani's blend of fiscal conservatism but moderation on social issues resembled that of Charlie Crist's appeal in the gubernatorial election. While Giuliani had led in most polls throughout 2007, his support had slipped as the nomination season began and other candidates—most noticeably McCain and Huckabee—began to gain momentum. Ultimately, the Florida primary shaped up as a contest between McCain and Romney. Romney played up his close ties with former governor Jeb Bush, even though Bush had not formally made an endorsement. Still, key Bush allies such as lieutenant governor Toni Jennings, congressman Tom Feeney, and former state party chair Al Cardenas were all early Romney backers. McCain, on the other hand, received the endorsement of senator Mel Martinez and, most significantly, governor Charlie Crist, the latter endorsing McCain just three days before the primary.[12]

McCain eked out a victory winning 36 percent to Romney's 31 percent. Finishing a distant third was Rudy Giuliani with 15 percent, with Huckabee fourth receiving 13 percent. The Crist endorsement may have proved important, as exit polls showed that of the 42 percent who said the endorsement was important, 54 percent backed McCain. Of most significance was the fact that McCain's victory was dependent on his strong support among Latino voters (both Cuban and non-Cuban). McCain actually lost the white vote to Romney (34 percent to 33 percent), but offset this by winning 54 percent of the Latino vote, which constituted 12 percent of the Republican primary electorate.[13] This marks the first time any Republican candidate has lost the white vote and yet still prevailed in a presidential primary in Florida.

Perhaps the greatest effect of the Florida primary was to knock out Giuliani, who subsequently endorsed McCain. It also meant that it was McCain who went into "Super Tuesday" with the momentum a week later. Thus, Florida essentially winnowed out the Republican field, when just a week prior to it pundits noted there was "chaos" within the GOP primary electorate, with no clear front-runner and a possibility of a brokered convention. At least on the Republican side, the early primary had the very effect that was intended, and it marked a decisive phase in the GOP nomination process.

The General Election Campaign

Pre-convention Campaigning: Obama Plays Catch-up

Although Barack Obama did not effectively clinch the Democratic nomination until June 3, following the final Democratic primaries in South Dakota and Montana, the general election had started in Florida by the middle of May. The absence of a primary campaign in the Sunshine State, together with Obama potentially having problems with key voting blocs in Florida—most notably Latinos, Jews, and possible racial backlash voting in north Florida—raised questions as to whether Obama would seriously contest Florida's twenty-seven Electoral College votes. This was reinforced by the fact that in May, McCain led Obama by an average of 9 percentage points.[14] However, Obama signaled his intentions with a three-day visit to Florida, which included stops in Orlando and Miami as well as the Democratic strongholds of Broward and Palm Beach counties.[15] Other than private fund-raisers, these events marked the first campaign appearances by Obama in the state. In a preview of the intense battle to come in Florida, John McCain also appeared in Miami during the same week to shore up support among Cuban Americans. McCain criticized Obama for being willing to talk to foreign leaders without pre-conditions, and he said he would not sit down with Cuban president Raul Castro until free elections were held there. McCain also signaled the importance of the campaign in Florida when governor Charlie Crist was mentioned as a possible vice presidential candidate. Crist's credentials were further reinforced by a visit to McCain's ranch in Arizona.[16]

The pre-convention attention to Florida continued from both the Obama and McCain campaigns throughout the rest of the summer. The challenge for Obama was to build a statewide organization that could compete with the GOP's state party machine. To that end, beginning in early June, four hundred trained "fellows" from the Obama campaign sought to register and mobilize supporters—especially disgruntled supporters of Hillary Clinton. The effort was further bolstered by the appointment of Steve Schale as the state political director. Schale had come to prominence having masterminded the Democratic gains in the state House in the 2006 midterm elections.[17] Such an unprecedented grassroots effort by the Democrats clearly caught the GOP campaign by surprise, which arguably rested on its laurels from prior campaigns. As one Democratic strategist observed: "In the 15 years that I've been here, the Democrats' volunteer apparatus has atrophied to such an extent that it's helped Republicans maintain their power."[18] The Obama campaign had twenty paid organizers in Florida by June, compared to just two from the McCain campaign. Whereas McCain had not put up any television ads since January, during the GOP primary, the Obama campaign had spent five million dollars by the beginning of August according to the Wisconsin Advertising Project at the University of Wisconsin at Madison.[19] This early organizing and advertising by the Obama campaign, together with some measure of complacency by the McCain campaign, was likely consequential in the looming battle for Florida. By the end of July, a Real Clear Politics average of polls showed McCain's lead had evaporated, with the two candidates essentially tied. Heading into August, which would end with the Democratic National Convention, Florida was viewed as a battleground state by both campaigns, as evidenced by the fact that both candidates appeared in the Sunshine State on August 1, Obama in St. Petersburg and McCain in Orlando. Previewing the fall campaign to come, both candidates emphasized the economy, which was increasingly becoming the central issue of the campaign for Florida, as it was for the nation as a whole. McCain emphasized tax credits for families, and Obama touted middle-class tax cuts.

After the Conventions: Battleground Florida

Following the Democratic National Convention in Denver and the Republican National Convention in Minneapolis-St. Paul, both campaigns could find good and bad news out of Florida. For the Obama campaign, the fact that Florida was in play was important, given that McCain had been favored just a few months earlier. At the same time, Democrats could point to an impressive increase in voter registration. On the other hand, the fact that McCain was tied or slightly ahead in the polls in Florida, despite not being able to match Obama's summer TV ad blitz and grassroots infrastructure, encouraged Republicans that voters in Florida might be reluctant to vote for a northern liberal Democrat. Also, even though he had not been selected as McCain's running mate, governor Charlie Crist was clearly an asset to the campaign in Florida, having already made several appearances with McCain both inside and outside the state during the summer.

The post-convention strategies of Obama and McCain for Florida were in some ways similar to those of prior contests. Geographically, the Democrats have relied on maximizing their support in South Florida in addition to the strongly Democratic enclaves of Alachua and Leon counties in northern Florida. For the Republicans, the base is the southwestern Gulf Coast counties and the Panhandle and Northern counties. The counties of central Florida—especially the vote-rich "I-4 corridor"—are the battleground counties of the battleground state, where statewide elections are usually won or lost. As in prior elections racial groups were another essential part of forging a winning strategy. For the Democrats, turning out the black vote was crucial, and clearly the Obama candidacy stimulated unprecedented black voter registration. For the Republicans, maximizing the white vote was critical, with the target being around 60 percent of the white vote needed for victory. Latinos, who are perhaps the key to statewide success, were courted by both parties.

Perhaps the decisive moment in the battle for Florida—and indeed nationally—occurred in the middle of September when the economy became the dominant issue in the campaign. Indeed, it was during a speech at a rally in Miami that John McCain made the now infamous remark: "The fundamentals of the economy are strong." This was one day after the investment bank Lehman Brothers filed for bankruptcy and the beginning of what many commentators have referred to as the greatest financial crisis since the Great Depression. McCain's remarks, together with the "suspension" of his campaign the following week to return to

Washington, D.C., to deal with the economic crisis prior to the first presidential debate were certainly pivotal moments in terms of the direction of momentum in Florida. From August 1 until September 24, McCain had led or was tied in nineteen of the twenty-one polls taken in Florida. In contrast, from September 27 until November 2, McCain led or was tied in just seven of the forty-one polls.

The economic situation, combined with the organization put in place by the Obama campaign, clearly put McCain on the defensive in the Sunshine State, which rapidly became a "must-win" state for the GOP. While Obama's contesting of Florida was perhaps initially designed to force McCain to devote time and resources to the state that would otherwise have gone elsewhere, by the middle of October there was a sense that the Democrats could actually win Florida, and in doing so make it almost impossible for McCain to reach the required 270 Electoral College votes.[20] This was reflected by the saturation of all the major media markets by Obama ads at the end of September and early October, when the campaign spent $2.1 million in state TV buys compared to just $659,000 for McCain.[21] Such an advantage moved some state Republicans to openly question McCain's Florida campaign strategy with respect to resources devoted, overall message, and strategy. As McCain launched a "Joe the Plumber" tour of the I-4 corridor to blast Obama on taxes, former state GOP political director Jaime Milner observed that it was "sad when some guy named 'Joe the Plumber' comes up with a better message for the McCain campaign than the McCain campaign."[22]

The state GOP also pointed fingers at the Republican National Committee for not doing enough to assist the state party.[23] The perilous situation facing the McCain campaign was further reinforced when Governor Crist clearly did not want to be associated with a losing cause or one that was increasingly relying on negative ads such as those highlighting Obama's connection to 1960s radical William Ayers, a point emphasized in rallies in the state by McCain's running mate, Sarah Palin. Crist let it be known he would spend the final few weeks of the campaign focused on the economy of the state rather than campaigning full time for his party's presidential nominee.

Although Obama had clearly built an advantage in Florida from the end of September, the intense campaigning continued in the final stretch of the campaign, largely because opinion polls showed McCain was still competitive despite the criticisms leveled against his campaign. In the final two weeks of the campaign the importance of Florida was demonstrated by the fact that the presidential and vice presidential nominees of both parties held a combined total of fifty-one campaign events in the Sunshine state, twenty-nine for the Obama-Biden ticket and twenty-two for the McCain-Palin ticket.[24] This total does not include those events conducted by the spouses of the candidates and other campaign surrogates, which meant that not a day went by in the closing two weeks of the campaign in Florida without some sort of campaign event.

The central theme of the Obama campaign in the final phase was the importance of mobilizing Democratic voters, especially those who were newly registered and not habitual voters.[25] Indeed, registration figures showed Democrats leading Republicans by 657,775.[26] Obama also encouraged voters to take advantage of Florida's early voting laws, appearing at a rally with Hillary Clinton in Orlando on October 20, the first day of early voting, and the first joint appearance by the two rivals for the Democratic nomination since June.[27] To underscore the importance of Florida, Obama's thirty-minute "infomercial" shown on the Wednesday before the election on seven broadcast and cable networks concluded with Obama addressing a live campaign rally in Sunrise, in south Florida. This was followed the next evening by a late night rally in Kissimmee in central Florida, which featured the first joint appearance of the campaign between Obama and Bill Clinton, where Clinton, after having provided a less-than-enthusiastic endorsement of Obama previously, told a crowd of 35,000 that "Barack Obama represents America's future, and you've got to be there for him next Tuesday." Even more symbolism was perhaps attached to the first appearance by former vice president Al Gore for Obama in Palm Beach County, with Gore alluding to the disputed election of 2000: "Take it from me, elections matter. Every vote matters."[28]

Although trailing in the polls, the McCain campaign clearly realized the importance of winning Florida, with McCain returning to his experience to address foreign policy, noting at a roundtable discussion with military leaders at the University of Tampa that "the question is whether [Obama] has what it takes to protect America from Osama bin Laden, al-Qaida and other grave threats."[29] In addition, McCain and Palin both returned to the theme of taxes to attack Obama. This message was reinforced by a TV ad shown on the weekend before the election featuring former governor Jeb Bush asking voters: "Do we elect a president who'll raise your taxes, or fight for working families? A president who'll spread your income, or let you keep what's yours?"[30]

On the eve of the election, the final opinion polls suggested the vote would be close in Florida, with Obama holding a lead of just under 2 percent in an average of polls compiled by Real Clear Politics. Such a tight race saw both McCain and Obama return to Florida one final time for election eve rallies, Obama in Jacksonville and McCain in Tampa.

Results and Analysis

Voter Turnout

Voter turnout in Florida, based on the voting-eligible population, was 67.1 percent, the second-highest turnout rate of any of the eleven southern states, and higher than the nationwide turnout rate of 61.4 percent. This represented an increase over Florida's 2004 presidential election turnout (64.4 percent).[31] Among registered voters, turnout was 75.2 percent, compared to 74.2 percent in 2004. Overall, there was a 10 percentage point increase in the total votes cast in Florida, to just over 8.4 million in 2008 from 7.6 million in 2004. Interestingly, this increase was almost entirely a result of the increase of 698,530 (20 percent) in the Democratic total votes cast compared to just a 81,102 (2 percent) increase in the Republican total vote, suggesting a better mobilization of the vote for Obama, or possibly lack of enthusiasm among state Republicans for McCain.

Analysis: The Presidential Race

As the polls in the last week of the campaign had indicated, Florida produced a close contest, with Obama carrying Florida's twenty-seven Electoral College votes and defeating McCain by 2.8 percentage points, 51.0 to 48.2 (see Table 9.1). Obama's victory margin was less than that of the previous two Democratic victors in the state: Bill Clinton, who won in 1996 by 5.7 percentage points, and Jimmy Carter, who won by 5.3 percentage points in 1976. On the other hand, the fact that an African American from a northern state with a perceived liberal voting record had won Florida at all was a remarkable result. Moreover, the result again indicated how Florida was very much a microcosm of the nation, with Obama's statewide total being just 1.8 percentage points below his national share of the popular vote.

Geography. An analysis of the presidential vote by county reveals that Obama won a majority of the vote in just fifteen of Florida's sixty-seven counties. However, the counties he won contained mostly all of the large population centers of the state. Indeed, Obama won all but one of the seven largest counties with a total vote of over four hundred thousand,

Table 9.1 Results of 2008 Florida Presidential Election and Selected Congressional Districts

Candidate (Party)	Percent of Vote	Vote Totals
President		
Barack Obama/Joe Biden (D)	51.0	4,282,074
John McCain/Sarah Palin (R)	48.2	4,045,624
Others	0.8	63,046
Total Presidential Vote		8,327,698
U.S. House of Representatives		
Eighth District (Orlando; Winter Park; Orange Co.)		
Alan Grayson (D)	52.0	172,854
*Rick Keller (R)	48.0	159,490
Total District Vote		332,334
Sixteenth District (Port St. Lucie; St. Lucie Co.; Martin Co.)		
Tom Rooney (R)	60.1	209,874
*Tim Mahoney (D)	39.9	139,373
Total District Vote		349,247
Eighteenth District (Miami; Miami-Dade Co; Monroe Co.; The Keys)		
*Ileana Ros-Lehtinen (R)	57.9	140,617
Annette Taddeo (D)	42.1	102,373
Total District Vote		242,990
Twenty-First District (Miami-Dade Co.; Hialeah; Pembroke Pines)		
*Lincoln Diaz-Balart (R)	57.2	137,226
Raul L. Martinez (D)	41.1	99,776
Total District Vote		237,002
Twenty-Fourth District (Seminole Co.; Orange Co.; Volusia Co.;"Space Coast")		
*Suzanne M. Kosmas (D)	57.2	211,284
Tom Feeney (R)	41.1	151,863
Total District Vote		363,147
Twenty-Fifth District (Miami-Dade Co.; Monroe Co.; Collier County)		
*Mario Diaz-Balart (R)	53.1	130,891
Joe Garcia (D)	46.9	115,820
Total District Vote		246,711

Key: *=incumbent, D=Democratic Party, R=Republican Party.

Source: Compiled by the author from data obtained from the Florida Secretary of State Elections Division, http://election.dos.state.fl.us/elections.

and even the county he lost—Duval County—was lost by just 1.9 percentage points. The movement of Florida's "mega" counties toward the Democratic Party in presidential elections is of great consequence, particularly as these counties supply almost half of the votes cast statewide. Table 9.2 shows the pro-Democratic movement in these counties since 1988. A major explanation of the decline of Florida from a safe Republican state in presidential elections toward one that is now a battleground —and maybe Democratic leaning—state can be found by the partisan change in the most populous counties.

While Obama increased the Democratic vote by 3.9 percentage points over that received by John Kerry in 2004, there was a large degree of continuity in the structure of the vote across elections. This was evidenced by the fact that only four counties that were carried by George W. Bush in 2004 switched to Obama in 2008 (Hillsborough, Flagler, Osceola and Pinellas), and that the county-by-county correlation between the 2004 and 2008 Democratic vote was extremely high (Pearson's r = .96).[32] This suggests there was an across-the-board surge to Obama in Florida, and indeed his percentage of the vote went up in fifty-two counties relative to John Kerry's vote in 2004, while it declined in fifteen counties, mostly in the Panhandle. By dividing the state into six discrete geographic regions, Obama's areas of strength—and relative weakness—can be better discerned (see Table 9.3).

Table 9.2 Partisan Change in Florida's "Mega" Counties in Presidential Elections, 1988–2008 (in percent)

	1988	1992	1996	2000	2004	2008
Miami-Dade	R +11	D +4	D +19	D +7	D +6	D +16
Broward	R +0.5	D +21	D +35	D +36	D +35	D +35
Palm Beach	R +12	D +11	D +24	D +27	D +21	D +23
Hillsborough	R +20	R +5	D +3	R +3	R +7	D +7
Pinellas	R +16	D +0.4	D +9	D +4	R +0.1	D +8
Orange	R +37	R +11	R +0.2	D +2	D +0.2	D +19
Duval	R +26	R +13	R +6	R +16	R +16	R +2
Percentage of Statewide Vote Cast by "Mega" Counties	52.3	50.9	49.5	49.3	48.8	48.2

Note: Cell entries show the winning party and the margin of victory.

Source: Compiled by the author from data obtained from the Florida Secretary of State Elections Division, http://election.dos.state.fl.us/elections.

Table 9.3 Florida 2008 Presidential Election Vote by Region

	Obama (D)	McCain (R)	Change in Democratic Vote from 2004	Total Votes Cast	Statewide Vote	Increase in Total Votes Cast from 2004
Panhandle	39.5	59.5	+2.2	691,826	8.2	8.7
North	43.3	55.9	+4.0	1,159,074	13.8	13.2
East Central	50.3	48.9	+5.4	2,011,050	23.9	14.8
West Central	51.4	47.6	+4.5	1,355,519	16.2	7.6
Southwest	44.9	54.1	+4.0	985,390	11.7	8.0
Gold Coast	61.9	37.7	+3.1	2,187,885	26.1	8.0
Statewide	51.0	48.2	+3.9	8,390,744	100	10.3

Note: County breakdowns for regions are as follows. Panhandle: Counties of Bay, Calhoun, Escambia, Franklin, Gadsden, Gulf, Holmes, Jackson, Jefferson, Leon, Liberty, Okaloosa, Santa Rosa, Wakulla, Walton, Washington; North: Counties of Alachua, Baker, Bradford, Clay, Columbia, Dixie, Duval, Flagler, Gilchrist, Hamilton, Lafayette, Levy, Madison, Marion, Nassau, Putnam, St. Johns, Suwannee, Taylor, Union; East Central: Brevard, Indian River, Lake, Martin, Orange, Osceola, Polk, Seminole, St. Lucie, Sumter, Volusia; West Central: Counties of Citrus, Hernando, Hillsborough, Pasco, Pinellas; Southwest: Counties of Charlotte, Collier, DeSoto, Glades, Hardee, Hendry, Highlands, Lee, Manatee, Monroe, Okeechobee, Sarasota; Gold Coast: Counties of Broward, Miami-Dade, Palm Beach.

Source: Compiled by the author from data obtained at the Florida Secretary of State Elections Division, http://election.dos.state.fl.us/elections.

Obama increased the Democratic vote in every region compared to Kerry's performance in 2004, even in the Republican strongholds of the Panhandle, the North, and the Southwest. By keeping the McCain vote to below 60 percent in these regions, and then sweeping the Democratic base of the Gold Coast counties with 61.9 percent of the vote, Obama needed to essentially split the two vote-rich Central Florida regions, which he did, winning 50.3 percent in the East Central region and 51.4 percent in the West Central region. Indeed, Obama recorded his highest vote increase compared to Kerry in the East Central region (up 5.4 percent), which also recorded the largest overall total vote increase of any of Florida's regions (up 14.8 percent). As it has been in previous elections, Central Florida proved to be the decisive battleground region.

Race, Gender, Age, and Income. Given the presence of the first African American candidate for a major party nomination on the ticket, race was clearly going to be an important factor in Florida, as elsewhere in the South. Despite forecasts of a radically different electorate in 2008, the racial composition of Florida's electorate was almost identical to 2004, with whites constituting 71 percent of the electorate, Latinos 14 percent, and blacks 13 percent. As Table 9.4 shows, a racial gap in voting behavior did exist, with Obama winning 42 percent of the white vote (the highest share of the white vote in any of the eleven southern states), about the same share of the white vote that Obama received nationally (43 percent). Obama's performance among whites was the same as Kerry's in Florida in 2004, suggesting there is a natural ceiling on the white vote that can be won by a Democratic presidential candidate regardless of short-term factors such as issues, candidate attributes, and economic conditions. The importance of minorities in southern politics is demonstrated in Florida, with Obama winning the black vote by a whopping 96 percent to McCain's 4 percent, a margin that was generally repeated across the South and the nation. This represented a 10 percentage point increase over the vote achieved by Kerry in 2004. The crucial racial group in Florida was Latinos, with Obama winning 57 percent of the vote compared to 42 percent for McCain, essentially a reversal of 2004 when George W. Bush bested Kerry 56 percent to 44 percent. This increase can be attributed to the growth of Florida's non-Cuban Latino population, as evidenced by the pro-Democratic movement in Osceola and Orange counties, where Obama increased the vote by 12 and 9 percentage points respectively compared to Kerry's performance. Both of these Central Florida counties have witnessed a large increase in their Latino population, and the outcome demonstrates the growing importance of the non-Cuban Latino vote. However, the increase in the Democratic vote in Miami-Dade County suggests that Obama also made inroads among the traditionally Republican Cuban American vote.

Despite a concern in the Obama campaign that women who had supported Hillary Clinton in the Democratic primary might defect to McCain, there was no gender gap in 2008, with Obama winning 51 percent of men and 52 percent of women. Even when controlling for race, the gender gap did not emerge among white voters, with Obama winning 42 percent of the vote among white men and women. The only noticeable gender gap was actually among Latinos, with Obama winning among men by 60 percent to McCain's 40 percent, but among women Obama won by half that margin, 55 percent compared to 45 percent for McCain.

The potential of a large generational gap in voting behavior had been discussed widely, especially given the targeting of the youth vote by the Obama campaign and the existence of an older electorate in Florida. Table 9.4 does provide some initial support for a generational gap in Florida, with 61 percent of voters aged eighteen to twenty-nine voting for

Table 9.4 Florida Exit Poll Results Reporting Demographic and Political Factors in the 2008 Presidential Vote (in percent)

Voter Characteristics/Attitude	Obama	McCain	Percentage of Category
Race			
White	42	56	71
Black	96	4	13
Latino	57	42	14
Gender			
Male	51	47	47
Female	52	47	53
Gender, Controlling for Race			
White Males	42	55	35
White Females	42	57	36
Black Males	95	5	5
Black Females	97	3	8
Latino Males	60	40	6
Latino Females	55	45	8
Age			
18–29	61	37	15
30–44	49	49	25
45–64	52	47	37
65+	45	53	22
Income			
Under $15,000	66	33	8
$15–30,000	62	37	12
$30–50,000	59	39	19
$50–75,000	47	52	23
$75–100,000	39	58	14
$100–150,000	40	58	12
$150–200,000	45	54	7
$200,000+	51	48	5
Income, Controlling for Race			
White under $50,000	48	51	24
White over $50,000	38	61	47
Non-white under $50,000	84	16	15
Non-white over $50,000	65	34	14

Table 9.4 (continued)

Voter Characteristics/Attitude	Obama	McCain	Percentage of Category
Party Identification			
Democratic	87	12	37
Republican	12	87	34
Independent	52	45	29
Ideology			
Liberal	91	8	19
Moderate	57	41	47
Conservative	21	77	35
Approval of Bush			
Approve	9	90	28
Disapprove	69	29	70
Which Issue Mattered Most?			
Economy	56	43	62
Terrorism	8	92	10
Iraq 60	39	10	
Health Care	73	25	8
Energy Policy	38	61	7
National Economic Conditions			
Excellent/Good	24	76	7
Not So Good/Poor	53	45	92
Vote on Amendment 2 (Marriage as Union between Man and Woman)			
Yes	35	64	61
No	74	24	39
Which Candidate Quality Mattered Most?			
Can Bring Change	92	7	34
Shares My Values	30	69	26
Experience	6	93	23
Cares about People	69	28	14

Note: Obama and McCain totals may not add up to 100 as other party candidates have been omitted.

Source: National Election Pool-Edison/Mitofsky Exit Poll (Florida), November 4, 2008.

Obama compared to 45 percent among those over sixty-five, with the other two age groups more or less evenly divided. However, this was not dramatically different from 2004, when Kerry received 58 percent of the youngest age group and 47 percent among the oldest. Moreover, when controlling for race (not shown in Table 9.4), the relationship between age and vote choice completely washes out for both white and black voters.[33] For example, among white voters Obama received 44 percent among those in the eighteen-to-twenty-nine group, 38 percent among the thirty-to-forty-four age group, 43 percent in the forty-five-to-sixty-four group and 43 percent among those over sixty-five. The only group where generational differences were evident was among Latinos, with 76 percent of the eighteen-to-twenty-nine age group voting for Obama, the thirty-to-forty-four age group split 50–50 between Obama and McCain, and Obama winning 62 percent of the vote among the forty-five-to-sixty-four age group. The dominance of the Latino youth vote for Obama, which was also evident nationally, certainly presents a potential for growth in Democratic support among Latinos through generational replacement of the electorate.

A modest degree of social class–based voting was evident in Florida, with Obama easily carrying each income group below fifty thousand dollars and McCain winning among those with incomes over fifty thousand dollars except for those earning more than two hundred thousand dollars a year. However, all income groups—except for those earning one hundred thousand dollars to one hundred and fifty thousand dollars, where Obama's support was down four percentage points compared to Kerry—registered an increase in support for Obama compared to 2004. Voters in this income group may have been swayed by the final weeks of the campaign where McCain and Palin emphasized taxes and labeled Obama's tax plan as "socialism." Interestingly, however, voters in the two highest income groups did not respond in the same way, and indeed voters with a household income of over two hundred thousand dollars—who in all likelihood would actually pay more in taxes under Obama—actually registered the largest increase in support for Obama among income groups, up 10 percent compared to the support received by Kerry.

Given that minority voters are more likely to be in the lower income categories, the relationship between income and vote choice should be examined while also controlling for race. This is particularly important given that a source of potential vote defection for Obama may have been caused by racial backlash among white, working-class voters. However, although McCain won white voters with household incomes under and over fifty thousand dollars, Obama actually did better among whites earning less than fifty thousand dollars, where he trailed McCain by just 3 percentage points. In contrast, McCain led Obama 61 to 38 percentage points among white voters earning more than fifty thousand dollars.

Party Identification and Ideology. Despite the presence of two presidential candidates who may have had the potential for broadening the appeal of their respective parties, the 2008 presidential vote in Florida essentially came down to appealing to the base. Indeed, when examining party identification, both Obama and McCain received support from 87 percent of their respective party identifiers. For Obama the loyalty of Democrats was slightly higher than in 2004, when Kerry won 85 percent of Democrats. The fear that Obama might also lose some support from "Hillary Democrats" was not borne out, with just 18 percent of white Democrats defecting and voting for McCain. In only two other southern states (North Carolina and Virginia) were the defection rates of white Democrats lower than in Florida. Republicans were not as loyal to McCain as they had been to Bush, who had received more than 90 percent of the vote from GOP identifiers in both 2000 and 2004. Again, this may be indicative of the Republican base being less enthused about McCain than Bush. Compounding McCain's problem was that Republicans made up 34 percent of the electorate in 2008, 7 percentage points less than in 2004, which was the lowest share in any of the past four presidential elections in Florida. Crucial to Obama's success in winning Florida was his performance among independents, winning this swing group 52 to 45 percent. Although Kerry carried independents by a larger margin in 2004 (57 percent to 41 percent), Obama gained more votes from independents as they made up a larger share of the electorate in 2008, 29 percent as compared to 23 percent in 2004. Interestingly, Florida was the only southern state in which independents gave a majority of the vote to Obama. This suggests that independents in the Sunshine State better resemble the national profile of independents than in the other southern states.

Ideology was also again strongly related to vote choice, although liberals were more cohesive behind Obama (91 percent to 9 percent) than were conservatives behind McCain (77 percent to 21 percent). While McCain's vote among conservatives did not approach the 83 percent won by Bush in 2004, it was identical to that received by Bush in 2000, suggesting that 2004 marked an unprecedented mobilization of conservatives in Florida by the GOP. As they were nationally, moderates were a crucial swing group won by Obama, 57 to 41 percent, almost identical to the margin won by John Kerry.

Issues and Candidate Qualities. As they were nationally, the economy and change were the two most important short-term factors at work in Florida. The economy was the dominant issue in Florida, with 62 percent citing it as the issue that most mattered. In 2004, just 16 percent mentioned the economy/jobs as the most important issue. Moreover, 92 percent of voters in Florida had a pessimistic view of the national economy. When the low approval ratings of President Bush are also considered— 70 percent disapproved of his performance—Obama clearly benefited from retrospective voting. It is also not a surprise that against this backdrop, 34 percent of Florida voters cited "change" as the candidate quality that mattered most. This was compared to just 23 percent of voters who cited "experience" as the most important quality, which was clearly McCain's strongest attribute.

One final point to note is that while economic issues were clearly front and center of the campaign in 2008, cultural issues were not completely relegated to irrelevance in Florida, as evidenced by the vote on the constitutional amendment to define marriage as a union between a man and a woman. The amendment passed, 62 percent to 38 percent, clearing the required 60 percent threshold for the passage of constitutional amendments. Interestingly, a substantial minority of those voting "yes" on the amendment also voted for Obama (35 percent), more than those voting "no" who also voted for McCain (24 percent). A separate exit poll reveals that blacks and Latinos, who were central to Obama's winning electoral coalition, were actually more likely to be in favor of the amendment, with 71 percent of blacks and 64 percent of Latinos voting "yes," compared to 60 percent among whites.[34]

Analysis: U.S. House and State Legislative Elections

While the presidential election in Florida was clearly the main event in the Sunshine State, there were some changes in the composition of the congressional delegation, with the Democrats gaining two seats from the Republicans while the GOP gained one Democratic-held district. The Florida congressional delegation still favors the Republicans, with fifteen GOP members of the House compared to ten Democrats, but the five-seat deficit is the smallest since 1990.

Both of the Democratic pick-ups were in Central Florida districts, suggesting the possible influence of Obama's coattails in these districts given his strong showing in Central Florida. In the Eighth District, four-term incumbent Republican Ric Keller was defeated by the Democratic

challenger Alan Grayson, an attorney who prosecuted war profiteers, fil-
ing law suits against, among others, Halliburton. Grayson, who spent two
million dollars of his own money, took 52 percent of the vote to Keller's
48 percent. Keller was possibly damaged by the fact that he had pledged
to serve just four terms when he was first elected in 2000. The fact that
he won just 53 percent of the vote in the GOP primary pointed to his
potential vulnerability. However, he also was not helped by a district that
was becoming increasingly Democratic, with a Democratic advantage of
almost ten thousand in party registration.[35] This suggests that the district
may be difficult for the Republicans to win back in a future election.

The Twenty-fourth District delivered perhaps one of the most shocking
—although not entirely unexpected—results with three-term incumbent
Republican Tom Feeney being defeated by former state House member
Suzanne Kosmas. The district, largely drawn by Feeney in his capacity of
speaker of the Florida state House during the post-2000 census redistricting, is heavily Republican, and, unlike the Eighth District, still has a GOP
advantage in party registration of almost fifteen thousand. This had
allowed Feeney to win the district easily in prior elections, and he was not
even opposed by a Democrat in 2004. However, Feeney faced ethics
charges after a 2003 golfing trip to Scotland paid for by former lobbyist
Jack Abramoff. Furthermore, the public interest group Citizens for
Responsibility and Ethics in Washington named Feeney as one of the "20
Most Corrupt Members of Congress."[36] This forced Feeney to air a TV
ad where he offered an apology for his actions. Sensing blood, the Democratic Congressional Campaign Committee identified Kosmas as the type
of moderate Democrat who could win the district and poured in one mil-
lion dollars on TV ads.[37] Feeney's mea culpa clearly did not work, and
Kosmas won the seat by a convincing margin, 57 percent to 41 percent.
However, Kosmas may have her work cut out to hold the seat against a
Republican other than Feeney in the 2010 midterm elections.

One of the only Republican gains nationally took place in the Sixteenth
District, where one-term Democratic incumbent Tim Mahoney was easily beaten by Republican challenger Tom Rooney, 60 to 40 percent, the
largest losing margin of any incumbent in 2008. Ironically, Mahoney,
who had defeated the disgraced Mark Foley in 2006, was himself the subject of character questions after it emerged that he had paid "hush money"
to his mistress.[38]

Three districts that did not change hands, but were considered potential Democratic pick-ups, were the Miami majority-Latino districts held
by Ileana Ros-Lehtinen (FL-18), Lincoln Diaz-Balart (FL-21), and Mario

Diaz-Balart (FL-25). While these are usually considered ultra-safe Republican seats with Ros-Lehtinen and Lincoln Diaz-Balart having held the districts since 1989 and 1993, respectively, there were some suggestions that the once-solid GOP support among Cuban Americans might be eroding.[39] Indeed, had it not been for Democratic prospects in the two Central Florida districts it is possible that the Democratic Congressional Campaign Committee may have made more of a play for the South Florida seats. In the end, Ros-Lehtinen and Lincoln Diaz-Balart had comfortable victories, winning 58 percent and 57 percent of the vote, respectively, although in Diaz-Balart's case this was his lowest share of the vote since first winning the district in 1992. However, his brother, three-term incumbent Mario Diaz-Balart, won with a much narrower margin of victory, 53 percent to 47 percent over his Democratic challenger, Joe Garcia, a former executive director of the Cuban American National Foundation. Diaz-Balart may take some solace from the fact that he won reelection despite the strong pro-Democratic tide in 2008. On the other hand, his district is also one that is becoming more Democratic in terms of party registration, with a GOP advantage in 2008 of just over three thousand. Diaz-Balart's district may continue to be targeted by the Democrats in future election cycles.

Finally, elections to the state legislature saw the Republicans hold on to their large majorities in both the state House (seventy-six to forty-four seats) and state Senate (twenty-six to fourteen seats), with the Democrats making a net gain of just one seat in the state House. For the Democrats this may have been considered something of a disappointment given the performance of Obama at the top of the ticket and given the gain of nine state House seats in the 2006 midterm elections. Still, Democrats would likely view any advances as welcome considering the party had lost ground in the state House in every election from 1992 to 2004. Democratic prospects for taking control of either chamber of the state legislature, however, remain rather remote for the foreseeable future.

Conclusions: Toward the Future

The 2008 presidential election again emphasized Florida's status as a battleground state. While not playing quite the decisive role it did in 2000, or even 2004—Obama would have been elected president even if he had lost Florida—the state was crucial to both the Obama and McCain campaigns. Obama's victory over McCain in Florida was without question historic, given that only southern Democrats have been able to carry the Sunshine State in the post–World War II period. However, Obama won not by attracting support from the Republican base, but rather by consolidating the Democratic base and, most crucially, by mobilizing groups that have been trending Democratic in recent elections. Most critically, Obama won with a diverse racial electoral coalition, one that will likely be a model for Democrats to reassemble in future statewide elections. The increase in the Democratic vote among Latinos—especially younger non-Cuban Latinos—should be a signal to Republicans in Florida that they can no longer win as a party that appeals exclusively to the white electorate. Likewise, declining support for the Republicans in the most populous counties of the state is a troubling development for GOP strategists looking ahead to regaining the state in 2012. In 2008, none of the seven largest counties could be considered "safe" for the Republicans, while in four counties—Broward, Miami-Dade, Orange and Palm Beach—Obama won by landslide margins. To explain away Obama's victory in Florida to short-term forces and a "bad" Republican year ignores the long-term demographic dynamics in the state that favor the Democrats.

On the other hand, the Republican Party still holds a majority of congressional seats and continues to dominate the state legislature. Interestingly, a party system where the presidency is competitive and the GOP dominates at the subpresidential level is a mirror image of the one that existed until the mid-1990s, that is, a solid Republican state in presidential elections with Democrats holding the majority at the state and local level.

The midterm elections of 2010 should provide an interesting indicator as to the nature of the evolution of Florida's party competition, with both a gubernatorial election and a U.S. Senate election. Looking further ahead to the 2012 election, Florida will remain a "must win" state for the GOP, regardless of who the party's nominee will be. Barack Obama's victory certainly gave the "blues" to the GOP in the Sunshine State in 2008, and a follow-up victory in 2012 will be an indication that Florida has become one very consequential "blue" breakthrough in the South.[40]

10.

North Carolina

Change and Continuity in 2008

Charles Prysby

Introduction

Reflecting electoral developments that were occurring in the South as a whole, North Carolina Republicans made great gains in the 1970s and 1980s, winning presidential, gubernatorial, and U.S. Senate elections for the first time in modern history. During these two decades, Republicans won four of the five presidential elections, four of the six Senate elections, and three of the five gubernatorial elections. As in other southern states, Democrats did better further down the ballot, but Republican gains were evident here, too. However, Republican advances were less dramatic after the 1980s, and North Carolina elections displayed a fairly stable pattern from 1992 through 2004. The state was competitive overall, but with Republicans having the advantage in federal elections and Democrats

Author's note: The following individuals shared their perspectives on the 2008 elections in North Carolina: Kerra Bolton and Caroline Valand (North Carolina Democratic Party), Chris McClure (North Carolina Republican Party), Mark Farinella (North Carolina Obama Campaign), Seth Effron (North Carolina Governor's Office), Ferrel Guillory and Thad Beyle (University of North Carolina-Chapel Hill), Ted Arrington (University of North Carolina-Charlotte), Rob Christensen (*Raleigh News and Observer*), and Paul Johnson (High Point Enterprise). I appreciate their willingness to share their insights and information with me. I, of course, am responsible for all of the facts and interpretations contained in this chapter.

having the advantage in state elections. Put simply, the Tar Heel political colors were federal red and state blue.[1]

The Republican advantage in federal elections from 1992 to 2004 is evident in Table 10.1. Republicans won all the presidential elections during this period, even in the years when they were losing nationally. Only in 1992 was the presidential outcome in doubt. Even in 2004, when then senator John Edwards was the Democratic vice presidential candidate, the state went Republican by a comfortable margin. U.S. Senate elections were fairly competitive races, as every election during this time period was won with less than 55 percent of the vote, but Republicans won five of the six Senate elections held between 1990 and 2004, including all three held in presidential years.[2] In U.S. House elections, the GOP first gained a majority of seats in the state in 1994, and it retained that majority through the 2004 elections, except in 1996, when the two parties evenly split the seats.

The Democratic advantage in state elections from 1992 to 2004 also is clear in Table 10.1. Democrats won all the gubernatorial elections and most of the council of state offices during this time period. Democrats

Table 10.1 North Carolina Election Results, Presidential Years, 1992–2008 (in percent)

	1992	1996	2000	2004	2008
Presidential Vote	50.5	52.5	56.5	56.2	49.8
U.S. Senate Vote	52.2	53.4	—	52.3	45.6
Percent of U.S. House Seats Won	33.3	50.0	58.3	53.8	38.5
Gubernatorial Vote	45.1	43.3	47.1	43.5	48.3
Percent of COS Offices Won	0	0	10	30	20
Percent of State Senate Seats Won	22.0	42.0	30.0	42.0	40.0
Percent of State House Seats Won	34.4	50.8	48.3	47.5	43.3

Note: Vote percentages are the Republican percentage of the major party vote. Other figures are the Republican percentage of seats or offices won. The COS (Council of State) offices include the governor, lieutenant governor, and eight other executive positions, all elected statewide. No U.S. Senate election occurred in 2000.

Source: Computed from data obtained from the North Carolina Board of Elections.

also controlled the state legislature during this time, save for a short period in the 1990s when Republicans were able to form the majority in the state house. Greater Democratic success in state rather than federal elections is a well-known feature of southern politics, but North Carolina Democrats were particularly successful in controlling state government in recent years, and this was despite the fact that the state holds its major state elections in presidential election years, unlike the rest of the South. Even with a presidential candidate who was carrying the state at the top of their ticket, North Carolina Republicans failed to score even one decisive victory in state elections in the 1990s or in the first decade of the twenty-first century.

The 2008 election results shattered the electoral pattern that characterized the 1992–2004 period. Democrats not only retained control of state government, they also won the presidential and congressional elections, as we can see from the data in Table 10.1. The victory in the presidential contest was the first for Democrats in the state since 1976. The victory in the U.S. Senate race was the first for Democrats in a presidential election year since 1968 and only the third since 1974. Finally, Democrats extended their majority in the U.S. House delegation, which they obtained in 2006, to eight of the thirteen seats. Striking change in federal election outcomes was accompanied by continuity in state election results. Democrats retained control of the governorship with their fifth victory in a row, extended their domination of the council of state offices, and maintained a solid grip on both houses of the state legislature.

Early in 2008, few political observers would have predicted this sweeping Democratic victory. Based on previous years, North Carolina seemed safe for John McCain even if he lost nationally, unless it was by a landslide. The incumbent Republican senator, Elizabeth Dole, was regarded as likely to be reelected; in fact, several prominent Democrats passed on the opportunity to run against her, suggesting that she was not perceived as highly vulnerable. Even the gubernatorial election was considered a tossup. The incumbent governor was ineligible to run again; the Democratic candidate, lieutenant governor Beverly Perdue, was not considered to be a dynamic campaigner; and the Republican candidate, Charlotte mayor Pat McCrory, was seen by many as the strongest GOP gubernatorial candidate in years. But while Republican hopes may have been high early in the year, there were few unhappy Democrats but many disappointed Republicans after November.

The principle goal of this study is to explain and interpret these election results. The central question is whether Democratic success in 2008 was produced by very favorable national conditions in that year or by significant lasting changes in the political landscape of North Carolina. If the Democratic victories were largely due to short-term forces, principally a very unpopular Republican presidential administration, then a Republican resurgence would likely come if and when these short-term political forces shifted in the other direction. If Democratic gains reflected long-term political developments in the state, Republican prospects in future elections would be less favorable.

The Presidential Election

The seeds of Obama's November victory in North Carolina were planted in the May presidential primary. Usually held near the end of the presidential primary season, the North Carolina primary played virtually no role in recent presidential nominating contests prior to 2008. In these recent earlier elections, both parties had effectively chosen their presidential nominees by the time of the North Carolina presidential primary, making the state irrelevant in the nomination contest. However, in 2008, the prolonged nomination battle between Barack Obama and Hillary Clinton for the Democratic nomination made the North Carolina presidential primary crucial. Obama's victory in the state helped him cement his delegate lead and capture the nomination. More important, at least for the general election contest, was the sizable organization effort mounted by the Obama campaign in the spring of 2008. That effort provided the foundation for an unprecedented fall organizational effort. Democrats included North Carolina in their list of targeted states and poured resources into the state. Obama made six trips to the state in the fall. Hoping he would prevail without heavy spending, McCain committed fewer resources to the state, partly because he had fewer resources available; but as polls showed the outcome in doubt, McCain paid attention to North Carolina, visiting three times in October. The preelection polls were accurate; the outcome was one of the closest in the nation. Obama won by about 14,000 votes out of a total of nearly 4.3 million cast.

There are three possible explanations for why the Democratic presidential candidate was able to carry the state in 2008 despite the failure to do so in every election from 1980 to 2004. First, it was a particularly good year for Democrats nationally, which helped Obama in almost every state. President George Bush's approval rating was dismal throughout 2008, never rising above 34 percent and dropping to 25 percent in early October, according to a Gallup Poll.[3] Although McCain attempted to separate himself from Bush, Obama did his best to tie the two together, and the Republican candidate suffered because of the foreign policy and economic failures of the Bush administration. Exit poll data show a close relationship between assessment of the Bush administration and the presidential vote. For example, nearly one-half of the voters thought McCain would continue the policies of President Bush, and 90 percent of this group voted for Obama.[4]

Table 10.2 shows the outcome of recent presidential elections in North Carolina and the nation. Clearly, election outcomes in the state are linked to the national outcome; Republicans did best in North Carolina when they were doing well nationally. However, the gap between North Carolina and the nation has varied. In 1996 and 2000, the state was around 7 percentage points more Republican than the country as a whole. It was less than 5 points more Republican in 2004 (perhaps because North Carolina Senator Edwards was on the Democratic ticket). In 2008, it was only about 3 points more Republican. Two conclusions can be drawn from these figures. First, if Obama had won nationally with only 51 or 52 percent of the two-party vote, he would not have carried North Carolina. Second, if North Carolina had been 5 points more Republican, as it was in 2004, McCain would have won the state despite his national defeat. Put another way, the Democratic share of the 2008 two-party presidential vote in North Carolina was 6.4 percentage points greater than it was in 2004. Almost 5 points of that change can be attributed to national change, while about 1.6 points came from the narrowing of the gap between the state and the nation.

Although the most important source of the Obama victory in North Carolina was the favorable national political landscape for Democrats, this is not the whole story. Obama's narrow victory in the state was due in part to the fact that North Carolina was only about 3 points more Republican than the nation in 2008. Why was this gap narrower than in previous elections? One possibility is the extremely vigorous campaign effort put forth by Obama in the state, an effort that began with the presidential primary, as discussed above. In the fall, the Obama campaign had forty-five field offices in the state. The paid staff numbered more than three hundred. Over twenty thousand volunteers were involved. These Obama campaign workers and volunteers engaged in extensive efforts to register new voters (especially African Americans), to contact and persuade potential but unreliable Democratic voters, and to get supporters to vote.[5] Exit poll data show that about one-third of voters reported being contacted by the Obama campaign; only one-fourth reported a McCain

Table 10.2 Presidential Vote in North Carolina and the Nation, 1988–2008 (in percent)

Presidential Vote	1988	1992	1996	2000	2004	2008
North Carolina	58.2	50.5	52.5	56.5	56.2	49.8
Nation	53.9	46.5	45.4	49.7	51.4	46.6
NC vs. Nation	+4.3	+4.0	+7.1	+6.8	+4.8	+3.2

Note: Entries are the Republican percentage of the two-party vote for president. The last row gives the difference between the Republican vote in North Carolina and in the nation.

Source: Computed from data in America Votes, various editions, the North Carolina Board of Elections website, and the CNN 2008 Elections website.

contact. Added to the Obama organization was the campaign effort of the state Democratic Party, and the two organizations appear to have worked well together. By all accounts, the extent of the Democratic effort far exceeded what either party had done in any previous presidential election.[6]

Ascertaining the true impact of this organizational effort is difficult. Some relevant evidence comes from registration figures.[7] From January to November 2008, Democratic registration increased by 471,000, compared to 211,000 for Republicans and 283,000 for unaffiliated voters. In November 2008, 21.6 percent of registered voters were black, compared to 20.2 percent in 2004. These figures suggest considerable success in registering Democrats and blacks, although it is possible the Obama candidacy would have spurred black registration even absent the unprecedented organizational effort. Voter turnout data also indicate that the Democratic organizational effort was effective in mobilizing supporters. Turnout in the state increased from 57.8 percent of eligible voters in 2004 to 65.8 percent in 2008, a far greater increase than occurred in the United States overall.[8] Thus, one reason why North Carolina was only about 3 points more Republican than the nation in 2008 probably was the stronger Democratic organizational effort compared to that of the Republicans. To the extent that this was a cause, then North Carolina may not be so similar to the country in future elections unless there continues to be a comparable Democratic advantage in campaign organization and effort. Campaign effort may be a short-term force that was very favorable to the Democrats in 2008, but it is one that might well be favorable to the Republicans in another year.

A final reason for the narrowing of the gap between the state and the nation in 2008 could be a changing political landscape in North Carolina.

North Carolina was one of the fastest growing states over the past several years. Its population increased by 7.6 percent since 2004. Much of the growth has occurred in the major metropolitan areas, particularly Charlotte and Raleigh-Durham. For example, Mecklenburg County (Charlotte) had a population increase of about 25 percent between 2000 and 2007, and Wake County (Raleigh) had an increase of 33 percent.[9] Obama did extremely well in these areas, capturing 62 percent of the vote in Mecklenburg County and 57 percent of the vote in Wake County.[10] Many of the newcomers to these areas are northern immigrants, who often are more moderate in their political orientations. Similar economic and demographic changes have been cited as sources of change in Virginia politics. These changes are likely to continue in North Carolina, so if they were a contributing factor to Democratic success in 2008, they are likely to provide further support for Democrats.

Underlying the significant change in the outcome of the presidential contest is substantial continuity in the sources of partisan support. Table 10.3 presents data on the relationship between presidential voting and two political orientations.[11] The patterns for party identification are very similar to those for 2004 and 2000. Democrats voted overwhelmingly for their party's presidential candidate. Republicans did the same. Independents were fairly evenly divided. The change in the election outcome in 2008 was produced by two slight shifts from 2004: Democrats were a slightly greater proportion of the electorate and defections among Democratic voters were slightly fewer. Similarly, the relationship between ideology and voting in 2008 is very similar to the 2004 pattern, although it is worth noting that the proportion of voters calling themselves conservative declined somewhat in 2008. While Obama stressed in his campaign that he would move beyond the bitter partisanship that characterized Washington politics, he did no better than Kerry in attracting votes from North Carolina conservatives, Republicans, or even independents.

The demographic and social sources of voting in the 2008 presidential election also were similar to those in previous elections (see Table 10.4). Blacks were far more Democratic in their presidential voting than whites, just as they were in 2000 and 2004; in fact, the 60-point gap between whites and blacks in their presidential vote is almost exactly what it was in 2004, when Kerry received 85 percent of the vote from blacks and 27 percent from whites. As in previous elections, gender, religion, and socioeconomic status were related to voting. The gender gap was somewhat larger in 2008 than in 2004, while differences along income and educational lines were somewhat smaller. The one striking change in

Table 10.3 North Carolina Voting by Selected Political Orientations, 2008 (in percent)

Variable	Voting for Obama	Voting for Hagan	Voting for Perdue
All Voters	50	53	50
Party Identification			
Democrats (42)	90	90	88
Independents (27)	39	39	37
Republicans (31)	4	10	9
Ideology			
Liberal (19)	87	89	85
Moderate (44)	63	64	63
Conservative (37)	15	19	19

Note: Entries are the percentage of voters in the specified category who voted for the Democratic presidential, senatorial, and gubernatorial candidates (Obama, Hagan, and Perdue). The figures in parentheses indicate the percentage of all respondents in that category. For example, the data for party identification indicate that 42 percent of the voters were Democrats in 2008 and that 90 percent of Democrats voted for Obama. Only the percentages for the Democratic candidates are shown; these were essentially two-candidate races, so the proportion of the vote not going to the Democratic candidate went almost entirely to the Republican candidate.

Source: National Election Pool 2008 North Carolina Exit Poll.

the demographic patterns is the strong relationship between age and voting. Young voters were far more likely to vote for Obama; in 2004, they were only somewhat more likely to vote for Kerry.

Congressional Elections

Kay Hagan's victory in the U.S. Senate election was almost as much of a surprise as Obama's victory in the presidential contest. Hagan was a highly regarded state senator, but she lacked statewide name recognition. Elizabeth Dole was an incumbent with strong name recognition throughout the state. An April statewide poll showed her with a 58 percent approval rating.[12] Still, she had potential vulnerabilities, the most important of which was the fact that she spent little time visiting the state or even being visible in the state media during her term.[13] She also was regarded as a lackluster campaigner. Combined with a very unfavorable year for Republicans, these vulnerabilities led to her defeat. Key to Hagan's victory was her ability to amass substantial campaign funds, and her ability to do this depended

Table 10.4 North Carolina Voting by Selected Demographic and Social Variables, 2008 (in percent)

Variable	Voting for Obama	Voting for Hagan	Voting for Perdue
All Voters	50	53	50
Race			
White (72)	35	39	36
Black (25)	95	96	95
Gender			
Male (46)	43	47	47
Female (54)	55	55	52
Income			
Under $50,000 (50)	57	58	57
$50,000 and Over (50)	43	48	46
Education			
No College Education (32)	52	55	55
Some College (27)	45	47	47
College Degree (41)	51	52	47
Age			
Under 30 (18)	74	71	71
30–64 (66)	46	49	48
65 and Older (16)	43	45	40
Religion			
White Evangelical (44)	25	31	30
Other (56)	68	69	66

Note: Entries are the percentage of voters in the specified category who voted for the Democratic presidential, senatorial, and gubernatorial candidates (Obama, Hagan, and Perdue). The figures in parentheses indicate the percentage of all respondents in that category. For example, the data for race indicate that whites were 72 percent of the electorate in 2008 and that 35 thirty-five of whites voted for Obama. Only the percentages for the Democratic candidates are shown; these were essentially two-candidate races, so the proportion of the vote not going to the Democratic candidate went almost entirely to the Republican candidate.

Source: National Election Pool 2008 North Carolina Exit Poll.

greatly on support from the national party. Dole was identified by the Democratic Senate Campaign Committee as someone who could be defeated, and they heavily supported Hagan's campaign. Dole substantially outspent Hagan, but the committee spent heavily on ads in North Carolina, which made up for Dole's financial advantage.[14]

The Democratic campaign emphasized Dole's ineffectiveness and lack of attention to the state. One ad had two elderly men sitting in rocking chairs on a front porch discussing Dole's ineffectiveness, with hints that she was too old for the job.[15] Another ad criticized Dole (who held a seat on the Senate banking committee) for doing little to prevent the financial crisis that plagued the nation.[16] Dole responded with attack ads of her own, many of which stressed that Hagan was too liberal. One ad may have backfired. Late in the campaign, a Dole ad linked Hagan to a prominent atheist who hosted a fund-raising event for Hagan; the ad ended with a picture of Hagan and another woman's voice saying that there is no God (but giving the impression that Hagan was making the statement).[17] Hagan protested vehemently, stating that she was very active in her church and that the ad deliberately misrepresented her position. News coverage of the controversy seemed to benefit Hagan. What had been a very tight race in the polls turned into a surprisingly easy victory for Hagan.

The outcome of the Senate election was undoubtedly affected by the presidential race in the state. The Obama organizational effort was well coordinated with the Democratic Party and with the campaign efforts of other candidates. Obama campaign activities to register Democrats, to contact and persuade potential Democratic voters, and to get Democrats to the polls benefitted Hagan and other Democrats as well. Exit polls showed that 90 percent of Obama voters voted for Hagan.[18] Added to this was the very favorable national climate for Democrats, which made Dole's support for Bush and solid Republican voting record in the Senate into something she hesitated to emphasize. The result was a Democratic victory. While few pundits predicted this outcome early in the year, it was not unimaginable. Although Republicans won five of the last six Senate elections held before 2008, all were competitive contests, as discussed earlier. Thus, in a year with strong short-term forces pushing in a Democratic direction, a small underlying Republican advantage in federal elections could be overcome in a particular election.

Change characterized the Senate election, but there was more continuity than change in the U.S. House elections in 2008. Table 10.5 has the results of these elections, along with the 2006 outcomes and the 2004 presidential vote in the district, which is provided as a measure of the underlying partisanship in the district. Every incumbent ran for reelection in 2008, and all but one won. The lone loser, Eighth District Republican Robin Hayes, was defeated by Larry Kissel. Even this seat switch was hardly surprising. In 2006, Kissel barely lost to Hayes, even though the national Democratic Party did not target Hayes and therefore did not provide financial support to Kissel, who undoubtedly would have won with greater resources. In 2008, Democrats did not make the same mistake. Kissel received national party support, spent more heavily, and won. This seat pickup, combined with one in 2006 (Democrat Heath Shuler defeated an incumbent Republican in the Eleventh District), gave the Democrats eight of the thirteen House seats. Given the basic partisanship of the districts, as measured by the 2004 presidential vote in each district, Democrats probably have reached their upper limit in House seats. The

Table 10.5 Congressional Election Outcomes in North Carolina, 2006–2008 (in percent)

Congressional District	2004 Presidential Election (% Repub.)	2006 U.S. House Election (% Repub.)	2008 U.S. House Election (% Repub.)	2008 District Winner (# previous terms)
1	42	0	30	Butterfield (2)
2	54	33	33	Etheridge (6)
3	64	69	66	Jones (7)
4	44	35	37	Price (10)
5	66	57	58	Foxx (2)
6	69	71	67	Coble (12)
7	56	27	31	McIntyre (6)
8	54	50	45	Kissel
9	63	67	62	Myrick (7)
10	67	62	58	McHenry (2)
11	57	46	36	Schuler (1)
12	37	33	28	Watt (8)
13	52	36	34	Miller (3)

Note: Entries under election results are the Republican percentage of the two-party vote. Butterfield is listed as having served two previous terms, but he also served a short part of a third term, having been elected in a special election in July 2004, to replace the incumbent, who resigned from office. Price is listed as having ten previous terms, but these were not all consecutive; he served four terms, was defeated in 1994, and then elected again from 1996 on.

Source: Calculated from data provided by the North Carolina Board of Elections website and from data in Michael Barone and Richard E. Cohen, *The Almanac of American Politics 2008* (Washington, D.C.: National Journal Group, 2007).

five remaining Republican seats are all in districts won by Bush in 2004 by over 60 percent; each would almost certainly would be won by a Republican even if the incumbent failed to run for reelection. On the other hand, five of the Democratic House seats (Districts Two, Seven, Eight, Eleven, and Thirteen) are not solidly Democratic. The incumbent Democrat in each case may be able to win reelection, but each district could switch in an open seat election, particularly in a good year for the GOP.

State Elections

Continuity prevailed in state elections in 2008, but just barely so in the case of the gubernatorial election. Despite Democratic victories in the past four gubernatorial elections, the contest between Bev Perdue and Pat McCrory was expected by many observers to be very competitive. McCrory had been elected mayor of Charlotte, the largest city in the state, seven times. He was seen as a pragmatic Republican who could attract moderate and independent voters. He received the endorsement of most of the major newspapers in the state. Most pundits regarded him as a good campaigner, and he convincingly defeated three more conservative candidates in the Republican primary. Lieutenant Governor Perdue had the advantage of winning statewide office twice, experience that McCrory lacked, but lieutenant governor is not a powerful office in North Carolina. She also was not regarded as a dynamic or inspiring campaigner; five debates were held between McCrory and Perdue, and the consensus was that she lost each of them. Moreover, the lengthy control of state government by Democrats was in some ways a burden for Perdue. Over the past several years, a number of scandals and episodes of mismanagement in state government elicited prominent stories in the media. Some of these events had occurred well before 2008, and Perdue was not a central figure in them, but there was an opportunity for Republicans to argue that Democrats had been in power for too long and had become corrupt. McCrory promised a change in the old way of doing things and tried to paint Perdue as someone who would continue the status quo in Raleigh. McCrory also emphasized creating a better business climate in the state, which included lowering income, business, and estate taxes.[19] Perdue criticized McCrory for supporting school vouchers, claiming they would harm the public school system.[20] She also ran ads arguing that McCrory would divert funds for roads in rural North Carolina to transportation projects in Charlotte; these ads may have helped her in eastern North

Carolina.[21] Perdue also had more to spend on ads. Through the end of September, she raised over $15 million, compared to just $5.4 million for McCrory.[22] In a year that was more favorable to Republicans, McCrory might have prevailed, but 2008 was not that year.

Perdue's source of support was very similar to that of Obama and Hagan, as we can see in Tables 10.3 and 10.4. She did better among blacks, women, lower-socioeconomic status voters, and younger voters. About 90 percent of Obama and Hagan voters also voted for Perdue. However, a comparison of support for Perdue and Hagan reveals some of the reasons why the gubernatorial race was closer. Perdue did slightly less well than Hagan among Democrats and independents and among liberals and moderates. Core Democratic groups were not quite as strong in their support for Perdue as they were for Hagan. Fortunately for Perdue, the favorable year for Democrats and the effectiveness of the Democratic campaign effort resulted in a strong turnout of Democrats. In past years, Democratic gubernatorial candidates won in spite of their party's presidential candidate. In 2008, Perdue may have Obama to thank for her success.

Continuity clearly characterized other state elections. Democrats continued to claim the majority of the council of state offices, adding the office of state auditor to increase their total to eight of the ten offices. In addition to the governor and lieutenant governor, Democrats held other important statewide offices, such as attorney general and secretary of state. After 2008, Republicans held only two council of state offices: secretary of agriculture and secretary of labor. Democratic success in these lesser statewide offices is significant not only for control of the executive branch but also because these offices are good springboards to higher offices. Democrats also maintained their control of both houses of the state legislature. The distribution of seats after 2008 was hardly different from what it was before the election. Democrats therefore entered 2009 with solid control of state government, control they have maintained almost continuously since the 1992 elections. Republicans could take some comfort in the fact that many of the council of state races were close contests and that they were slightly better off in the state house after the election, but the GOP was clearly the minority party in state government.

Conclusion

A strong national Democratic tide helped to propel Democrats in North Carolina to victory. For the first time in the post-civil rights era, the party won the presidential, U.S. Senate, and gubernatorial elections in the same year; in fact, the party had not even won a gubernatorial and senatorial election in the same year since 1968. Twenty years ago, few pundits would have predicted that North Carolina Democrats would have nearly complete control of state government, a majority of U.S. House seats, and half of the U.S. Senate seats in 2009, but that is exactly where the state stood following the 2008 elections. But if the 2008 victories depended greatly on this national tide, what is the forecast for politics in the state? Future elections will be subjected to different tidal forces, and outcomes could shift considerably. Republicans could easily win back the Senate seat that they lost, as Hagan would be up for reelection in 2014, which would be the midterm election of the second Obama term (assuming his reelection in 2012), and midterm elections in the second term of a president historically are unkind to the party in the White House. Several of the U.S. House seats held by Democrats are in districts that have a fairly even partisan split. When these seats become open, they could change party hands. Some of the incumbents could be beaten by a strong Republican in a good year for the GOP. Even the long control of state government by Democrats could be precarious. The gubernatorial and several other statewide council of state races were very competitive contests. While the Democrats have solid majorities in both houses of the state legislature, their seat margins are much greater than their popular vote margins; a fairly small shift in the popular vote could produce considerable seat change.

However, the Democratic victories in 2008 could also reflect long-term shifts in Tar Heel politics. The rapid growth of the state, especially in major urban areas, may be working to the advantage of the Democrats. Even though they are a more affluent group, the newcomers to the state may be politically more moderate voters, who are both unreceptive to appeals based on social conservatism and accepting of a greater government role in such areas as health care, education, and environmental protection. The fact that young voters were so heavily Democratic in 2008 is another favorable sign for Democrats. This group also was disproportionately Democratic in 2004, although not to the same degree that it was in 2008. Of course, just because young, first-time voters cast a Democratic ballot in 2008 does not necessarily mean that they will continue to vote Democratic. Many of these voters undoubtedly lack a strong party identification. But they are starting out with an initial affinity for Democrats, and if this is reinforced in subsequent elections, these voters could develop clear identifications with the Democratic Party. Once party identifications are formed, they tend to be fairly stable, so the voting patterns of this age cohort should be examined in future elections. In sum, 2008 may have been nothing more than a year in which there were very strong short-term forces favoring the Democrats, but it also could be the start of some new developments in North Carolina politics. At this point, we can only wait for the results of future elections to assess these possibilities.

11.

Tennessee

Cracker Barrel Realignment

Ronald Keith Gaddie,
with the assistance of Michael D. Jones

Introduction

Tennessee presents an interesting case when considering the 2008 election. Before the 2008 campaign, it had nearly elected to the U.S. Senate the first southern black senator since Reconstruction, Harold Ford Jr. Rep. Ford would provide a contrast to Barak Obama in the early days of the campaign. These comparisons arose based on Ford's efforts to emphasize his crossracial appeal to garner white, southern votes, and also on the role of code-wording and implicit racial appeals in his narrow loss to Chattanooga mayor Bob Corker. Until Obama emerged as a presidential candidate in late 2006, it was an ongoing debate regarding which man was the more prominent mainstream black politician in the United States. Like Ford, Obama did not succeed in winning the hearts, minds, and votes of most Tennesseans. However, also like Ford, Obama did run ahead of most other Democrats in Tennessee who recently sought a seat in the U.S. Senate or the presidency. Their race left them relatively undistinguished from their white Democratic counterparts. In the case of Obama, however, it is possible to discount any role of race in determining voter preferences, though it requires that one point the finger at another explanation—evangelical Christianity.

Tennessee in Presidential Elections

Tennessee is historically the most competitive southern state for Republicans. In 1920 and 1928 the state cast its electoral votes for Republicans. In 1948, Tennessee did not bolt over the Democratic National Party's inclusion of a civil rights plank. Instead, Tennessee Democratic party leadership split over supporting the Dixiecrats, with E. H. Crump and his Memphis-based machine favoring the bolt while moderate elements from Nashville and surrounding middle Tennessee stayed with Harry Truman and the national party.[1] The civil rights rift presaged a realignment of Tennessee. Political scientist Peter Nardulli considers the period of 1948–52 to be a period of critical realignment away from the presidential Democrats in Middle and West Tennessee.[2] This assessment is reasonable, as Republicans won Tennessee in three straight presidential elections before 1964 (1952, 1956, 1960) and would also carry the state in eight of the eleven elections subsequent to 1964 (all but 1976, 1992, and 1996).

The Grand Divisions

To understand Tennessee is to understand geography. It is a long, skinny state, an outgrowth of a cession of claims by the former Carolina colony to the United States. As V. O. Key described it, Tennessee is

> a narrow ribbon of real estate stretching from North Carolina to the Mississippi. From Bristol, in the far northeast, to Memphis, in the southwest, about equals the distance from Hartford, Connecticut to Cleveland, Ohio. Tennessee's far western counties are but northward projections of Mississippi; its eastern mountain counties share both the topography and spirit of western North Carolina and southwestern Virginia. Between West Tennessee and East Tennessee lies Middle Tennessee, a fertile bowl, sometimes called . . . "the dimple of the universe," whose principal city is Nashville.[3]

The historical geography of Tennessee lent itself to greater Republican competitiveness than the rest of the South. At mid-century, Key observed that "[t]o the problems of political management inherent in three distinct geographical sections are added patterns of political behavior deposited by the Civil War." East Tennessee, mountainous and heavily white, had little truck for secession in the days leading up the Civil War, and people there were "staunch unionists [who] resisted secession."[4] The east sided with the Union, and there was countersecession sentiment like that in what is now West Virginia. After Reconstruction and through the Jim Crow era, Tennessee politics in the grand division of the East was Republican, and in the Reconstruction era East Tennessee Republicans dominated government and also engaged in payback for their repression by the Confederates. The Civil War alignment lingered as counties that opposed secession in 1861 were the most Republican counties nine decades later.

East Tennessee was the most Republican part of the South for a century. Republicans held one congressional district from 1867 forward, and a second from 1880 forward. Republican success, when it did come, was usually due to marrying east Tennessee votes with votes from Nashville and Middle Tennessee. The machine of congressman Carroll Reece made occasional corrupt bargains with the Crump machine of Memphis, but those deals did not preclude sending notable numbers of Republican lawmakers to the legislature in Nashville.[5] The New Deal realignment crushed the nascent Republican competitiveness of the 1920s, but sufficient GOP strength remained in east Tennessee.[6] The emerging Republican Party of the 1950s was a grassroots outgrowth of traditional Mountain Republicanism.[7]

Until the 1960s, West Tennessee remained the tough nut for Republican presidential politics. Large rural black populations and the reinforcement of segregation by the Democratic Party lent a Deep South flavor to the politics of the region. Memphis was the voting anchor, dominated for a half-century (until the 1950s) by the powerful Crump machine.[8] Republicans lacked party organization, voter identification, or an issue of affinity with which to attract conservative the rural whites of west Tennessee. The Goldwater campaign of 1964 changed this, offering a Republican States' Rights voice in the face of the Johnson administration's integrationist efforts.

Analysis of historic presidential elections in Tennessee reveals remarkable regional and local stability for over a century. Factor analysis of county voting patterns for president reveal that the basis of the two-party vote was stable from 1892 to 1968, with a second dimension of politics based on the antebellum system and a third that exists in the post-reconstruction era and structures Republican, Socialist, and Populist bases of support together. A new dimension emerges in 1972 that obliterates the old, severe sectional distinctions between west, middle, and east.[9]

The History of Racial Polarization in Tennessee Presidential Elections

John Lyman Mason notes that there are racial divisions in the politics of Tennessee between white Republicans and black Democrats.[10] However, his perception was that there was a lack of racial tension in the state, relative to other Southern states. The lack of racial tension in turn attracted out-of-state and foreign investment. This included General Motors—which built the original Saturn plant in middle Tennessee—and the Japanese automaker Nissan. Such was not always the case.

Tennessee's integration experience was less colorful and deadly than for her Deep South neighbors Alabama and Mississippi, though Tennessee had a history of both racial segregation and voting discrimination. The historic black belt poked into Tennessee in Fayette and Haywood counties of west Tennessee. The small black population is largely located in the westernmost of the three grand divisions of the state, with the largest numbers in Shelby County (Memphis) followed by metropolitan Nashville. Tennessee discrimination against blacks was relatively benign compared to Mississippi and Alabama. Tennessee political scientist David Brodsky observes that Tennessee historically placed "few obstacles in the path of potential African-American voters," noting the lack of a literacy test in particular.[11] Tennessee newspaperman Jennings Perry contrasted Tennessee with neighboring Kentucky, declaring them to be at highly similar (except for the practice in Tennessee of the poll tax).[12] Tennessee instituted a poll tax on men between the ages of twenty-one and sixty in 1890, but by 1948 had abandoned the practice of enforcing the poll tax and repealed the tax in 1953. Some Tennessee towns used a form of literacy test and were permitted to use local registration requirements ("Dortch's Law"), which caused some disfranchisement. The use of the poll tax in Tennessee did have a racially discriminatory effect, disproportionately affecting blacks.[13] The interaction of poll tax and Dortch's Law implementation through time meant black voters were disproportionately disfranchised by the laws. The poll tax was three times more likely to disfranchise a black voter.[14]

The effects of rural disfranchisement of blacks were offset in Memphis by the Crump machine. As early as 1949, V. O. Key observed that there were no real impediments to black voting in the cities, and as early as 1920 black voters had been actively sought in Nashville politics. Indeed, there is an irony to race, corruption, and Tennessee politics. Political machines like the Crump machine of Memphis wooed black voters with jobs and other patronage, and paid poll taxes for black voters in exchange for their ballots on election day for machine candidates. They also promised local government services in Memphis that were beneficial to the segregated black community. The Crump machine was far from publicly benevolent, however, when it came to changing the political status quo, delivering what Key termed "efficient government, a clean city . . . but all without freedom or liberty."[15]

As was often the case with a machined black vote, Crump's use of black votes did not necessarily deliver black preferences. Crump supported the Dixiecrat ticket in 1948. And while Strom Thurmond and Fielding Wright received just 13.5 percent of the vote in Tennessee, they rolled up substantial vote totals in Shelby County and other counties in the southwest corner of the state.

After the 1950s, political conflict in Memphis centered on the efforts of blacks to attain political access and fairer treatment. The Crump machine's power statewide was broken by Estes Kefauver and Frank Clement. By the 1960s, the crumbling of the machine in local politics resulted in strikes by black municipal workers and demands for better, integrated schools (an April 1968 strike by the black sanitation workers brought Martin Luther King Jr. to Memphis).

In the 1960s, as blacks emerged as an independent political force, there was a realigning effect on Tennessee politics. David Brodsky notes that the 1964 Goldwater candidacy was coincident to an effort to purge black "post-office" Republicans and to reconstruct the state Republican Party as a "lily-white" organization.[16] By the end of the decade, racially polarizing issues gravitated out of the Democratic primary and into general election politics. Bill Brock's successful effort to unseat Senator Al Gore Sr. trotted out a modernized version of racial threat that would be repeated—the "southern strategy"—to divide whites from the Democratic Party. Brock won an unprecedented majority of the white vote in the western grand division (where a majority of blacks in Tennessee resided). Tennessee politics subsequently evolved to economic and social issues not directly related to race, leading to an early departure of the politics of race.[17]

At the time of the passage of the Voting Rights Act, discrepancies in black and white voting existed. These differences were insufficient to suppress overall voter participation to a level that would trigger coverage by Section Five of the Voting Rights Act. Ironically, Crump's previous collection of black voters in the 1930s and 1940s, the abandoning of the poll tax, and the presence of a viable Republican opposition throughout most of the twentieth century ensured higher voter participation by the 1960s. The result kept Tennessee free from federal election oversight.

Religion and Politics in Tennessee

One cannot speak of southern politics in the last quarter century without addressing matters of faith. The South has more religious participation and a culture more entrenched in Protestant evangelical faith than any other part of the United States. The evangelical foundation of religious life in Tennessee is important because the latest realignment of southern politics has its origin the rise of Republicanism among evangelical Christians. Among the proxy measures of evangelical religious adherence is frequency of church attendance—most frequent churchgoers (more than once a week) are typically Protestants, who in Tennessee are most often evangelical Christians.

This is evident in Tennessee, where the dedication to religious exercise is largely a function of the Protestant tradition, especially through the Southern Baptist Convention. More recently, independent nondenominational evangelical churches have provided the greatest source of growth in adherents. These evangelical faiths encourage both active worship and proselytizing that provides a powerful basis for grassroots organizing. As indicated in Table 11.1, most Tennesseans attend church with some frequency.[17] Majorities across race report attending more than monthly attendance. Among those who attend at least once a week, the most frequent churchgoers are African Americans. Very few Tennesseans report never attending church, regardless of race. Variations in attendance from year to year among those who do attend appear to fall within sampling error, indicating a stable, churchgoing electorate.

Of the 9,634 religious congregations of all faiths in Tennessee in 2000, nearly three quarters—7,156—are evangelical congregations. Of the estimated 2.9 million religious adherents of all ages, over 2.1 million attend evangelical congregations.[18] This number is inclusive of more social-gospel oriented black congregations as well as conservative white congregations, and should not be viewed as an indication of political, social, or even theological homogeneity.

Exit poll data in Tennessee show consistently higher support for Republicans among evangelical whites than others in the electorate.[19] This relationship is evident in varying degrees across major statewide and congressional offices and especially in presidential voting over the last several decades. As we will see, it is faith in addition to race that structures the presidential election in Tennessee.

Table 11.1 How Often Do You Attend Religious Services? (in percent)

	Once a week or more	Once or twice a month	Less than once a month	Rarely	Never
Black					
2004	66.3	14.5	7.2	8.4	3.6
2002	68.7	10.4	4.5	13.4	3
1998	56.6	22.6	na	15.1	4.7
1994	60.2	21.2	na	11.5	5.3
1993	62.3	23.4	na	9.1	5.2
White					
2004	50.4	15.1	7.7	19.5	7.4
2002	50	17.4	5.2	20.7	6.2
1998	51	16.3	na	23.2	9
1994	51.9	15.5	na	24.5	7.8
1993	47.7	18.9	na	26.6	6.5

na=information not available.

Source: Ronald Keith Gaddie and Michael D. Jones, "Tennessee: A Quiet Sort of Inequality," in *New Voices of the Old South: How Women and Minorities Influence Southern Politics,* ed. Todd G. Shields and Shannon G. Davis (Tallahassee: Florida State University John Scott Daily Florida Institute of Government, 2008), Table 10.

The 2008 Presidential Primaries in Tennessee

Tennessee was one of twenty-four states to take part in the Super Tuesday primary on February 5, 2008. The Volunteer State has participated in Super Tuesday since its inception, first giving most of its delegates to favorite son Al Gore in 1988. John Kerry was the first nonsoutherner to win Tennessee's delegates on Super Tuesday.

Early polling showed Tennessee as a strong primary state for Hillary Clinton. Trial heats in early 2007 showed Senator Clinton besting John Edwards, Barack Obama, and Al Gore in the state, though the inclusion of Gore in an Insider Advantage trial heat poll cut Clinton's lead by about 10 points. Two weeks prior to the February 5 primary, polling placed Clinton (34 percent) with a double-digit lead over Obama (20 percent) and Edwards (16 percent). With Edwards's primary-eve withdrawal from the contest, polling showed a remarkable migration of voter preferences toward Clinton, followed by Obama. Clinton opened up a sizeable lead over Obama, 55 percent to 35 percent, in the last independent poll by pollster Scott Rasmussen on February 2. As in Oklahoma and Arkansas, the exit of Edwards led to a migration of white primary voters largely toward Clinton. On primary day, Clinton carried 53.8 percent of the vote to 40.5 percent for Obama and took forty of sixty-eight pledged delegates. Of the inactive candidates still on the ballot, only Edwards attracted more than 1 percent of the vote. In West Tennessee, Obama did best in Shelby (Memphis), and the rural, former black-belt counties that make up the southwest corner of Tennessee. In Middle Tennessee, Obama carried Davidson (Nashville), Williamson, and Marshall counties to the south on the I-65 corridor; in white, east Tennessee, Obama carried only Hamilton County (Chattanooga) with an 8-point plurality.

African American voters made up an estimated third of the Democratic primary electorate, and that vote went heavily for Obama. Exit polls indicate that an estimated 77 percent of blacks voted for Obama, thereby providing the bulk of his support, as in other southern primary states. Exit poll data indicate Obama had far less racial crossover appeal in the Democratic primary, pulling just 25 percent of the white vote. Senator Clinton swept the nonurban core and rural counties outside the old black belt, where the older, white, and less-educated electorate resembled the demographic of her support in many other states across the nation.

On the Republican side of the primary, southern evangelical Republicans continued to propel the candidacy of Arkansas's former governor Mike Huckabee. The evangelical-marathoner edged John McCain 34.5 percent to 31.8 percent, with Mitt Romney trailing at 23.6 percent. Governor Huckabee won just over a third of the total primary vote, but about four in ten evangelical voters, who provided his margin over McCain in the three-cornered primary.

One of the interesting features of the 2008 presidential election in the South in general is the disjunction between Obama's performance in primaries versus the general elections in the southern states. Obama won three southern states in the general election: Florida, North Carolina, and Virginia, all of which are covered in part by the amended Voting Rights Act of 1965. He lost eight southern states, six of which are wholly covered by the Voting Rights Act and two of which are not—Tennessee and Arkansas. Of the ten southern states that held binding presidential nomination contests authorized by the Democratic National Committee (all but Florida), Obama won eight, all covered in whole or part by the Voting Rights Act. Obama lost the delegate counts only in Arkansas and Tennessee.[20] If one looks at the Obama vote shares in the other southern states, the dominant nature of his candidacy in the South is evident: South Carolina, 55 percent; Mississippi, 61 percent; Alabama, 56 percent; Georgia,

66 percent; Louisiana, 57 percent; Virginia, 64 percent; North Carolina, 56 percent. Black voters constituted majorities or near-majorities of the turnout in all of these primaries. Tennessee and Arkansas stand as peculiar exceptions, southern states where Obama had no success within the party or among the general electorate.

General Election Success

Across the larger South, Barack Obama commanded 46.7 percent of the two-party presidential vote and won fifty-five Electoral College votes. Tennessee went with the South and against the nation, casting 57 percent of its votes for John McCain. This should come as no surprise to Volunteer State political observers, or anyone who watched the polls. From the moment that an Obama nomination was evident to most political observers —just after the Super Tuesday primaries—poll tracks indicated that a McCain-Obama matchup would conform to the pattern for recent Tennessee presidential elections. As indicated in Table 11.2, no poll taken from February 11 through the end of October showed McCain with less than a double-digit lead. McCain's largest lead, reported in a Rasmussen poll during the convention season, showed McCain up by 25 points. Some evidence of movement due to the credit crisis is observable, as the average McCain lead shrank from 19 points from April to September to 15 points after the market collapse.

Table 11.2 Poll Tracks in Tennessee, President, 2008 (in percent)

Polling House	Release Date	McCain (R)	Obama (D)
MTSU	February 23	50	36
SurveyUSA	February 28	54	38
Ayres-McHenry	March 9	53	36
Rasmussen	April 3	58	31
Rasmussen	June 24	51	36
Ayres-McHenry	August 12	51	36
Rasmussen	August 20	60	35
MTSU	September 27	48	36
Mason-Dixon	September 24	55	39
Rasmussen	September 29	58	39
Rasmussen	October 16	54	42
Research 2000	October 22	54	38

Source: Realclearpolitics.com.

State media were divided in interpreting these data. In Knoxville, the local papers supported the McCain candidacy, while in Chattanooga the *Times Press* was skeptical of both the GOP ticket and the voters of Tennessee: "[M]any of Tennessee's McCain supporters are among those in the so-called Red states who are still falling for the baseless McCain/Palin attacks on Mr. Obama's character, patriotism and, implicitly, his race, while ignoring the harm they and their families would continue to endure from the economic policies that Mr. McCain would continue from the Bush administration."[21] The Chattanooga paper subsequently endorsed Obama for president, and the Democrat carried Hamilton County in the general election.

Tennessee's most lasting contribution to the 2008 presidential campaign in the minds of some observers may be the reminder that the mindset that led to the founding of the Ku Klux Klan 140 years ago is still with us. On October 27, Tennessean Daniel Cowart and Arkansan Paul Schlesselman were arrested and subsequently indicted on weapons charges and threatening a presidential candidate. The two had planned to murder eighty-eight black people and then engage in a suicide attack on Obama, driving a speeding car and firing guns while wearing white ties, white tails, and white top hats. They were arrested outside Memphis after a shooting at a rural black church. The day before the election, someone stabbed and then hanged an Obama face-decorated pumpkin on the campus of Middle Tennessee State in Murfreesboro. It is worth noting that these acts pale when compared to nineteenth century political violence in Tennessee.

The Obama-Biden ticket received almost unanimous support from black voters across the South, and Tennessee was no exception (see Table 11.3). According to the National Election Pool exit polls, between 92 percent and 98 percent of African American voters supported the Democratic ticket in the various southern states. Among white voters, the Democratic ticket posted its strongest support in Florida (42 percent), Virginia (39 percent), and North Carolina (35 percent), and its weakest figures among whites in Mississippi (11 percent), Alabama (12 percent), and Louisiana (14 percent). All of the Rim South states except Texas offered at least 30 percent support to Obama, while no Deep South state showed more than 26 percent white support for the Democratic candidate.

Tennessee vote share for Obama ranked low among southern states. The Democrat's 42.1 percent was good enough to tie for eighth among the eleven southern states, ranking only ahead of Alabama and Arkansas and equaling Louisiana. The white vote share for Obama, however, ranked

Table 11.3 Comparing Obama's Tennessee Performance to the Rest of the South (in percent)

State	OBAMA VOTE SHARES			SHARE OF TURNOUT		
	Total percent	Black percent	White percent	Black percent	White percent	Latino percent
Alabama	39	98	12	29	65	4
Arkansas	39.7	94	30	12	83	3
Florida	51.2	96	42*	13	71	14
Georgia	46.7	98	23	30	65	3
Louisiana	42.1	94	14	29	65	4
Mississippi	43.1	98	11	33	62	4
N. Carolina	50.1	97	35	23	72	3
S. Carolina	45.3	96	26	25	71	3
Tennessee	42.1	94	34	12	84	2
Texas	44.1	98	26*	13	63	20
Virginia	52.3	92	39	20	70	5

*Does not include Latino vote; Latinos went an estimated 57 percent for Obama in Florida, 63 percent in Texas.

Source: Charles S. Bullock III and Roland Keith Gaddie, The Triumph of Voting Rights in the South (Norman: University of Oklahoma Press, 2009).

fourth among the eleven southern states at 34 percent, behind only North Carolina (35 percent), Virginia (39 percent), and Florida (42 percent).

Despite Obama's poor popular showing and the weak geographic distribution of his support in Tennessee, he nonetheless ran better among southern whites in Tennessee than in most of the South. The reason for his failure is in part attributable to simple demographics: black voters only constituted about 12 percent of the electorate in Tennessee, which is the lowest black share in any southern state.[22] If we compare the black vote share in Tennessee to the 23 percent in North Carolina and the 20 percent in Virginia, we can reach a reasonable conclusion: if the black electorate were comparable in numbers in Tennessee and the white vote held constant, Obama would have carried the Volunteer State. The alternative requires a 10-point shift in the preferences of white voters to over 43 percent of the white vote.

The other matter of note is the general continuity, in the aggregate, of the presidential vote from 2004 to 2008. According to exit polling, in Florida, Georgia, and Tennessee white voters all stood pat in their preferences from 2004 to 2008.[23] An examination of exit polls in Tennessee reveals this constancy—the white preference for Democrats was effectively unchanged from 2000 to 2004 to 2008, as was the degree of black preference for Democrats for president (see Table 11.4). The estimated preference of the black vote, indeed, is consistent back to 1992. White preferences, however, shifted 18 points more Republican from 1992 to 2004, but remained relatively constant from 2004 to 2008. In the aggregate, there is no indication of a weakening of the Republican white vote due to the Obama candidacy. The Obama candidacy also only runs about three points weaker among whites than the Harold Ford candidacy for the Senate in 2006.

Changes in the Tennessee Election Pattern

The substantial Obama national victory illuminated the divergence of most of the nation with the South in presidential politics. In particular, national attention focused on the swath of counties running from central Oklahoma, through Arkansas, Tennessee, northern Alabama, and southeastern Kentucky to West Virginia that voted more Republican in 2008 than in 2004. These counties were largely rural, largely possessed of large white populations, and not very affluent. As shown in Tennessee (see Figure 11.1), this arc of counties cuts across all of the grand divisions of the state, but they are largely outside the major metropolitan areas of Tennessee.

Table 11.4 NEP Exit Poll Estimates of White and Black Voter Preferences, 1992–2008 (in percent)

Year	Office	Party	Black	White
2008	President	D	94	34
		R	6	63
2004	President	D	91	34
		R	9	65
2000	President	D	92	36
		R	8	60
1996	President	D	90	42
		R	10	51
1992	President	D	96	42
		R	3	47
2006	U.S. Senate	D	95.0	40.0
		R	4.0	59.0

Source: 2008 National Election Pool.

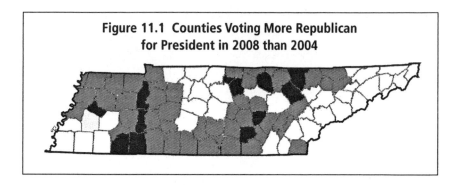

Figure 11.1 Counties Voting More Republican for President in 2008 than 2004

As shown in Table 11.5, which reports results of a regression analysis, the 2004 general election vote for president demonstrated a racial structure, but not an evangelical Christian structure[24]. John Kerry's vote share generally increased as the black share of the potential electorate increased (b = .532), which is not surprising. The evangelical Christian coefficient was not significant and not even in the expected direction. Things change for Barack Obama in 2008. The Democratic nominee enjoys a stronger return on black voters than Kerry (b = .668). However, the Obama vote share falls with the increase in concentration of evangelical Christians in the electorate—and the fit of the model is substantially better than in 2004.

So what of all the shifting and sorting going on in Figure 11.1? Of the ninety-five counties in Tennessee, nine showed net gains of Democratic strength from 2004 to 2008, and they are among the most populous in the state, the most heavily black, or both: Shelby, +5.9 percent (most populous, second most black—Memphis); Davidson, +5.1 percent (second most populous, eighth most black—Nashville); Montgomery, +4.5 percent (ninth most populous); Madison, +2.5 percent (sixth most heavily black); Haywood, + 2.5 percent (most heavily black, 50.5 percent); Williamson, +2.5 percent (sixth most populous); Rutherford, +2.3 percent (fifth most populous); Hamilton, +1.7 percent (fourth most populous, Chattanooga); and Knox, +0.73 percent (third most populous, Knoxville).

Another eighty-six counties showed Republican gains over 2004. Thirteen counties were at least 10 points more Republican for president in 2008 than in 2004, and sixty counties were at least five points more Republican. The county with the largest Republican gain was Scott County (Huntsville), an Eastern Tennessee county that lies just south of McCreary County, Kentucky, and which has a nearly 99 percent white population. Of the thirteen biggest GOP gainers, only two had black populations of

Table 11.5 WLS Estimates of the 2004 and 2008 Democratic Presidential Vote, and the Structure of Shifting Preferences in Tennessee

	Kerry 2004 percent	Obama 2008 percent	Δ '04-'08	Δ '04-'08
Intercept	25.283	41.013	15.730	6.515
Non-Hispanic Black Percent	.532 (.045)**	.668 (.043)**	.136 (.023)**	.128 (.023)**
Evangelical Percent	.119 (.074)	-.142 (.072)*	-.261 (.037)**	-.156 (.061)**
Roman Catholic Percent				.263 (.121)**
Adjusted R^2	.663	.817	.683	.695

(N = 95)
* p < .05
** p < .01
Note: Standard errors in parentheses.
Source: Computed by author.

more than 10 percent (Crockett and Trousdale) and five had less than 1 percent black population. None of the thirteen biggest GOP gainers had more than 12,500 ballots cast for president, and the average ballots cast per county was 6,914. Of the thirteen counties exhibiting the largest GOP gains, five were in West Tennessee, while four each were in Middle Tennessee and East Tennessee.

In Table 11.5, a pair of weighted least squares regressions is estimated for the net change in the Democratic vote at the county level from 2004 to 2008. The initial estimation controls for the percent of non-Hispanic black population and the percent of evangelical adherents in each county. The model explains 68 percent of the variation in the change in Democratic vote and indicates that Obama made gains over Kerry where black populations were greater, likely reflecting increased mobilization of the African American electorate. However, Obama's gain is muted by large evangelical populations. I then respecified the equation to also control for the Roman Catholic population in the counties. While the overall Roman Catholic population of Tennessee is not great, four counties have over 10 percent Roman Catholic adherents (Cheatham, Maury, Shelby, and Williamson, with over 20 percent). While Roman Catholics have been a source of increased social conservative mobilization for over two decades, Catholics are also historically more racially tolerant. The Roman Catholic control is significant and in the expected positive direction, while not reducing the significance of the other two control variables.

Despite the continuity of the Obama vote relative to the Kerry vote in Tennessee, the election of 2008 constituted a further sorting of the Tennessee electorate on the basis of religion. First, when compared to the 2004 results, evangelical populations took on a statistically significant and negative relationship to the Democratic vote that was not evident in 2004 when Kerry ran. Second, the change in Democratic strength was structured by both race and by the proportion of the population that was evangelical. These counties—rural, smaller, whiter, and more evangelical—were consistent with the rhetoric of "real America" emphasized by the GOP ticket, and were the logical target of the 2008 Republican campaign.

Down-ticket Elections in 2008

Down-ticket political events were largely uneventful in the Volunteer State. Incumbent senator Lamar Alexander won reelection with 65 percent of the vote over Democrat Bob Tuke. Tuke, a lawyer and Marine Corps veteran who served in Vietnam, was past chair of the state Democratic Party and also chair of the Obama campaign in Tennessee. He emerged from a crowded Democratic primary field, winning the nomination with just 32 percent of the vote.

The much-anticipated arrival of a Republican majority in the state's House of Representatives promised to fell longtime Democratic Speaker Jimmy Naifeh of Covington. Naifeh, elected from the last black-belt district in Tennessee (Haywood and Tipton counties), was returned to office, though Democrats came up one seat short of their majority. His eighteen-year reign as speaker ended, though not in a total abdication of power. Democrats continued to organize the chamber when they used their forty-nine votes, plus the vote of Republican Kent Williams, to place Williams in the speaker's chair, thereby defeating the succession plans of Republican leader Jason Mumpower. The irony is that such scenarios had been suggested for toppling Naifeh in the past through the use of dissident Democrats allied with a cohesive Republican minority caucus.

The most intriguing race in the state was the congressional primary in District Nine in Shelby County. Incumbent Steve Cohen is a rarity, a white lawmaker representing a majority-black district. A former state senator, Cohen emerged from a crowded field in 2006 to succeed Harold Ford Jr. in the seat. In 2008, Cohen confronted African American lawyer Nikki Tinker in the Democratic primary. Tinker, who had lost to Cohen two years prior, ran a divisive campaign that attempted to simultaneously tie the Jewish Cohen to the Ku Klux Klan while also attacking him as not being Christian. In the end, Cohen prevailed over the negative diatribes in a walk with almost 80 percent of the vote.

Conclusion

In an election season where change was the watchword, Tennessee did not change. This is surprising considering that Tennessee would have seemed to be a potential pickup for Democrats in 2008. Recent political history had Tennessee casting votes for Democratic presidential candidates in the 1990s. The state has major urban centers that are centers of black political power (Memphis) and major progressive centers (Nashville). Demographically, Tennessee is a new South state with major industries and a diversified economy.

Nonetheless, Tennessee did not budge in the presidential election. And within the state a sorting of politics occurred where Republicans made gains in major rural areas while declining in three of the state's four urban centers. A deeper force was at work. The assumed suspect is race.[25] The reality is more compelling.

The analysis presented here indicates that the Obama shift in Tennessee was less a function of race than of religion and culture. The politics of the 2008 were structured by race and religion; so too were the shifts relative to 2004. The nature of the campaign waged in Tennessee and elsewhere, which placed a premium on cultural identity politics, activated evangelical Christian voters in rural and small-town counties to support the Republican ticket.

Was this a racial appeal vested within a cultural and religious appeal? The topical analysis presented here cannot answer that question. However, to get at the answer to the question requires students of southern politics, race and politics, and religion and politics to confront two lurking questions of southern politics that are disquieting:

1. How do historic differences in black and white evangelical faiths—with the former emphasizing social gospel and the latter emphasizing morality and obedience to authority relationships—lead to differing political preferences despite a similar relationship to Biblical scripture?
2. How might the uncomfortable historic relationship between southern Protestant evangelical denominations and institutions of segregation and white supremacy construct modern evangelical political rhetoric and preferences?

The rhetoric of social conservatism, designed to appeal to social conservatives and evangelicals, walks close to the rhetoric of racial separation. The initial aggregate analysis from Tennessee indicates that the vehicle of faith structures Tennessee's change. The question mark that remains is how that vehicle acted on racial attitudes and preferences that necessarily cannot be detected in polling.

12.

Texas

After the Bush Era

Brian Arbour and Mark McKenzie

Introduction

January 20, 2009, ushered in a new administration with the inauguration of Barack Obama, and to some, it ushered in a new political age. But in Texas, that date marked an end: the end to the Bush era in Texas politics. On that day, George W. Bush left office, returning to Texas to retire permanently from electoral politics. And for the first time since at least 1980, the most prominent Republican politician in the state of Texas will not be named George Bush.

Before 1980, political Texas was a very different place. In 1976, Democrat Jimmy Carter won the state, and the state political establishment was dominated by Democrats. At that point, only one Republican politician had won victory in a statewide election since Reconstruction (U.S. senator John Tower), and Republican representation in the state legislature and congressional delegation seemed a mere token.[1] In the intervening thirty-two years, the tables in Texas have turned. Republicans have won, and in recent years, won big. Republicans have won the presidency in Texas every election since 1980, have held the state's two U.S. Senate seats since 1993, and won majorities in the state Senate in 1998, in the state House in 2002, and in the state's congressional delegation in 2004. In short, the state today is solidly Republican.

195

In this chapter, we assess the 2008 election in the context of the Bush era in Texas politics. The Bush era made the state not only solidly Republican at present, but it has put the Republicans in a solid position for the near future. Nearly half of the state's 2008 voters (46 percent) were conservatives, helping Republicans to hold a major advantage among white voters and in rural and suburban Texas. The 2008 election provided some hopeful signs for Texas Democrats—gains in urban counties, and among Hispanic and young voters—but the Republican strengths are greater than the Democrats'. Republican political dominance of Texas will continue over the next decade unless Democrats can reduce the number of conservatives in the state and make gains among white and suburban voters.

The 2008 Election

The 2008 election was a continuation of the state's Republican trend. Table 12.1 shows that John McCain won the state easily, taking 55.5 percent of the statewide vote to pocket the state's thirty-four electoral votes. John Cornyn's numbers were similar; he garnered 54.8 percent of the vote to win reelection to the U.S. Senate. Republicans recaptured a House seat they previously held when Pete Olson defeated incumbent Democrat Nick Lampson in the Twenty-second congressional district,[2] and targeted Republican incumbents John Culberson and Michael McCaul won reelection.

Despite the Republican success at the top of the ticket, Democrats had several down-ballot successes. Incumbent Ciro Rodriguez held the congressional seat that he took from Henry Bonilla in 2006. Democrats netted three seats in the state House, (putting them two seats from a majority), defeated an incumbent Republican state senator for the first time in decades, and won the majority of courthouse races in the state's largest county (Harris) for the first time since 1994. Barack Obama also won three of the state's four largest counties, which Al Gore and John Kerry had not been able to do. These results have made Texas Democrats optimistic that they could win the state in the near future.

Primary Excitement

The year 2008 produced a bifurcated campaign in Texas. John McCain led Texas polls by a wide margin throughout the general election.[3] As a result, Texans participated in the general election campaign mostly by proxy, donating money and time that the campaigns could use in other,

Table 12.1 The Vote in Texas, 2008

	Candidate (Party)	Percent of Vote	Vote Totals
President			
	John McCain (R)	55.5	4,467,748
	Barack Obama (D)	43.7	3,521,164
Senate			
	John Cornyn (I)	54.8	4,326,639
	Rick Noriega (D)	42.8	3,383,890
U.S. House of Representatives			
Seventh District	John Culberson (I)	55.9	162,205
	Michael Skelly (D)	42.3	122,832
Tenth District	Michael McCaul (I)	51.5	113,567
	Larry Joe Doherty (D)	46	101,548
Twenty-second District	Pete Olson (R)	52.4	161,600
	Nick Lampson (D)	45.4	139,879
Twenty-third District	Lyle Larson (R)	44.7	76,800
	Ciro Rodriguez (I)	53	91,014
State Senate			
Tenth District	Kim Brimer (I)	47.5	140.613
	Wendy Davis (D)	49.9	147.561

Note: D=Democratic Party, R=Republican Party, I=Independent.
Source: Election results from the Texas Secretary of State.

more competitive states. But the primary was different. For two weeks, Texas was the center of the political nation's attention.

Texas held its primary on March 4. Conventional wisdom held that Texas would only ratify the nomination choice made by the states that held contests in January and on Super Tuesday, February 5. In the Republican nomination, this is essentially what happened. McCain won the most votes and delegates on Super Tuesday, and expanded his lead during the February primaries. McCain's perfunctory 13 point victory in Texas (and in Ohio, Vermont, and Rhode Island the same day) gave him enough delegates to clinch the Republican nomination.[4]

The Democratic nomination contest upset the predictions of conventional wisdom. Super Tuesday turned out to be a virtual tie. Barack Obama then ran off a string of eleven straight victories. Obama's February 19 victory in the Wisconsin primary indicated that he might be building momentum and that the Hillary Clinton campaign was foundering.[5] Most political observers thought that an Obama victory in Texas would knock Clinton out of the race. Even former president Bill Clinton raised the stakes, telling a crowd in Beaumont, Texas, that "[i]f she wins Texas and Ohio, I think she will be the nominee. If you don't deliver for her, then I don't think she can be."[6]

As election day approached, it looked like Texas might not deliver for Clinton. Polls showed Obama taking the lead,[7] and early vote patterns were favorable to Obama.[8] Clinton needed to reverse the momentum. To do this, the Clinton campaign turned the agenda to experience and foreign policy, via the now famous "three a.m." advertisement. The ad argued that when a phone in the White House rang suddenly at three o'clock in the morning, voters had to decide if the person who would answer that phone "already knows the world's leaders, knows the military—someone tested and ready to lead in a dangerous world."[9]

Polling averages show the trajectories of the two candidates changing in the last day or two of the campaign, with Clinton rising and Obama falling.[10] The momentum held on election night, as Clinton defeated Obama 50.9 percent to 47.4 percent in the Texas primary. Of course, to say Clinton "won" Texas depends, to paraphrase Bill Clinton, on what the definition of "won" is. Political observers learned that the Texas two-step was more than a country dance; it also described the Texas Democratic Party's unique primary-caucus hybrid. One-third of Texas's delegates are awarded by caucuses, and Obama's victory in the caucus meant he won the most delegates from Texas. But the national media focused on the primary victory, which kept Clinton alive. The *Boston Globe* headlined Clinton's victory as a "red-phone resurgence."[11]

General Election Stasis

The primary results produced three themes that were important going into the general election. The first was Obama's weakness in the Hispanic community. The network exit polls show that he won only 32 percent of the vote among Texas Hispanics, compared to 66 percent for Clinton.[12] The second was Obama's weakness in rural Texas. Obama only won 9 of the state's 177 rural counties.[13]

The third was the remarkable turnout for the Democratic primary, in which 2,874,968 million voters, 23 percent of registered voters, cast ballots.[14] That number is 42,264 *more* than the number of votes cast for

John Kerry in the 2004 general election.[15] "Is Texas still a red state?" veteran Texas journalist Paul Burka asked. He noted, "The strength of the Democratic vote in the March 4 primary was so unexpected, so complete a departure from our recent history, that the numbers are potentially the most significant development in Texas politics in thirty years."[16]

Did the boom in Democratic turnout in the primary change the nature of the general election campaign as Burka speculated? In short, the answer in 2008 was no. For example, the turnout increase in the primary election did not presage an increase in the general election. In fact, turnout in the 2008 general election (45.3 percent of Texas's voting-age population) was slightly lower than in 2004 (46.1 percent of the voting-age population). Furthermore, neither campaign seriously contested the state. While McCain, Obama, Joe Biden, and Sarah Palin made numerous appearances in other, more competitive rim South states—North Carolina, Virginia, and Florida—they skipped Texas for the most part. McCain made no appearances in Texas after the Republican National Convention. Palin went to the state on October 3 for a pair of fund-raisers one day after the vice presidential debate. While in Texas, Palin stressed issues that might likely resonate with Texas's conservative voters, criticizing Obama's views on the wars in Afghanistan and Iraq and promoting energy independence.[17] Obama last appeared in the state on July 31 for a pair of Houston fund-raisers. Biden went to Texas on September 12 for a fund-raiser in San Antonio, though another scheduled fund raiser that day in Austin was cancelled due to Hurricane Ike.[18]

Paid media campaign activity was limited in Texas. Both campaigns bought advertisements in El Paso, but these ads were designed to persuade voters in Las Cruces and other parts of southern New Mexico. In the rest of the state, whatever ad buys voters saw were part of national ad buys.

In newspaper endorsements, Obama captured three of the state's largest five newspapers. Not surprisingly, the liberal editorial boards of the *Austin American-Statesman* and *Fort Worth Star-Telegram* endorsed Obama, and the more conservative editorial boards of the *San Antonio Express-News* and the *Dallas Morning News* went for McCain. The surprise was the moderate to conservative editorial board of the *Houston Chronicle*. They endorsed Obama, which was the first time they had endorsed a Democratic presidential candidate since 1964. While newspaper endorsements of presidential candidates matter little in terms of actually influencing voters in their final decisions for president, the fact that the *Houston Chronicle* endorsed a Democratic candidate for president for the first time in a generation does illustrate a somewhat changed political climate in the state compared to the Bush era.

In terms of campaign organization, neither candidate had organizations designed to "win" the state, given that it is reliably Republican. Both campaigns sought and received plenty of money from Texans. The Obama campaign raised $17.7 million in Texas for both the primary and general election campaign, while the McCain campaign raised $17.6 million.[19] Neither campaign created large organizations in the state. The Obama campaign opened offices in Texas, where volunteers made phone calls to voters in other, more competitive states.

Issues and Texas Voters

Texans did not differ from most Americans as a whole in their views of what issues were most important. Where Texans differed was in who they thought could deal with those issues. Table 12.2 shows that in both Texas and the nation, the economy was the most important issue (63 percent in the national exit poll and 54 percent in the Texas exit poll). In Texas, these economic voters slightly favored McCain; nationally, they favored Obama.

Another key difference between the Texas and the national electorate was on the issue of energy policy. Texas has a long history as an oil-producing state, and Texans who considered energy the most important issue favored McCain heavily, 67 to 31 percent. Nationally, Obama had a slight advantage among these voters, 50 to 46 percent.[20]

Table 12.2 Which One of These Five Issues is the Most Important Facing the Country?

	NATIONAL			TEXAS		
	percent Total	McCain	Obama	percent Total	McCain	Obama
Most Important Issue						
Economy	63	44	53	54	51	48
Health Care	9	26	73	12	42	57
Iraq	10	39	59	11	49	48
Energy Policy	7	46	50	10	67	31
Terrorism	9	86	13	10	92	7

Source: Exit polls were conducted by Edison Mitofsky Research for the National Election Pool Results taken from http://www.msnbc.msn.com/id/26843704.

Some observers thought immigration policy would hold great importance in the 2008 election, especially in Texas. The state has the nation's
longest border with Mexico, a long history of immigration across the Rio
Grande, a large and growing Hispanic population, and a large community of immigrants, both documented and undocumented. Despite these
expectations, the issue disappeared, both nationally and in the state. Most
state Republican leaders in Texas do not want to touch the immigration
issue. President Bush, Governor Rick Perry, and most of the state's Republican establishment oppose taking a hard line against illegal immigration,
in part because the business community benefits from this labor market.
These views are a continuation of George Bush's immigration stance when
he was governor and are not necessarily out of sync with the Texas public. A University of Texas poll taken October 15–22, 2008, showed that
while Texans were divided over the issue, a plurality of respondents (over
46 percent) leaned toward the view that "illegal immigrants who have
lived and worked long enough in the U.S. should be allowed to keep their
jobs and apply for legal status." Just fewer than 40 percent of respondents
leaned toward the view that immigrants should return to their native
land.[21]

In the end, most issues paled in importance to economic issues. As
University of Texas political scientist Bruce Buchanan said, "the economic
issues sucked all the oxygen away from all the other issues."[22]

Congressional Elections in Texas

Over the last two decades, House campaigns in Texas have been relatively
calm. This calm is the result of successful efforts by redistricters in the
state to create safe districts for their party. Democrats created enough safe
districts in the 1990s to retain their majority in the congressional delegation, despite the burgeoning Bush Republican trend in the state. Republicans got control of the redistricting process after the 2002 elections and
redrew the map favorably, producing a Republican majority in the delegation after a series of easy victories in the 2004 election.[23]

Entering the 2006 cycle, expectations were that Texas would stay out
of the national spotlight on House campaigns. However, Democrats did
score two upset wins, wins that Republicans regarded as the product of
ballot circumstances, and not the true preferences of voters. Nick Lampson
won District Twenty-two against nobody—Republicans were unable to
replace Tom DeLay on the ballot upon his resignation, and had to support a write-in campaign from Shelly Sekula-Gibbs (a write-in unfriendly

name if there ever was one). Ciro Rodriguez won District Twenty-three over incumbent Henry Bonilla in a post-November election mandated by a federal court after the U.S. Supreme Court ruled that Texas had diluted the impact of Hispanic voters in south Texas, violating the Voting Rights Act.[24] This low-turnout election reflected the level of enthusiasm of the Democratic base and the despondency of the Republican base after the Democratic wave of 2006.

Republicans aimed to return both of these districts to their Republican roots in 2008. In the Twenty-second they nominated Pete Olson, a former staffer for senators Phil Gramm and John Cornyn. Strong Republican voting patterns made this "arguably the best Republican takeover opportunity in the country,"[25] and these predictions were borne out on election day, with Olson defeating Lampson 52 to 45 percent. In the Twenty-third, Republicans also had high hopes for Bexar (San Antonio) County Commissioner Lyle Larson against Rodriguez. Larson's campaign fizzled, though, raising just over $800,000 (compared to Rodriguez's $2.3 million) and losing 56 to 42 percent.

Despite the Republican trend in the state, Democrats found two surprising pickup opportunities, which slipped onto the edge of the national radar. The Tenth District was drawn in 2004 to be a Republican stronghold, so much so that no Democrat ran for the new seat that year. But the district (centered in suburban Austin and Houston) proved less reliably Republican than anticipated. Television judge Larry Joe Doherty raised more than a million dollars in his challenge to incumbent Michael McCaul. The Seventh District is the most traditionally Republican district in the state, represented by George H. W. Bush in the 1960s, and by Ways and Means chairman Bill Archer for the following three decades. Changes in Harris County have made this seat less securely Republican. Wind energy executive Michael Skelly, who gave his campaign a million dollars,[26] provided the first credible Democratic campaign in the district in years. Incumbent John Culberson won, but the 56 to 42 percent margin was closer than the typical election in this district. McCaul also won, but by a closer margin than expected—54 to 43 percent.

The next real drama in the Texas House delegation is not likely to occur until after the 2010 redistricting cycle. With Texas now expected to gain four House seats and Republicans almost assuredly in charge of the process, the question will be how Republicans can maximize their partisan advantage while still complying with Voting Rights Act regulations and legal challenges that require maximizing representation of the state's rapidly growing and Democratic leaning Hispanic population. If Republicans want to gain three of the four seats, they may have to do so by creating two Hispanic majority seats, and trying to "crack" the district of the state's only white Democrat elected in a white-majority district, Lloyd Doggett. Republicans were unsuccessful in their attempts to target Doggett in the last round of redistricting.

Changes in Texas Since 1976

From its founding to the end of World War II, Texas was a solidly Democratic state. Only in 1928, when the Democrats nominated the urban, Catholic, and "wet" Al Smith, did Texans give their electoral votes to Republicans. In 1952, however, two-party politics emerged in the state, at least at the presidential level. Texas gave a majority to Republican (and native son) Dwight Eisenhower in both 1952 and 1956. Figure 12.1 shows these changes by measuring the trend in the Republican presidential vote in Texas since World War II, by subtracting the Republican nominee's vote share in Texas from his national vote share. While the state

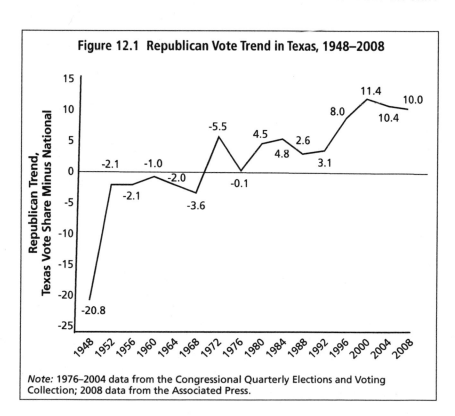

Figure 12.1 Republican Vote Trend in Texas, 1948–2008

Note: 1976–2004 data from the Congressional Quarterly Elections and Voting Collection; 2008 data from the Associated Press.

went solidly for Harry Truman, the state only had a slight Democratic lean from 1952 to 1968. In 1972, the state moved strongly toward Richard Nixon and the Republicans.[27]

In the 1976 election, Texas was not only the nation's third-biggest electoral prize, but also one of the closest. President Gerald Ford and governor Jimmy Carter both campaigned hard to win the state,[28] with Carter prevailing with 51.1 percent of the Texas vote. Ford nearly matched his national vote share with 48 percent of the vote. Texas stood near the center of the nation politically.

This did not last. In 1980, Texas gave its electoral votes to Republican Ronald Reagan (and his Texan running mate George H. W. Bush), and has not voted for a Democratic nominee since. Through the Reagan and Bush runs for president, Texas voters leaned more Republican than the nation as a whole. As Republican leadership in the state passed from the elder to the younger George W. Bush, the state moved strongly toward the Republicans. In 1996, Bob Dole won 8 percent more in Texas than he did nationally; George W. Bush won the state by 11.4 percent more than his national total in 2000 and 10.4 percent more in 2004. Despite losing a "favorite son" candidate from the Republican ticket in 2008, Republican erosion was small. John McCain exceeded his national vote share by 10 percent. After 28 years, the Bush era has moved the state strongly and solidly into the Republican column.

The biggest change has been the stark partisan shift in the rural parts of the state. Figure 12.2 divides the state into three parts—urban, suburban, and rural[29]—and compares the Republican vote trend (again local Republican vote share minus the Republican nominee's national vote share) across time. In the 1976 election, the state's urban counties were its most Republican, as they gave Gerald Ford a slight majority. In both suburban and rural Texas, Jimmy Carter won a greater share of the vote than he won nationally.

This pattern quickly changed. Rural and suburban Texas both moved strongly toward the Republicans. The suburbs moved quickly through the Reagan elections, moderated for the George H.W. Bush campaigns, and moved strongly toward Republicans in 1996 and 2000. For rural Texas, the full shift took longer. Rural Texas was comparatively favorable to Democrats from 1980 to 1992, but moved strongly against Bill Clinton in 1996, and stayed with George W. Bush in his two presidential runs. In Texas's cities, the Republican trend has been relatively slight. Urban Texas drifted only slightly toward the Republicans throughout the Bush era. In 2008, Texas's cities moved sharply toward the national average.

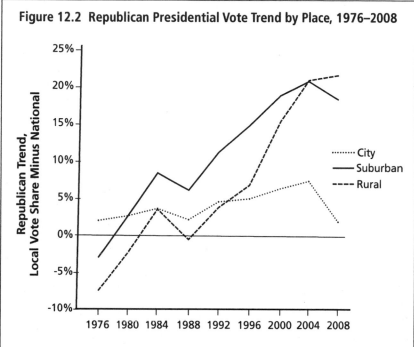

Figure 12.2 Republican Presidential Vote Trend by Place, 1976–2008

Note: 1976–2004 data from the CQ Elections and Voting Collection. 2008 Data from the Associated Press. Rural: counties not designated by the US Census Bureau as part of a metropolitan area. Urban: counties that host the "named" city of a metropolitan area. Suburban: counties that are part of a metropolitan area, but do not host the named city.

Throughout the Bush era in Texas, the political strength of the state reversed. Rural areas provided strong margins to Jimmy Carter. By 2008, they were the backbone of Republican dominance in the state. Suburban counties have also moved strongly into the Republican column since the Carter election. Texas's urban counties were its most Republican in 1976; today, they are the least Republican, and they moved heavily towards the Democrats in 2008, providing some ray of hope for Democrats.

Democratic Optimism

The 2008 election marked yet another victory for Texas Republicans. And despite the national trend towards the Democrats and the excitement created by the campaign of Barack Obama, Texas Democrats were not able to make substantial gains overall among the electorate.

Below the surface of these Republican wins, the 2008 election provided hopeful signs for Texas Democrats. Democrats gained a net of three seats in the state House, bringing the partisan makeup of the body to seventy-six Republicans and seventy-four Democrats. Democrats made a gain in the state Senate for the first time since 1982. Democrats won county and judicial races in Harris County for the first time since 1992. Obama won in three of the state's four largest counties: Harris, Dallas, and Bexar; each had gone for Republicans in the last three presidential elections.

The results of the 2008 election show that Democrats are gaining among three parts of the state electorate: Hispanics, young voters, and urbanites. This particular set of strengths gives Texas Democrats optimism for 2010, 2012 and beyond.

There were good reasons why the Hispanic vote would be up for grabs in 2008. George W. Bush was remarkably successful among Texas Hispanics, winning a majority of their vote when reelected governor in 1998 and splitting their votes in his two presidential runs. And, as noted, Obama lost Texas Hispanics two to one to Clinton in the primary. But the general election was a different story. Obama won 63 percent of Texas Hispanics. This 13 percent improvement over John Kerry's performance mirrored the 14 percent national shift of Hispanics toward Obama. With the growth in the Hispanic population nationally and in the state, Bush's "architect" Karl Rove argued after the election that "[i]f this trend continues, the GOP will find it difficult to regain the majority."[30] Bush and Rove explicitly pursued the Hispanic vote in Texas and nationally in an effort to build a long-standing Republican majority. The results of the 2008 election indicate that their great political fear—that Democrats would dominate this growing demographic group to their electoral benefit—may be coming true.

The second area of growth for Texas Democrats is among young voters. Among voters age eighteen to twenty-nine, Obama won 54 to 45 percent, which was a 14 percent gain over John Kerry's margin in 2004. Obama also made substantial gains among voters ages thirty to forty-four; he improved 16 points over John Kerry's performance, losing only 46 to 52 percent. Of course, young age cohorts also tend to have more minorities than older cohorts, so this trend reinforces Democratic strength among Latinos. But the big gains among young voters indicate that the Texas electorate could well be changing. Young Texans have different political views than their parents and grandparents.

The third area of growth for Texas Democrats is in the state's urban areas (see Figure 12.3). As mentioned above, Obama won victories in

Harris, Dallas, and Bexar counties. The Democratic presidential nominee had not won Dallas or Bexar counties since 1996, and had not won Harris County since 1964. Obama also won Travis County (Austin). While Kerry won here also, Obama improved 8 points over Kerry. Of the state's five largest counties, Obama won all but Tarrant (Fort Worth). Figure 12.3 shows the trend in each of these urban counties.

Further analysis shows that Democratic gains have come from finding new voters. Obama gained 27.1 percent more votes than Kerry did in these five counties, while McCain lost only 4.7 percent of Bush's 2004 totals. Exit poll results reinforce the Obama gains in urban areas. Respondents who lived in cities with populations greater than five hundred thousand gave Obama a 55 to 44 percent majority, which was a 16 point improvement over John Kerry. Obama increased the Democratic vote share in cities with populations between fifty thousand and five hundred thousand to 47 percent, a 15 point increase from 2004. Texas may be an ocean of red, but some blue islands have emerged. Obama still ran behind his national totals (much less his national totals in urban areas) in Texas's metropolitan counties, but only by 1.1 points.

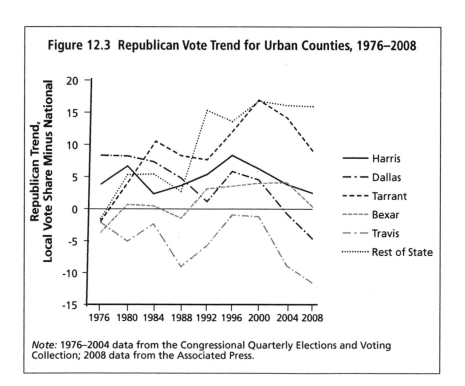

Figure 12.3 Republican Vote Trend for Urban Counties, 1976–2008

Note: 1976–2004 data from the Congressional Quarterly Elections and Voting Collection; 2008 data from the Associated Press.

The effects of this increased Obama strength in urban counties can be indirectly seen in the lower ballot judicial races (see Table 12.3). In previewing the 2008 election, *Texas Monthly* focused on down-ballot races because "that's where the action is. . . . The presidential race matters because it drives, or fails to drive, turnout."[31] In many ways, the votes in judicial races seemed to mirror the presidential race in the five most urban counties in 2008. Table 12.3 illustrates how closely judicial votes tracked the presidential vote in these counties. Many of these races were won by Democrats, no doubt helped along by Obama, and these victories were significant prizes for the party. Since 1994, Republicans had captured all the courthouse races in the state's four largest counties—Tarrant (Fort Worth), Dallas, Bexar (San Antonio), and Harris (Houston). In 2006, Dallas County turned back to the Democrats; their candidates won every contested county race that year, ousting a series of long-term incumbents. The 2006 Dallas results reflected the changing demographics of an ever more diverse county and the pro-Democratic national wave. As 2008 came, Democrats captured a majority of the judicial races in Harris, Dallas, Bexar, and Travis counties. So Texas Democrats can look at the results from 2008 with some degree of optimism. Their party has established a base in some of the ascendant areas of the state's population. They can see a path to growth over the long term that could change the state.

Republican Strengths

The results of the 2008 election have prompted some to see Texas as a potential target for Democrats in the 2012 presidential election. Howard Dean told Democratic bloggers "that states such as Georgia and Texas might be attractive targets for Democrats at the presidential level in 2012."[32] The *Los Angeles Times* wrote, "strategists believe the large and growing Latino population there remains untapped, along with a large black electorate, which could make Texas competitive with a major investment of time and money from an Obama-led Democratic Party."[33] Could the nation's largest Republican state, and the home of the last two Republican presidents, really go "blue" in 2012?

We are skeptical. Our analysis of the 2008 election returns shows that the Republican Party holds great strengths in Texas and that the Democrats have a steep climb to win Texas anytime soon. Our argument for Republican optimism is simple: Republicans have been winning in Texas and won in 2008 by large margins. While Barack Obama made

Table 12.3 Vote Share of Presidential Candidates and District Judges, 2008 (in percent)

	REPUBLICANS		DEMOCRATS	
	McCain	Mean GOP District Judge	Obama	Mean Dem. District Judge
Harris County	49.3	49.2	50.8	50.8
Dallas County	42.3	41.6	57.7	58.4
Tarrant County	55.9	55.4	44.1	44.6
Bexar County	47.2	48.3	52.8	51.7
Travis County	35.0	38.2*	65.0	61.8*

Note: Percentages are all two-party vote share. "Mean GOP (Dem.) District Judge" is the mean vote share for all Republican (Democrat) district judge candidates in that county.
Source: Data are from the appropriate County Clerk's office.
*Travis County had one state district judge race that was contested.

gains relative to John Kerry, those gains were mostly in line with the national movement toward the Democrat. Further, among three sets of voters—whites, rural voters, and suburbanites—Republicans developed major strengths during the Bush era, and the 2008 results show little erosion in this strength. For the near and medium term, these strengths mean that Republicans win the state with great ease.

Republican strength among white voters is the bedrock of Republican political success in the state. Exit polls from 2004 and 2008 show why Republicans have such a strong grip on the state—they dominate the white vote. The results presented in Table 12.3 show that George W. Bush won 74 percent of the white vote in the state in 2004. Four years later, John McCain won 73 percent of the white vote. Nationally, McCain lost 3 percent off Bush's 2004 share of white voters.

McCain did well in Texas even among the groups of white voters that Obama won nationally. For example, Obama won young (age eighteen to twenty-nine) white voters nationally, but McCain won them solidly in Texas, 69 percent to 30 percent.[34] Obama lost white college graduates nationally by a 51 percent to 47 percent margin. But among these voters in Texas, McCain routed him, 74 percent to 25 percent. Nationally, white independents split nearly evenly between McCain and Obama. In Texas, they favored the Republican by a whopping 72 percent to 27 percent margin. Obama even lost 20 percent of whites who identified themselves as Democrats. Republican strength among white voters helps create a conservative lean to the state. Forty-six percent of Texans identified their ideology as conservative in 2008, 1 percent more than in 2004, and 12 points more than the national electorate. While McCain lost 5.5 points statewide from George W. Bush in 2004, nearly all of that erosion came from minority voters, and almost none of it came from white voters.

Republican strength in Texas is also bolstered by the party's performance in rural areas. As noted, Obama did poorly in rural Texas during his Democratic primary contest against Hillary Clinton. This continued in the general election. McCain won 68.5 percent of the vote in Texas's rural counties, just one percent less than George Bush. When compared to the national (and statewide) trend, rural Texas turned into an even stronger part of the Republican base. The exit polls found that McCain ran particularly strong in Texas's small cities (with populations between ten thousand and fifty thousand), winning 69 percent to 30 percent. This was a 10 point improvement over George Bush's performance in these same towns.[35]

In fact, in many areas, John McCain did better than George W. Bush did in 2004. Throughout the state, McCain outperformed Bush—despite the national trend away from Republicans and without the favorite son effect—in 98 of the state's 254 counties. Most of the places where McCain outperformed Bush were in rural Texas. McCain outperformed Bush in only two of the state's twenty-five urban counties and in eighteen of the state's fifty-two suburban counties. But in rural Texas, McCain outperformed Bush in 78 of 177 counties, just over 44 percent. In particular, McCain ran better than Bush in rural East Texas. The Arizonan outperformed the Texan in 34 of the 46 these counties.[36] In rural West Texas, McCain improved on Bush in forty-four counties (out of ninety-seven). Rural Texas is at the end of the "McCain belt," the series of counties that stretches down the Appalachian Mountains, and then across the highland South, and into Oklahoma and Louisiana.[37]

The third area of Republican strength in Texas is the suburbs. In suburban counties, McCain won 65 percent of the vote. This number is down from 69.4 percent in 2004, but is still higher than in 1996, the last time the Democrats took the White House, when Bob Dole won 60 percent of the suburban vote. In fact, John McCain won *every* suburban county in the state. As a result, suburban counties provided nearly 31 percent of McCain's 4.5 million statewide votes.

What path could Democrats follow to overcome these Republican strengths and win in Texas in the near future? One thing is clear, Democrats

Table 12.4 Exit Poll Results, 2008 (in percent)

	National Percent Total	McCain	Obama	Texas Percent Total	McCain	Obama	Difference McCain
All White Voters	74	55	42	63	73	26	22
Whites By Age							
18–29	11	44	54	9	69	30	25
30–44	20	57	41	19	71	27	14
45–65	30	56	42	26	74	25	18
65+	13	58	40	10	78	20	20
Whites by Education							
College Graduates	35	51	47	33	74	26	23
No College Degree	39	58	40	30	72	25	14
Whites by Income							
Income >$50K	49	56	43	46	74	25	18
Income <$50K	25	51	47	17	70	27	19
Whites by Party							
Democrats	23	14	85	12	20	78	6
Independents	29	49	47	22	72	27	23
Republicans	23	91	8	29	95	5	4
Population of Area (All Voters)							
City Over 500K	11	28	70	27	44	55	16
City 50K to 500K	19	39	59	16	52	47	13
Suburbs	49	48	50	41	61	37	13
City 10K to 50K	7	53	45	10	69	30	16
Rural	14	53	45	6	55	44	2
Ideology (All Voters)							
Liberal	22	10	89	15	12	86	2
Moderate	34	39	60	39	45	53	7
Conservative	45	78	20	46	78	21	0

Source: Exit polls were conducted by Edison Mitofsky Research for the National Election Pool Results taken from http://www.msnbc.msn.com/id/26843704.

cannot rely on demography. We calculate that Obama won 75 percent of the vote among nonwhites in the state. Assuming that Democrats win the same share of the white and minority vote in subsequent elections, a Democrat will not win Texas until the electorate is only 51 percent white. In 2008, the state population was 48 percent white, but the electorate was 63 percent white. So if the white share of the electorate remains 15 percent greater than their share of the population, they will have to make up 36 percent of the state's population for the electorate to be 49 percent minority. Population projections indicate that Democrats would have to wait until the 2020s for this to happen.[38]

If Democrats are going to make gains in the state any time in the next decade and a half, they will have to improve their performance among white Texans. Democrats will have to reshape the ideological views of Texans. As noted, 46 percent of Texans say they are conservative, and only 15 percent say they are liberal. Assuming that Democrats cannot win nearly every moderate vote in the state, they must reduce the number of conservatives to have a fighting chance. And if the problems of the Bush administration did not encourage Texans to reconsider their ideology, it is hard to see what Texas Democrats might come up with over the next few years.

Thinking geographically, Texas Democrats need to improve their performance in the state's urban areas even further. Nationally, Obama won big cities 70 percent to 28 percent. As shown, he is a long way from that in Texas. The increase in the state's minority population has been centered in its urban areas, which indicates that Democrats have room to grow. And Democrats must expand their appeal into Texas's suburban counties. Obama won only 37 percent of the vote in the state's suburbs. Since suburbs casts 41 percent of the state's votes, this weakness is crippling to Texas Democrats. There were a few glimmers of hope for Democrats in 2008. Obama came close in Fort Bend County—the home of Tom DeLay —garnering 48.6 percent of the vote, and Democrats won an open state House seat in Williamson County, outside of Austin. But these glimmers were few and far between.

What has the Bush era produced in Texas? A stable Republican majority, focused on white voters, and cemented by the conservatism of the state's voters. To win Texas in 2012, Barack Obama would need a massive national landslide, of a Reagan 1984 or Johnson 1964 quality. The data show that it is unlikely the state will move strongly toward the national average in the upcoming decade. In the long term, the growth of the Hispanic population in the state provides the Democrats an advantage. But Hispanics are neither uniformly Democratic nor uniformly part of the Democratic base. George W. Bush showed that a talented and popular Republican politician can peel a set of these voters away from the Democrats. To win in the future, Texas Democrats have the difficult task of not only holding on to the new, and not necessarily stable, elements of their own political base, but also finding a way to chip off members of the Republican's more solid base. That the Democratic task is so difficult is ultimate tribute to the political success of the Bush era in Texas.

13.

Virginia

The New Math of Blue Virginia

John J. McGlennon

Introduction

Barack Obama's victory in Virginia was a critical element in the Democrat's electoral strategy. In position to win every state carried four years earlier by his party's standard-bearer, the Illinois senator needed to add only fifteen electoral votes to prevail. Demographic and electoral trends highlighted a handful of states that offered particular promise, and none may have been more surprising than Virginia.

Almost from the moment polls closed on the 2004 presidential election, Virginia became the focus of debate over where Democrats could best hope to reverse their narrow loss and retake the White House in 2008.[1] Virginia seemed an unlikely prospect at first, as the only southern state to withstand the regional appeal of Democrat Jimmy Carter in 1976, and one of a handful of states with the longest GOP winning streaks in Presidential contests.[2]

A New Dominion?

Realignment was evident in the Old Dominion even as John Kerry fell short of George Bush. Kerry became the first Democrat since Lyndon

Johnson in 1964 to carry Fairfax County, the largest political jurisdiction in the state, and home to one of every eight state residents. Central cities and affluent suburbs limited Bush to the same level of support as he had in 2000, even as he increased his national share of the vote by some 3 percent.

In the three years leading to the 2008 contest, Virginia's movement toward the Democrats became evident. In 2005, Virginia elected a Democratic governor, Timothy Kaine, to succeed one-term-limited governor Mark Warner. Warner's triumph in 2001 had been more personal than partisan, as he had to share power with an enlarged Republican majority in the state legislature. Kaine's win was originally seen as a ratification of Warner's leadership style, but in fact, Kaine outperformed his mentor in a number of areas of the state, particularly the vote-rich Northern Virginia and Hampton Roads suburbs.

In 2006, former Republican governor and first-term U.S. senator George Allen was ousted by Democrat James Webb in one of the closest contests of the year. Though Allen damaged himself with campaign missteps, including a disparaging comment to a dark-skinned Webb campaign volunteer that was caught on camera and widely disseminated on the Internet (the so-called "Macaca Moment")[3], he had been polling weakly throughout the summer and fall, and voting patterns tended to match the results from 2005. Finally, in 2007, Democrats overcame a three-seat deficit and a highly partisan redistricting map to regain control of the state Senate. Again, the victory was built on Democratic wins in Northern Virginia and Hampton Roads.

At eleven Eastern Standard Time on election night, the news networks awarded Obama victory in Virginia and enough other states to proclaim him the next president. The Democratic win in the state, so hard for both parties to envision even in the face of public opinion polls giving Obama an edge throughout the last month of the campaign, had become reality in a record-shattering turnout.

The Nomination Contest

Virginia, often called the Mother of Presidents, had three favorite sons in the early stages of the presidential contest. George Allen, just off a successful chairmanship of the National Republican Senatorial Campaign Committee, emerged in 2005 and 2006 as a leading contender for the GOP: a former governor and sitting senator with a new national fundraising base, appeal to the Christian Right and business-oriented Republicans, without deep ties to the Bush administration.

Governor Mark Warner was attractive to Democrats looking for a centrist alternative to Hillary Clinton, as a successful businessman who had worked across party lines to address Virginia's fiscal crisis. Former governor James Gilmore, who had served as Bush's Chair of the Republican National Committee in 2001, presented himself as a staunch fiscal conservative who would resist tax increases, as he had done in Virginia.

Ultimately, Allen's shocking loss in 2006 eliminated him as a candidate. Warner found little room in a contest where Clinton and Obama commanded almost all the attention. Gilmore was unable to raise any significant campaign money, attracted little support in his own state, and had to fold early in 2008. The latter two wound up in a mismatch to succeed senator John Warner, with Mark Warner (no relation to John Warner) the overwhelming winner.

The Virginia Primary

By primary day in Virginia on February 12,[4] the Republican contest for president was largely decided, and the Democratic contest was reduced to Clinton and Obama. Maryland and the District of Columbia voted on the same day, in a regional contest dubbed the "Potomac Primary" by the media. Despite rain in much of the state and icy roads in Northern Virginia, record numbers of voters flocked to the polls.

Republican front-runner McCain had a nearly insurmountable lead in the delegate hunt, but his remaining challenger, former Arkansas governor Mike Huckabee, hoped for an upset by attracting support in rural areas and among evangelical and fundamentalist voters. Though Huckabee swept the western half of the state and attracted 41 percent of the vote, McCain won a bare majority in the winner-take-all race for delegates.

Obama won all three primaries, but his performance in Virginia was stronger than expected. Earning 64 percent of the Democratic vote, he carried cities and suburbs along with rural areas in all but the western section of the state, along the Appalachian mountain range.[5] His victory was spearheaded by Governor Kaine, the first major elected official outside of Illinois to endorse Obama, in February 2007.

Voter turnout for the primary put to rest the images of Virginia as a low-interest, low-turnout state. V. O. Key had famously written of Virginia: "By contrast Mississippi is a hotbed of democracy."[6] In this primary, however, more than 1.4 million people cast votes, with two-thirds, or nearly one million, requesting a Democratic ballot. The combined increase more than doubled the previous high turnout, although this marked the first time since 1988 that both Virginia parties had held binding primaries on the same date.

The General Election Campaign

Any doubt that the Old Dominion would be a central focus of the fall campaign was put to rest quickly. Virginians figured prominently on the vice presidential lists of both candidates, with Obama seeming to look deeply into the state for a potential running mate. McCain's camp floated the name of Seventh District Congressman Eric Cantor, the deputy whip of the House of Representatives (since promoted to minority whip for the 111th Congress).[7]

Obama's search included three prominent Virginians: Mark Warner, Webb, and Kaine. Warner, with his Senate campaign in full swing, and Webb both withdrew from consideration. Kaine was widely reported to be one of three finalists as Obama narrowed his choices.[8] The governor had developed a warm personal relationship with Senator Obama throughout the campaign, but Virginia's centrality to the campaign strategy made his appeal even stronger.

Though ultimately Obama settled on Delaware Senator Joe Biden, his schedule demonstrated that he saw Virginia as a critical target for his campaign. At virtually every stage of the general election campaign, Obama returned to the state. The nomination contest was settled, and Obama headed for Virginia. Right before and after the Democratic convention, the standard-bearer made trips to the commonwealth. On election-eve, Obama visited both Virginia Beach and Prince William County.

Although he focused attention on Northern Virginia and Hampton Roads, Obama was not hesitant to venture into more difficult territory. His visit to Lebanon, in southwestern Virginia, made national headlines when Obama said that the GOP's post-convention image-shaping was like putting "lipstick on a pig," a comment some took to be a swipe at Alaska Governor Sarah Palin, McCain's running mate.[9] Late in the campaign, Obama spoke at James Madison University in Harrisonburg, a traditionally Republican community that Obama noted had not seen a Democratic presidential candidate since Stephen Douglas contested Abraham Lincoln in 1860. Obama easily carried the city. Biden and Michelle Obama made several stops in the state as well, with the latter devoting special attention to the families of servicemen and women in visits to military-heavy Hampton Roads.

The McCain campaign, either because it did not recognize the challenge Obama was making in Virginia or because it had other, more pressing states to keep in play, largely left the field uncontested until late in the campaign. At that point, both McCain and Palin made a number of visits, including a late stop by McCain to the southwestern corner of the state. Their efforts came after warnings and complaints by GOP officials of the danger of losing a state that had been safely theirs for decades.

Controversy emerged when state party chairman Jeffrey Fredrick was quoted in *Time* magazine exhorting volunteers in Prince William County to defeat Obama because, according to Frederick, Obama and Al-Qaeda terrorist leader Osama bin-Laden "both have friends who bombed the Pentagon."[10] The reference was to Obama's membership on a foundation board with former Weather Underground radical William Ayres, who had participated in bombings (not of the Virginia-located Pentagon) when Obama was a child.

Despite the growing evidence of Obama's strength, few Virginians were sure of the outcome. Republicans expressed optimism that whatever signs of a close race might be showing up in polls, eventually Virginia would return to its normal "red" status. Democrats, disappointed more than once as what appeared to be close races turned into GOP victories, took the polling with a grain of salt, and Governor Kaine cautioned that the state was likely to be decided by a paper-thin margin.

Public Opinion Polling

Polling did provide evidence of Obama's appeal throughout the summer and fall. Eleven published polls conducted by several survey organizations between June and the end of August showed McCain and Obama to be within 1.5 percent of each other on average, with Obama slightly ahead. Three polls gave McCain a 1 percent lead, while seven put Obama's advantage between 1 and 5 points. The remaining survey reported a tie.[11]

September polling was more inconsistent, due to McCain's "convention bounce," as twenty-one surveys of this "battleground" state produced results varying from a McCain edge of 9 percent to an identical lead for Obama. The average lead was a scant 0.3 percent for McCain for the month, reinforcing the view that Virginia's drift toward the GOP had begun.

The final month of the election, though, with Obama's campaign lifted nationally by the crisis in the financial markets, produced thirty-one polls of Virginia voters, not a single one finding the GOP ahead. Obama's average lead of 6.5 percent was outside the margin of error, and virtually identical to the Democratic margin in the presidential vote.

Media and Advertising

Spending by candidates and parties in 2008 was exceptionally high in Virginia, a state that had rarely seen political ads in Presidential contests. With Obama raising unprecedented amounts of money for the election, he was able to outspend McCain's publicly funded campaign by a wide margin (about $2.4 million to $600,000 in one October week alone).[12] The advertising advantage was not so lopsided when expenditures by the parties and interest groups were taken into account, but it is clear Obama held the upper hand on television.

Stories from major newspapers, television networks, magazines, and Internet sites focused on Virginia as one of the key states to determining the election. The NBC News program, *Today*, spent a week looking at four critical states: Virginia, Florida, Michigan, and Pennsylvania. The national focus on the state prompted extensive coverage by the local newspapers and television stations as well. TV news covered campaign events live, broadcasting major portions of the candidates' speeches and reporting on the latest developments.

Participation

With the spotlight fixed on the Old Dominion, participation surged among the state's voters. Virginia was among the handful of states with the highest increases in participation, jumping by 7.1 percent over 2004.[13]

The surge was foreshadowed throughout the year by the heavy turnout in the primary and large increases in voter registration, especially among young people. Overall, voter rolls topped five million for the first time, with a net increase of 436,000 over the previous year. This nearly 10 percent increase was notable for a number of reasons, especially the characteristics of new registrants. [14]

Registration

Registration increases were highest in college or university towns and in areas with concentrations of minority voters. Williamsburg, a small city of 12,000, where half the population are students at the College of William & Mary, led the state with a 20 percent increase in registrants, though much of that was driven by a student campaign in May for a seat on the city council. Still, Charlottesville and other university towns also surpassed the state average. Petersburg and Richmond, both cities with African American majorities and flat population statistics, had large increases in registration rates, along with Northern Virginia's inner suburbs of Alexandria and Arlington. Norfolk, Hampton, and Newport News also experienced sharp increases in registration, particularly in heavily black precincts.[15]

In general, registration lagged in the rural southwestern part of the state. Lynchburg was a notable exception, because of efforts to register students at Liberty University, a center of the Evangelical Christian movement founded by the Rev. Jerry Falwell. In 2004, an active effort to register rural and religiously motivated voters swelled rolls even in areas that were losing population.

The increased registration reflected efforts by both the Obama campaign and minority-voter mobilization organizations. Both targeted areas with high African American populations and low voting participation. One such organization, the Community Voters Project, claimed credit for registering 85,000 minority voters across the state. Young people were a main target of Obama's effort, with highly organized campus drives.[16] The State Board of Elections reported that 60 percent of new registrants were under the age of thirty-five.

Absentee Voting

Skeptics cautioned that getting voters registered did not necessarily mean they would show up at the polls on election day. In fact, to an unprecedented level, voters chose to show up before November 4, casting 506,672 absentee ballots either by mail or in person at designated sites in the four weeks preceding the election. Compared to a previous high of 222,059 in 2004, this was a remarkable achievement, given Virginia's relatively restrictive absentee rules. With a normal 5 percent or less rate, the fact that more than 13 percent of votes were cast early again reflected an Obama campaign strategy, and was particularly notable in his strongholds.

In Fairfax, more than one hundred thousand votes were absentees, or about one of every five votes cast. More than 30 percent of Arlington County voters were absentees. Among the rural western counties carried by McCain, absentee voting was usually well below double digits, perhaps up from previous elections, but not close to the state average.

Total Turnout

The 3,752,858 votes cast in the general election represented a new record, surpassing the 2004 vote by just fewer than 530,000, an increase of more than 16 percent. The increases were particularly striking in the areas that Obama had targeted: college towns, central cities, Northern Virginia, and Hampton Roads. Increases in voter participation included 29 percent in the city of Charlottesville (University of Virginia), 30 percent in Fredericksburg (University of Mary Washington) and Montgomery County (Virginia Tech), 34 percent in Harrisonburg (James Madison University) and a breathtaking 57 percent in Williamsburg (William & Mary).

Cities with large minority populations saw large jumps. For example, Petersburg was up 31 percent, Richmond increased 25 percent, Norfolk gained 24 percent, and Newport News had 20 percent more voters.

Both McCain and Obama had shown weakness in the southwestern region of the state during the primary, but with few minority voters, the area was more difficult for Obama. McCain had lost the region to Huckabee in the GOP primary, but was conceded to have the general election advantage. Lack of enthusiasm for the two candidates produced anemic turnout. Mountainous Alleghany County saw less than a 2 percent increase after having surged by a third between 2000 and 2004. Grayson County in the far southwest increased by a modest 5 percent, while Scott and Tazewell counties both saw their overall turnout drop slightly.

The southwestern Ninth Congressional District had the lowest vote of the state's eleven districts, the only one to fall below 70 percent of registered voters. The slight numeric increase was largely the result of Virginia Tech's Montgomery County. Many of these communities had come close to "maxing out" their turnout potential with the Republican/Christian Right efforts in support of George W. Bush's reelection, but as components of the 2008 electorate, white rural voters were down, and urban young and black voters were up.

Results: Obama Becomes First Democrat to Carry Virginia in Forty-four Years

The results in Virginia may have been accurately forecast, but the scope of the win was still dramatic and surprising. On election night, news organizations resisted declaring the state for Obama during the first hours after the seven o'clock poll closing and the early reporting rural areas gave McCain backers some temporary optimism. At eleven that evening, as California polls closed, Virginia joined a torrent of states in the Obama column as the city and suburban vote propelled the Democrat to a comfortable 52.6 to 46.3 percent victory. (See Table 13.1.)

With 1,959,532 votes to McCain's 1,725,005, Obama won a majority and topped the showing of John Kerry and George Bush in 2004, to become the highest presidential vote-getter in Virginia history. McCain edged out Bush by about eight thousand votes to claim second place on the list, but Obama bested Kerry's total of 2004 by a little more than a half million.

Obama's victory was broad and deep, claiming six of the eleven congressional districts while narrowly losing two others. He scored landslides in cities across the state, swept Northern Virginia, and won Hampton Roads comfortably. He improved on Democratic performance in suburban areas. Only among the rural, white southwest voters did he seem to drop back to "normal" Democratic performance. His vote was built on young people, minorities, urban and suburban residents, a strong desire for change, and a deep concern about the economy. In addition, Obama benefited from both a Democratic advantage among the electorate and a campaign organization that was more effective in contacting and motivating voters.

Race and Gender. According to exit polls conducted by major news organizations,[17] Obama won Virginia by carrying overwhelming majorities among minority voters and drawing two out of every five white voters (see Table 13.2). Among African Americans, 20 percent of the voters, Obama won a 92 to 8 percent. McCain lost the Latino vote (5 percent) by a decisive 65 to 34 percent, but won among white voters, who comprised 70 percent of the total, by a 60 to 39 percent margin. Obama's performance among whites was 7 percent better than John Kerry's, though exit polls showed no difference in the racial composition of the electorate.

Obama won among both men and women, by 4 and 7 percent respectively. The same small difference appeared across racial groups, with McCain faring slightly better among men than women regardless of race. *Age.* The surge of young people was reflected in exit polls. Young (eighteen to twenty-nine) voters comprised 17 percent of the vote in 2004, but jumped to 22 percent in 2008, and delivered nearly 60 percent to Obama. Among young white voters, however, McCain prevailed 56 to 42 percent. Young black voters seemed to turn out in larger numbers than the overall share of blacks in the electorate. Exit poll reports break down their

Table 13.1 Virginia Election Results

	Candidate	Vote	Percent
President			
	Barack Obama (D)	1,959,532	52.62
	John McCain (R)	1,725,005	46.33
	Ralph Nader (I)	11,483	0.30
	Bob Barr (L)	11,067	0.29
	Chuck Baldwin (C)	7,474	0.20
	Write-in	6,355	0.17
	Cynthia McKinney (G)	2,344	0.06
U.S. Senate			
	Mark Warner (D)	2,369,327	65.03
	James Gilmore (R)	1,228,830	33.72
U.S. House			
First District	Bill Day (D)	150,432	41.75
	Robert Wittman (R)*	203,839	56.57
Second District	Glenn Nye (D)	141,857	52.40
	Thelma Drake (R)*	128,486	47.46
Third District	Robert Scott (D)*	239,911	97.01
Fourth District	Andrea Miller (D)	135,041	40.36
	Randy Forbes (R)*	199,075	59.51
Fifth District	Tom Perriello (D)	158,810	50.08
	Virgil Goode (R)*	158.083	49.85
Sixth District	Sam Rasoul (D)	114,367	36.61
	Bob Goodlatte (R)*	192,350	61.57
Seventh District	Anita Hartke (D)	138,123	37.09
	Eric Cantor (R)*	233,531	62.72
Eighth District	James Moran (D)*	222,986	67.94
	Mark Ellmore (R)	97,425	29.68
Ninth District	Rick Boucher (D)*	207,306	97.06
Tenth District	Judy Feder (D)	147,357	38.83
	Frank Wolf (R)*	223,140	56.80
Eleventh District	Gerald Connolly (D)	196,598	54.68
	Keith Fimian (R)	154,758	43.04

Key: D=Democratic Party, R=Republican Party, I=Independent, L=Libertarian Party, C=Constitution Party, G=Green Party.

Source: Virginia State Board of Elections,
https://www.voterinfo.sbe.virginia.gov/election/DATA/2008/
07261AFC-9ED3–410F-B07D-84D014AB2C6B/Official/1_s.shtml.

Table 13.2 Virginia Exit Poll Results, 2008 (in percent)

	Obama	McCain	Advantage
Gender			
Male (46)	51	47	4 Obama
Female (54)	53	46	7 Obama
Race			
White (70)	39	60	21 McCain
African American (20)	92	8	84 Obama
Latino (5)	65	34	31 Obama
Age			
18–29 (21)	60	39	21 Obama
30–44 (30)	51	47	4 Obama
45–64 (38)	51	48	3 Obama
65 and Older (11)	46	53	7 McCain
40–49 (23)	48	50	2 McCain
50–64 (26)	52	47	5 Obama
Income			
Less than $50K (30)	62	37	25 Obama
$50–100K (35)	52	48	4 Obama
$100K Plus (35)	46	52	6 McCain
White Evangelical/Born Again			
Yes (28)	20	79	59 McCain
No (72)	64	35	29 Obama
Most Important Issue			
Economy (58)	54	45	9 Obama
Iraq (12)	60	39	21 Obama
Energy (10)	51	46	5 Obama
Terrorism (9)	13	86	73 McCain
Health Care (7)	76	23	53 Obama
Political Ideology			
Liberal (21)	90	9	81 Obama
Moderate (46)	58	41	17 Obama
Conservative (33)	18	80	62 McCain
President Bush Approval			
Approve (27)	10	90	80 McCain
Disapprove (72)	68	31	37 Obama
Somewhat Disapprove (22)	32	68	36 McCain
Strongly Disapprove (50)	84	15	69 Obama

continued >

Table 13.2 (continued)

	Obama	McCain	Advantage
Party Identification			
Democratic (39)	92	8	84 Obama
Republican (33)	8	92	84 McCain
Independent (27)	49	48	1 Obama
Campaign Contact			
Obama Only (22)	81	19	62 Obama
McCain Only (10)	15	84	69 McCain
Both Campaigns (28)	42	57	15 McCain
No Contact (38)	53	46	7 Obama
Place of Residence			
Urban (23)	62	37	25 Obama
Suburban (47)	51	48	3 Obama
Rural (29)	47	53	6 McCain

Source: http://www.cnn.com/ELECTION/2008/results/polls. Numbers in parentheses represent percentage of total sample in each category of respondents.

results along more than one scale, and while one set of results shows voters following a fairly consistent pattern (the older the voter, the higher the support for McCain), a second, more refined breakdown follows the general pattern except for those between the ages of forty to forty-nine and fifty to sixty-four. The first group, who came of age politically during Ronald Reagan's presidency, delivered a majority of their vote to McCain. The older group, the fabled "baby boomers," interrupt the trend by producing a 6-point Obama margin.

Income. Again, exit polls provide options for examining the relationship between income and vote, and in general, lower-income voters supported Obama heavily and more affluent voters backed McCain, but by smaller margins. For example, among those earning less than fifty thousand dollars, Obama enjoyed a lead of 25 percent, while among those earning fifty thousand dollars to one hundred thousand dollars, he still had an advantage, but only 4 percent, while among those earning over one hundred thousand dollas McCain was preferred by a 6 percent margin. With Obama's strong advantage in Northern Virginia, the wealthiest area of the state, the divisions may have been much sharper in other regions.

Religion. Unlike some southern states, Evangelical Christians were not a dominant force in Virginia. Comprising 28 percent of the electorate, white evangelicals gave McCain a four to one advantage, but that was not enough to offset the rest of the electorate who favored Obama 64 to 35 percent.

Issues and Ideology. The Wall Street collapse of September and October drove other issues off the agenda for the presidential contest, to Obama's benefit. With almost three in five voters citing the economy as their most important issue (Iraq, at 12 percent, was next), Obama enjoyed a nine percent advantage. He was also preferred among voters citing Iraq, energy policy (10 percent), and health care (7 percent). Only among those citing terrorism (9 percent) did McCain have the advantage.

Almost half the voters called themselves moderates, and this group preferred Obama by 17 percent. Among conservatives (33 percent of the total), McCain enjoyed an 80 to 18 percent edge, not quite the margin Obama claimed (90 to 9 percent) among the smaller (21 percent) group of liberals.

President Bush. Thirty-five percent, the plurality of voters, said the candidate quality they sought most in a president was the ability to bring about change. They preferred Obama by 92 to 7 percent. Dissatisfaction with President Bush and the state of the country under his leadership were handicaps that John McCain could never overcome. In a state that had voted for him twice by substantial margins, 72 percent of voters disapproved of Bush's performance in office, and this group gave Obama their support by a ratio of nearly two to one. Fully half of the electorate "strongly disapproved" of Bush, and among this group, Obama prevailed by a landslide, 84 to 15 percent. It is a reflection of the bipartisan rejection of the Bush presidency that the 22 percent who only "somewhat disapproved" preferred McCain by a margin of 68 to 32 percent.

Party Identification and Campaign Efforts. The rejection of President Bush carried over to his party, as Democrats claimed an advantage among Virginians. The party identification in 2008—39 percent Democratic, 32 percent Republican—reversed the order of the 2004 election, when the GOP led by a 39 to 35 percent margin. Both parties' adherents were loyal to their nominees, at 92 percent support, and independents split down the middle.

While dissatisfaction with their party may have kept some Republicans from the polls, it appears that the Democrats also did a better job of identifying and mobilizing their supporters. Half of all voters reported some contact from the Obama campaign, but only 38 percent reported hearing from McCain's campaign. Since more than a quarter had heard from both campaigns, the contrast between those who heard from only one was sharper. While 22 percent reported having heard from Obama alone, only 10 percent reported contact from just McCain.

Region and Community Type. As discussed above, Northern Virginia and Hampton Roads were the keys to Obama's win. Carrying the two largest regions of the state gave him a lead that could not be overcome by a declining vote in rural areas of central and western Virginia. Even here, Obama was able to win in many cities and to cut the GOP advantage in suburban and rural communities with racially mixed populations. Only in the overwhelmingly white, rural Appalachian region did Obama fail to improve on Kerry's performance (see Table 13.3).

Voters who lived in urban areas preferred Obama by a wide margin. The 23 percent who claimed urban residence gave the Democrat a 25 percent advantage. Turnout in these urban areas was up substantially in 2008, and in many cases, Obama's margin improved on Kerry's performance in a segment of the state where the 2004 standard-bearer did very well.[18]

In Richmond, Obama improved the Democratic share of the vote from 70 to 79 percent, and with a larger turnout, expanded the Democratic edge in the capital city from 30,000 to 55,000 votes. In Norfolk, the vote share rose 10 percent, and the margin increased from 17,000 to 38,000. The western city of Roanoke gave Obama a vote share 9 percent higher than Kerry, which increased his vote margin from 2,000 to 9,000. The adjoining cities of Newport News and Hampton, located in a section of Hampton Roads known as the Peninsula, produced a vote of 150,000 (versus 124,000 in 2004), and with each city increasing its Democratic vote by 12 percent, saw the edge jump from 11,000 for Kerry to nearly 50,000 for Obama. Danville and Martinsville, two economically distressed factory cities, narrowly preferred Kerry over Bush, but gave Obama margins of 19 and 28 percent, respectively.

Suburbanites also moved toward Obama. The heavily suburban nature of "NoVa" gave Obama the edge among suburbanites in exit polling. Given the recent powerful swing of the region toward the Democrats, it is easy to forget that the GOP had long relied on its support. Fairfax County had, in fact, not given the Democrats a presidential win from 1964, when Lyndon Johnson prevailed, until 2004, when John Kerry managed a 53 to 46 percent split and a 35,000 vote edge. Obama swept the county by 60 to 39 percent, producing a margin of nearly 110,000, or nearly half of his statewide advantage.

Table 13.3 Turnout and Vote in Selected Virginia Localities (in percent)

Locality	Turnout Gain '04-'08	Kerry	Bush	Obama	McCain	Dem Increase
University Towns						
Charlottesville	29	71.8	27.0	78.4	20.3	6.6
Montgomery County	30	44.8	54.2	51.7	46.8	6.9
Fredericksburg	30	54.2	45.0	63.6	35.3	9.4
Harrisonburg	34	42.9	55.9	57.5	41.2	14.6
Williamsburg	57	51.3	47.8	63.8	34.7	12.5
Central Cities						
Richmond	25	70.2	29.1	79.1	20.0	8.9
Newport News	20	52.0	47.4	63.9	35.3	11.9
Norfolk	24	61.7	37.4	71.0	28.1	9.3
Petersburg	31	81.0	18.7	88.6	10.2	7.6
Suburbs/Suburban Cities						
Chesterfield County	20	36.9	62.6	45.8	53.3	8.9
Henrico County	16	45.6	53.8	55.7	43.5	10.1
Hanover County	13	28.1	71.4	32.8	66.4	4.7
Virginia Beach	14	40.2	59.1	49.1	49.8	8.9
Chesapeake	17	42.3	57.1	50.2	48.9	7.9
Rural Southwest						
Carroll County	8	32.1	67.4	32.7	65.1	0.6
Lee County	-6	41.0	58.0	34.9	63.1	-6.1
Scott County	-2	33.4	65.0	27.6	70.7	-5.8
Tazewell County	-2	41.1	57.4	32.8	65.7	-8.3
Rural Racially Mixed						
Essex County	24	46.2	53.0	54.7	44.4	8.5
Halifax County	15	42.4	57.1	48.2	51.0	5.8
Northern Virginia						
Arlington County	16	67.6	31.3	71.7	21.2	4.1
Fairfax County	12	53.3	46.0	60.1	38.9	6.8
Loudoun County	29	43.6	55.7	53.7	45.4	10.1
Prince William County	23	46.4	52.8	57.5	41.6	11.1

Source: Virginia State Board of Elections and
http://www.cnn.com/ELECTION/2008/results/polls.

Fairfax had been moving toward the Democrats, but the transformation of the two fastest-growing counties of the region was more dramatic. Loudoun, one of the most rapidly expanding counties in the nation, and Prince William County had both produced comfortable margins for George W. Bush in 2000 and 2004, but began moving to the Democrats in 2005, and gave Obama wins of 9 and 16 percent, respectively. Both had seen their rapidly growing populations diversify far more than the traditional new suburb, and both were looking to government to address problems of growth, housing, education, and transportation.

In Hampton Roads, the state's largest "city," the urbanizing but still suburban Virginia Beach and its neighboring suburban cities of Chesapeake and Suffolk also improved their Democratic vote. Kerry had lost all three, coming closest in Suffolk. Obama carried two of the three, losing Virginia Beach by less than 1 percent. Combined with the votes from the central cities, the Democrats won the region easily. Even in the Richmond suburbs, long considered unassailable GOP turf, signs of erosion emerged. The three major suburban counties of Chesterfield, Hanover, and Henrico had all supported Bush in 2004 with a combined margin of 66,000 votes. Obama carried Henrico, the oldest and most diverse of the suburbs, with 56 percent and reduced the Democratic deficit in the three counties to 12,000, a margin that more than offset the Richmond city vote.

College cities and counties also produced much better results for Obama than Kerry. Increased turnout and movement to the Democrats resulted in landslides in Williamsburg, Fredericksburg, and Charlottesville, and flipped Harrisonburg city and Montgomery County from red to blue. In Lynchburg, the mobilization of Liberty students may have saved the city for McCain, as votes for both parties increased significantly.

Outcomes in rural counties varied. Those in the eastern and southern portions of the state and those with significant African American populations generally saw a surge for the Democrat, as reflected in votes in Essex, Halifax, and Southampton counties. Western counties with few black residents saw only modest gains at best for Obama, and in some cases, like Lee, Scott, and Tazewell counties, a decline in both Democratic percentage and absolute votes in places with little if any voter turnout increase. Despite Obama's visits, support from popular local figures (like bluegrass legend Ralph Stanley), and active endorsement from the United Mine Workers Union, McCain carried the southwest and the reliably Republican Shenandoah Valley handily, if without enthusiasm.

Democrats Gain in Other Contests

If there was any question about the partisan nature of the 2008 election, it was settled in contests for the United States Senate and House of Representatives (see Table 13.1). The upset victory by Senator Jim Webb in 2006 over George Allen had resulted in a nine to four Republican advantage in the commonwealth's congressional delegation. Coming out of the 2008 contests, Democrats claimed an eight to five advantage.

U.S. Senate

The fall campaign between two former governors to replace retiring Republican John Warner in the U.S. Senate provided little suspense. From the announcement that the Democratic Mark Warner would seek the seat, he had been the prohibitive favorite. Leaving office with broad public approval, and having made a generally positive impression in his exploratory presidential campaign, Warner outraised his Republican predecessor, Jim Gilmore, by a margin of six to one, and highlighted his support from prominent Republicans and independents. Warner's endorsements from former GOP legislative leaders in Richmond were particularly telling, as they contrasted Warner's "problem solving" approach to the confrontational style of Gilmore.

Given his landslide wins in two statewide races (for attorney general and governor) in the 1990s, his service as George W. Bush's first Republican National Committee chairman, and his own presidential campaign, Gilmore's performance may have seemed puzzling from outside the commonwealth. In Virginia, his candidacy elicited little enthusiasm. Among the Republican legislative and business establishment, there was some satisfaction in the opportunity to watch Gilmore suffer a humiliating defeat.

Warner had the luxury of a united party, crosspartisan support, and a prominence on the national stage. Obama selected him to deliver the national convention keynote address, the same showcase that had propelled the Illinois senator to political stardom. Warner's performance, laying out a path of pragmatic problem-solving keyed to technological and educational promotion, produced reviews more typical of such speeches, but afforded a relatively young politician a priceless introduction to the nation.

Gilmore could not seem to catch a break. Dismissed by more established Republicans as too partisan and ideologically rigid, he was challenged for the Senate nomination by a state legislator regarded as one of the most controversial officials in Richmond because of his sometimes extreme tactics in opposing abortion. Delegate Robert Marshall harnessed the support of the grassroots conservatives and antiabortion activists, delegates motivated by the long-shot Presidential candidacy of libertarian Texas congressman Ron Paul, and supporters of another state delegate, Jeff Frederick, who was challenging former lieutenant governor John Hager, for the state party chairmanship.

In effect, Gilmore's candidacy got caught up in a conflict between the two factions of the state party (pro-business, establishment office holders versus evangelical and antitax activists) without a firm hold on either group. Gilmore wound up winning the nomination by less than a 1-percent margin. He fared better than Hager, however, who lost the party chairmanship by a landslide. Hager, a former tobacco executive confined to a wheelchair who had won the second-highest post in state government in 1997 on his first run for office, epitomized one side of the cleavage in the party. After losing a close contest for the GOP nomination for governor in 2001, Hager accepted a position in Warner's cabinet, then was appointed assistant secretary of education by President Bush. When Hager lost the chairmanship, he was weeks away from becoming father-in-law to President Bush's daughter, Jenna.

The election outcome was overwhelming, as Warner carried all but four counties and two cities, outpacing Obama by 410,000 votes and nearly doubling Gilmore's total. Warner became the first Virginian to win more than two million votes.

U.S. House of Representatives

Democrats won an open seat in the House of Representatives and ousted two incumbent Republicans to take a six to five edge among the eleven House members. The open seat contest resulted from the decision of representative Tom Davis, a moderate from the Washington suburbs, to seek neither reelection nor the John Warner senate seat that he had openly coveted for years. Davis, a former chair of the National Republican Congressional Committee, was widely credited with encyclopedic knowledge of voting trends, both in Virginia and the rest of the nation. He decided not to seek the senate seat, citing concern that when the GOP decided to nominate its candidate in a convention rather than a primary, he would have little chance of winning among more conservative party activists. Undoubtedly, the prospect of facing Mark Warner in the fall was discouraging as well.

More surprising was Davis's decision to retire from the House, but it was not entirely unexpected. With a district rapidly becoming more Democratic and the prospect of a serious challenger, Davis understood his problems. In addition, he had thrown everything he could, from an endorsement by New York City mayor Michael Bloomberg to hundreds of thousands of dollars from his own reelection campaign fund, into his wife's 2007 race for reelection to a state senate seat that comprised a portion of his district. So thorough was her defeat that he may have lost his appetite for the 2008 race.

Republicans had expected difficulty competing for the Davis seat, and though their candidate raised and spent lavishly, Democrat Gerry Connolly, the chairman of the Fairfax County Board of Supervisors (Davis's launching pad into Congress fourteen years earlier), easily prevailed. They were not expecting to lose their two incumbents, Thelma Drake, seeking her second full term against Glenn Nye, a 34-year-old first-time candidate, and 14-year veteran Virgil Goode, who went down to defeat to another neophyte, lawyer Tom Perriello, by a paper-thin, 727 vote margin. Nye, a former foreign service officer, raised impressive funding, benefited from Obama's strong campaign in Hampton Roads, and gained the attention of national Democrats, who viewed Drake as a weak candidate. Hammering Drake for failing to support veterans' issues in a military-heavy district, Nye won comfortably, running ahead of Obama.

Perriello found an opening in some highly controversial statements by Goode on immigration (he objected, for instance to Mexican restaurants in the district displaying a Mexican flag) and Islam (perhaps not a great handicap in the largely rural district), and some hints of scandal (Goode was mentioned in a corruption case involving a defense contractor based in the district). Perriello also launched a creative and humorous advertising campaign designed to introduce himself and his ethnically distinctive name to voters, and he further benefitted from Goode's early dismissal of the challenge, followed by hyperbolic attacks when Goode realized its seriousness. Finally, Perriello was almost certainly carried over the finish line by the surge in turnout, especially among Charlottesville's student and academic population.

Summary

The victory of Barack Obama in Virginia was historic. Other Democrats had come close to winning the state, but not since Lyndon Johnson in 1964 had one succeeded. With a Republican presidential winning streak as long as any state's, skeptics could be excused for discounting the growing evidence of Democratic ascendancy. But with an engaged electorate, expanded by new young and minority voters, an emerging partisan advantage in other elections, unprecedented campaign spending, effective campaign organization, and a tarnishing of the Republican brand, Virginia's 13 electoral votes joined 362 others from across the country in electing the nation's first African American president.

While some marveled that "the capital of the Confederacy" had joined in this historic moment, Virginians had defied expectations before, as in their 1989 election of L. Douglas Wilder as the nation's first elected black governor. The shift of Virginia from what some saw as a rural/suburban dominated conservative bastion to what is now being described as a bluing reflection of yet another New South had been foreshadowed in contests for governor, senate, and the state legislature in the years between 2004 and 2008.

In fact, Virginia's tilt toward the Democrats is unmistakable, but it is driven by a combination of changes in the demographics of the electorate and by the Democrats' success in positioning themselves as moderate problem solvers. They have been aided by the GOP's internal strife and a continuation of its refusal to compromise to address issues that frustrate voters. Though the current direction of the state GOP, perhaps like the national party, appears to be toward a continuation of a narrower ideological focus, the dynamics of two-party politics suggest that the Republicans eventually will adapt to compete in this new political landscape. Whether that adaptation is sooner or later may determine whether Virginia remains a battleground in the next few years.

The designation of Governor Kaine as President Obama's Democratic National Committee chair ensures that the commonwealth will again be in the spotlight of national politics as it begins the 2009 gubernatorial election year, with the precedent of Gilmore's RNC tenure as a cautionary note on the ability of political fortunes to change quickly.

Conclusion

Don't Whistle Past Dixie Yet

H. Gibbs Knotts

Introduction

Fewer than forty-five years after Alabama governor George C. Wallace called for "segregation now, segregation tomorrow, segregation forever," the United States selected Barack Obama as the nation's first African American president. Perhaps most astonishingly, Obama won in Florida and North Carolina, and had a particularly strong victory in Virginia, the capital of the Old Confederacy.

Political observers and pundits have been divided into two camps when discussing Democratic prospects in the South. Some questioned the long term viability of Democratic success before, during, and after the 2008 contest. In 2006, political scientist Thomas Schaller published *Whistling Past Dixie: How Democrats Can Win Without the South.*[1] He contends that the South's social conservatism makes it very difficult for Democrats to win in the region. In the throes of the 2008 election campaign, Schaller took to the op-ed pages proclaiming that "Mr. Obama should not hope to capture the states in the country's most racially polarized region" and suggested that Obama "can write off Georgia and North Carolina for the same reasons that Mississippi is beyond reach—although the math in those states is slightly less daunting."[2] Of course, Obama did win in parts of the South, but his dominating 365–173 electoral vote margin meant he did not depend on any southern states for his victory. Without the fifty-five electoral votes in Florida, North Carolina, and Virginia, Obama would still have won by an eighty-two vote margin, giving some credence to this camp's position. After the election, reporter

235

Adam Nossiter wrote about how the South veered considerably from the national tide in 2008 and argued that "by leaving the mainstream so decisively, the Deep South and Appalachia will no longer be able to dictate that winning Democrats have Southern accents or adhere to conservative policies on issues like welfare and tax policy."[3]

Other observers interpreted the 2008 contest much differently, arguing that the South is changing and that the region is ripe for Democrats. In the midst of the primary battle between Obama and Hillary Clinton, Jack Bass wrote that "a half-century of Republican red-tide has crested, with signs of receding."[4] He emphasized recent Democratic congressional gains in the South and made the case that the current environment is favorable for Democrats. Bass argued that recent trends "suggest a region in transformation, with dynamic economic growth, an expanded black middle class, the arrival of millions of white migrants, the return of scores of thousands of African-American expatriates, and an emerging native white generation with little or no memory of racial segregation." Although Obama did not need Florida, North Carolina, and Virginia to win, his focus on these states forced the McCain campaign to spend valuable time and resources in areas that should have been safely Republican. By focusing on some southern states, Obama also chose a more centrist path to the presidency and likely increased his ability to win in more moderate areas of the country including the battleground states of the Midwest.

Given these differing views about the future direction of southern politics, it is a good time to take a broad look at the 2008 election. This chapter begins by placing the 2008 presidential contest in a historical perspective. Next, the chapter focuses on voter turnout in the 2008 election before moving to a discussion of the congressional contests. Following this, the chapter provides an overview of recent demographic shifts in the South, focusing specifically on factors that will likely benefit Democrats as well as the changes that favor Republicans. The chapter then examines the role of race in the 2008 election and the lessons about racial voting that can be learned for both political parties. The chapter concludes with some final thoughts about the future of southern electoral politics.

The 2008 Presidential Contest

It seems cliché to remark that the 2008 presidential election was "historic." There is the obvious: a biracial one-term U.S. Senator with a Kenyan father, a mother from Kansas, and a middle name of Hussein is an unlikely person to win a popular election in the United States. The epic primary battle against a talented female political rival likewise contributed to the campaign's lore. The 2008 presidential election was also historic because of the ways the Obama campaign harnessed the power of technology for electoral success. With the help of campaign manager David Plouffe and chief strategist David Axelrod, the Obama campaign built an unprecedented database of supporters and raised half a billion dollars on the Internet.[5] Targeted e-mail and text messages gave backers a sense of ownership in the campaign.

Taking nothing away from the historic nature of the Obama campaign, it is imperative that observers of the 2008 contest remember the broader trends in American politics. In short, this was a difficult year for Republicans, even in the South. The national economy was in freefall, the country lingered in protracted wars in Iraq and Afghanistan, and the incumbent Republican president's popularity ratings were among the lowest ever recorded for a president.

Despite the challenging national conditions for Republicans, recent history in the South limited the prospects for Democratic electoral success in the region. Obama won three states in a region that has been a stalwart for the Republican Party since Richard Nixon's "southern strategy." The Republican domination was particularly evident in the elections of 1984, 1988, 2000, and 2004, when Republicans garnered all of the Electoral College votes from each of the eleven states of the Old Confederacy.

To put this Republican domination in historical perspective, Figure C.1 compares the success of Republican presidential candidates in the South and non-South between 1980 and 2008. In every election, Republicans fared better in the South than outside the South. Moreover, the growing gap between the two lines indicates that Republican presidential candidates have done increasingly better in the South than in the non-South. Although Obama won three southern states, the largest difference between Republican support in the South and non-South occurred in the 2008 election. This gap is a strong sign for future Republican prospects in the South.

Even with the successes of Republican presidential candidates in the South, political strategists like James Carville continued to make the case that the region was winnable for the Democrats.[6] For many of these individuals, the path to victory involved the nomination of a southerner who would appeal to the region's white moderates. Arkansas governor Bill Clinton fit the mold of the Democratic Leadership Council's call for a moderate Democratic alternative to northeastern liberals. In the 1992 election, Clinton won his home state of Arkansas as well as Georgia,

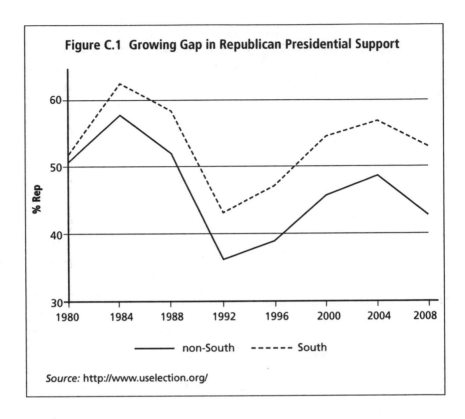

Figure C.1 Growing Gap in Republican Presidential Support

non-South ——— South - - - - -

Source: http://www.uselection.org/

Louisiana, and Tennessee. In his 1996 reelection bid, he won again in Arkansas, Louisiana, and Tennessee, lost in Georgia, but added Florida to the Democratic column. Clinton's success, along with a string of liberal-leaning Democratic nominees such as Walter Mondale, Michael Dukakis, and John Kerry, gave more credence to this winning formula for Democrats.

Since Clinton, however, southern Democrats have had less success in presidential contests. One of the major factors in Al Gore's 2000 defeat was his inability to win in the South, which was highlighted by his loss in his home state of Tennessee. North Carolinian John Edwards represented the most recent hope for southern Democrats but suffered two consecutive primary defeats and failed to deliver his home state as the vice presidential nominee in 2004.

The circumstances of the 2008 presidential election caused Democrats to update their playbook. Without a southerner atop the ticket, many believed that the region would greet the Obama candidacy with the same lack of enthusiasm as it did Walter Mondale, Michael Dukakis, and John Kerry. However, Obama consolidated the Democratic base and competed in different territory than previous Democrats. Florida was again a battleground state, but North Carolina had not voted for a Democrat since 1976 and Virginia had not supported a Democrat since the 1964 contest between Lyndon Johnson and Barry Goldwater.

Voter Turnout in the South

Most evidence suggests that higher turnout helps the Democrats, particularly in the South.[7] To better understand voter turnout in the South, Figure C.2 displays voter eligible turnout in the South and non-South for presidential elections between 1980 and 2008.[8] Voter turnout was lower in the South than in the non-South in every presidential election between 1980 and 2008. However, turnout in both the South and non-South has increased considerably since a low point in 1996, and the gap in voter turnout between the South and non-South has gotten smaller in nearly every election cycle. By 2008, turnout in the South and non-South was

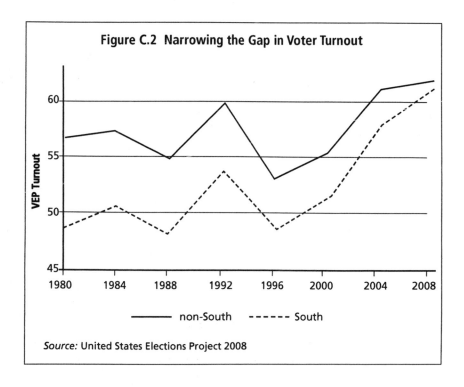

Figure C.2 Narrowing the Gap in Voter Turnout

Source: United States Elections Project 2008

virtually identical. It will take some time to better understand the nature of the higher turnout, but the enthusiasm generated by the Obama candidacy likely motivated many new participants. The challenge for Democrats is to engage these new voters in future political contests.

To further explore the electoral effects of voter turnout, Figure C.3 compares voter turnout across the southern states. Virginia had the highest voter turnout in the South, followed closely by Florida and North Carolina. Not surprisingly, these were the three states that moved to the Democratic column in 2008. These states received visits by all the major candidates, and they were also bombarded with political advertising, volunteers, and elaborate get-out-the-vote efforts. Voter turnout in six of the eleven southern states lagged the overall turnout in the United States of 61.6 percent, but voter turnout was up rather substantially in the South compared to turnout rates in 2004.[9] With the exception of Arkansas, all southern states had increases in voter turnout compared to 2004, and eight southern states increased above the overall national increase of 1.5 percent.

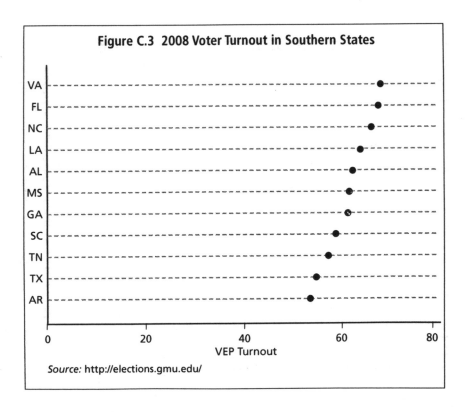

Figure C.3 2008 Voter Turnout in Southern States

Source: http://elections.gmu.edu/

The 2008 Congressional Contests

In addition to winning the presidency, Democrats added eight U.S. Senate seats and twenty-one U.S. House seats nationally in 2008.[10] In the South, Democrats added two Senate seats (North Carolina and Virginia) and also picked up three House seats.[11] These contests were likely aided by the organizational strength and advertising dollars of the Obama campaign.

To put these numbers in historical perspective, Figure C.4 displays the percent of the southern House and Senate delegations that was Republican between 1980 and 2008. Republicans usually did better in Senate contests than House contests, but success in both chambers increased at similar rates over time. The biggest increase in Republican success occurred in the historic 1994 midterm elections. There was another jump in the Republican percentage that coincided with the 2004 reelection of George W. Bush. With the Democrats regaining control of both branches of Congress in 2006, the percentage of Republicans in Congress decreased in the last two election cycles.

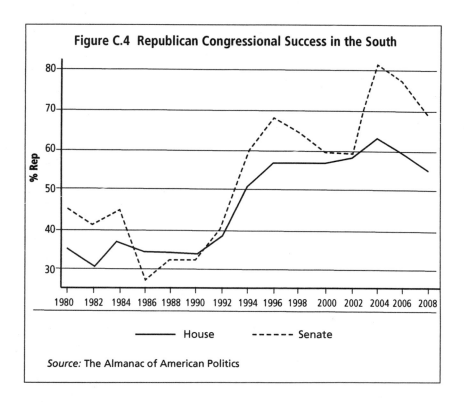

Figure C.4 Republican Congressional Success in the South

House ──────   Senate ------

Source: The Almanac of American Politics

The overall story though is the continued dominance of the Republican Party in southern congressional elections. The South is very fertile ground for GOP congressional candidates. Southerners' appetite for limited government, particularly in Washington, likely explains much of this trend. The findings provide a few good signs for Democrats, however. For instance, the Republican seat percentage has decreased in both the House and Senate since 2006.

The South's Changing Demography

Sorting out the South's political environment requires a close examination of the region's changing demographic profile. For sure, the South remains demographically different than other regions and generally has a higher percentage of African Americans, a lower percentage of high school graduates, lower household incomes, lower housing values, and a higher percentage of people in poverty.[12] Of all eleven southern states, only Virginia has a median family income above the national average of $50,046. Alabama, Louisiana, Arkansas, and Mississippi rank in the bottom 20 percent of states.

Population growth, however, has occurred at a much greater rate in the South than in the non-South over the last few decades, and the conventional wisdom suggests that a wave of newcomers, especially the white migrants and African American expatriates mentioned by Jack Bass, is good for Democrats.[13]

Figure C.5 shows population growth in the South between 1980 and 2006. Six of the eleven southern states grew at rates higher than the overall United States population increase of 32 percent. Florida, Georgia, Texas, North Carolina, and Virginia saw enormous increases in population between 1980 and 2006. Increases in Arkansas, Alabama, Mississippi, and Louisiana were much smaller. Louisiana experienced the lowest level of population growth. Population in the Bayou State actually declined by 4.1 percent between 2000 and 2006, due in large part to the devastation of Hurricane Katrina. In total, six of eleven southern states exceeded the national average in growth. Obama generally did better in states experiencing higher levels of population growth and much worse in states that were growing at lower rates. Winning in areas with growth is a good sign for Democrats and provides some evidence that the region's political dynamics are shifting away from Republican dominance.

Another potential advantage for Democrats in the South is the region's racial diversity. Hispanics, and particularly African Americans, support

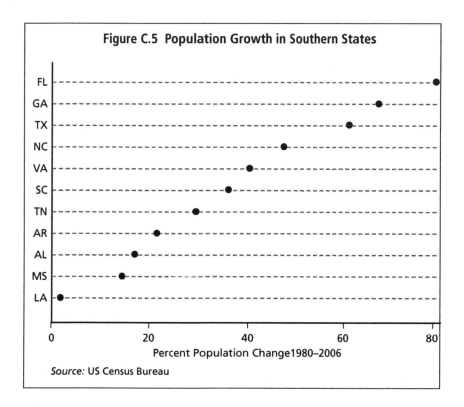

Figure C.5 Population Growth in Southern States

Percent Population Change1980–2006

Source: US Census Bureau

Democratic candidates at high levels. The size of the region's African American population changed dramatically during the last hundred years. In 1920, 77 percent of all blacks in the United States lived in the South. After decades of out-migration because of racial discrimination and promising job prospects outside the South, just 45 percent lived in the region by 1980.[14] Recent evidence, however, indicates that blacks are returning to the region.[15] Georgia, North Carolina, and Florida have experienced the largest recent increases in African Americans and the South is currently the only region experiencing a net increase in black population.

Figure C.6 compares the racial diversity across the southern states. Mississippi, Louisiana, Georgia, and South Carolina have the largest nonwhite populations in the South. In fact, all of these states rank in the top ten nationally in percent nonwhite population. Across the South, eight of the states have a higher percentage nonwhite population than the national average of 24.9 percent. Census reports indicate that the South is the only region to experience increases in each of the following groups: blacks, Asians, Hispanics, and non-Hispanic whites.[16]

Interestingly, Democratic presidential candidates have not done well in the southern states with the highest nonwhite populations. Although Clinton won Louisiana in 1992 and 1996, none of the states at the top of this list were competitive for the Democrats in 2008. A further influx of nonwhites to the region, however, could change this dynamic and provide an improved electoral environment for the Democratic Party.

Another political consideration for both parties is the economic makeup across the South. Republicans are generally thought to be the party more favorable to business, although there are a number of southern Democratic governors who would be considered progrowth. The *Forbes* magazine "Best States for Business" ranking considers business costs, labor, regulatory environment, economic climate, growth prospects, and quality of life.[17] Based on this list, the southern states of Virginia, Texas, and North Carolina ranked first, second, and third respectively. Florida and Georgia were also ranked in the top ten nationally. However, three southern states were ranked among the worst for business; Alabama, Mississippi, and Louisiana were in the bottom ten.

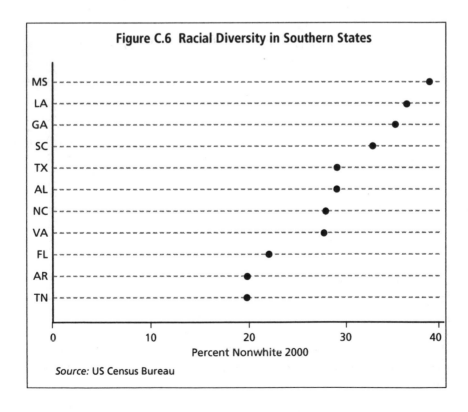

Figure C.6 Racial Diversity in Southern States

Percent Nonwhite 2000

Source: US Census Bureau

Another economic indicator that may have political implications is a state's connection to the "new economy." In North Carolina, for example, the Obama campaign did particularly well in Research Triangle Park, a haven for the high-tech industry. The Information Technology and Innovation Foundation ranked states on twenty-nine indicators gauging how well the state is structured for the new economy.[18] Virginia ranked in the top ten nationally and Texas, Georgia, Florida, and North Carolina were in the top half of states. Once again, several southern states ranked among the lowest, including Alabama, Arkansas, and Mississippi.

Interestingly, Obama did better in the states considered more favorable for business and more poorly in the states at the bottom of the list, indicating a troubling sign for Republicans. These results may be an indicator that people are beginning to trust Democrats more with economic issues. They could also be a sign of backlash against the troubling economic conditions ascribed by many to the Bush administration. As with the "Best States for Business" ranking, Obama did much better in the states at the top of the list than in the states at the bottom. As southern states improve conditions for business and focus on the creation of new economy jobs, prospects could improve for the Democrats.

Race and Southern Politics

The politics of the South certainly revolves around more than "the position of the Negro," but racial politics has a long history in the region.[19] Race was the driving force in the politics of the 1960s as southern demagogues capitalized on white fears of integration. These tactics became more covert in the 1970s as Nixon's law and order campaign appealed to the "silent majority."[20] During the 1990s, southern politicians like Jesse Helms played on racial fears to win elections. In the famous 1990 "hands" ad, white hands opened a rejection letter as the narrator states "you needed that job, but they had to give it to a minority because of a racial quota." In a 2006 example of racial campaigning, the Republican National Committee ran an ad where a white woman talks about meeting Tennessee Democrat Harold Ford Jr., who is black, at a Playboy party and says, "Harold, call me."

The 2008 election provided the first ever opportunity to vote for an African American at the top of the ticket. Southern blacks voted nearly unanimously for Obama, but the differences in white support for Obama varied considerably across the South. Overall, 42 percent of white voters in Florida supported Obama, followed by 39 percent of white voters in

Virginia, and 35 percent of white voters in North Carolina. Conversely, 10 percent of white voters in Alabama, 11 percent of white voters in Mississippi, and 14 percent of white voters in Louisiana cast ballots for Obama.

What is less clear is whether whites made the decision to vote for Obama based on race. One way to begin to address this question is by comparing white support for Obama in 2008 to white support to Kerry in 2004. Figure C.7 shows the relationship between white support for Kerry and white support for Obama in each of the eleven southern states. There was substantially more white support for Obama than for Kerry in North Carolina, Virginia, and to a lesser extent in South Carolina. Arkansas, Louisiana, and Alabama had much less white support for Obama than the Kerry white vote would have predicted.

Another way to address this question is by looking at the racial context in various states. According to the racial threat hypothesis, when whites are around higher percentages of blacks they are more likely to embrace racially charged opinions. This hypothesis has held up through

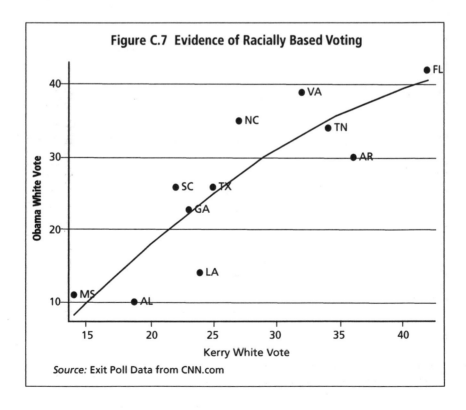

Figure C.7 Evidence of Racially Based Voting

Source: Exit Poll Data from CNN.com

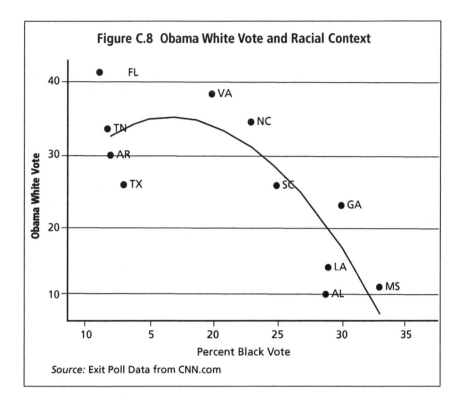

Figure C.8 Obama White Vote and Racial Context

Source: Exit Poll Data from CNN.com

years of scrutiny, and the evidence suggests that racial context generally affects a range of political and policy positions.[21] To investigate this hypothesis, Figure C.8 shows the percent of whites in each state supporting Obama compared to the percent black vote in that respective state. The line of best fit leads to some interesting findings about relationship between white support for Obama and the relative size of the black vote. In the upper left quadrant of Figure C.8, the line of best fit actually increases slightly, indicating that the white vote for Obama went up as the percent black vote increased. However, once a state has a percent black vote of about 15 percent, the line slopes downward dramatically. The four states with the highest percent black vote—Alabama, Louisiana, Georgia, and Mississippi—also had the lowest white support for Obama.

Looking Forward

This broad view of the 2008 elections in the South uncovers good news for both Republicans and Democrats. Republicans can feel confident that at the presidential and congressional levels, the region remains firmly aligned with the GOP. The South is the most Republican region in the country, and the gap in Republican presidential support between the South and non-South increased to its highest level in 2008. Republican congressional strength across the South is also quite strong and far exceeds support for Republicans outside the region. There is also evidence that in areas, with high black populations, which exist across the South, white support for Democratic candidates is generally low.

The 2008 contest provides some positive signs for the Democrats as well. Although higher than in the rest of the country, the South's support for McCain was down from the 2004 vote for Bush. Likewise, support for congressional Republicans in the South declined from a high in 2004. Increasing voter turnout in the South should also benefit the Democratic Party. Voter turnout in the South has continued to move closer to turnout outside the South, and southern voter turnout in 2008 was nearly identical to non-South turnout levels. High levels of population growth in the South should also improve Democratic prospects in the region. Democrats are generally doing better than Republicans in high-growth states and Republicans are generally doing better than Democrats in low-growth states. Finally, as southern states embrace the "new economy," prospects for the Democrats should also increase.

Another theme that emerges from this examination of the 2008 election is the clear lines of division across the Old Confederacy. A more moderate and progressive South exists in Virginia, North Carolina, and Florida. Democratic prospects in these states are strong, and the recent success of the Obama campaign means that Democratic candidates for the U.S. House and the U.S. Senate will likely be in friendly territory. More traditional and conservative conditions exist in Mississippi, Louisiana, and Alabama. Republicans should continue to do well here, and Democrats will likely view electoral success in these states as a long shot.

Both political parties should also continue to target areas within particular states. McCain advisor Nancy Pfotenhauer talked about the "real Virginia," a dig at D.C. suburbs in burgeoning northern Virginia. Democrats will find more electoral success in the region's urban areas with growing and diverse populations. These variations across states demonstrate just how fragile electoral coalitions can be. For example, McCain would have won North Carolina 52 to 48 percent without the Research Triangle Park counties of Durham, Orange, and Wake.[22] Future Democratic hopefuls can certainly win in Virginia, North Carolina, and Florida, and should target states with similar political and demographic profiles.

Additional time and money might also mean that future Democrats would have a chance in states like Tennessee, Texas, Georgia, and maybe even South Carolina. By campaigning in the South, Democrats put pressure on Republicans to defend their base. Moreover, crafting appeals to moderate southerners forces candidates to hone a message that maximizes national appeal. Given the recent successes of the Obama campaign, the likelihood of close contests in the future, and a host of promising trends, Democrats would be well served to avoid the temptation to whistle past Dixie.

Notes

Introduction

1. V. O. Key, Jr. *Southern Politics in State and Nation* (New York: Alfred A. Knopf, 1949).

2. Donald S. Strong, *The 1952 Presidential Election in the South* (Tuscaloosa: The University of Alabama Bureau of Public Administration, 1955).

3. See, for example, Alexander Heard, *A Two-Party South?* (Chapel Hill: University of North Carolina Press, 1952); Donald S. Strong, *Urban Republicanism in the South* (Tuscaloosa: The University of Alabama Bureau of Public Administration, 1960); Bernard Cosman, *Five States for Goldwater: Continuity and Change in Southern Presidential Voting Patterns* (Tuscaloosa: University of Alabama Press, 1966); William C. Havard, ed., *The Changing Politics of the South.* (Baton Rouge: Louisiana State University Press, 1972); Numan V. Bartley and Hugh D. Graham, *Southern Politics and the Second Reconstruction* (Baltimore: Johns Hopkins University Press, 1975); Jack Bass and Walter DeVries, *The Transformation of Southern Politics: Social Change and Political Consequence Since 1945* (New York: Basic Books, 1976); and Alexander P. Lamis, *The Two-Party South,* expanded editon (New York: Oxford University Press, 1988).

4. William C. Havard, "Southern Politics: A Prelude to Presidential Politics in 1984," in *The 1984 Presidential Election in the South: Patterns of Southern Party Politics,* ed. Robert P. Steed, Laurence W. Moreland, and Tod A. Baker (New York: Praeger, 1986): 3.

5. For a well-written overview of this growing body of literature, see Harold W. Stanley, "Presidential Elections and the South," in *Writing Southern Politics,* ed. Robert P. Steed and Laurence W. Moreland (Lexington: University Press of Kentucky, 2006): chap. 9.

6. Earl Black and Merle Black, *Politics and Society in the South* (Cambridge: Harvard University Press, 1987); *The Vital South: How Presidents are Elected* (Cambridge: Harvard University Press, 1992); and *The Rise of Southern Republicans* (Cambridge: Harvard University Press, 2002). *The Vital South* is especially relevant to the present discussion.

7. Joseph Aistrup, *The Southern Strategy Revisited: Republican Top-Down Advancement in the South* (Lexington: University Press of Kentucky, 1994).

8. Alexander P. Lamis, ed., *Southern Politics in the 1990s* (Baton Rouge: Louisiana State University Press, 1999).

9. David Lublin, *The Republican South: Democratization and Partisan Change* (Princeton, NJ: Princeton University Press, 2004).

10. See, for example, Black and Black, *Politics and Society in the South;* Black and Black, *The Rise of Southern Republicans;* Richard K. Scher, *Politics in the New South: Republicanism, Race, and Leadership in the Twentieth Century*

(Armonk, NY: M.E. Sharpe, 1998); Charles S. Bullock III and Mark J. Rozell, eds., *The New Politics of the Old South* (Lanham, MD: Rowman and Littlefield, 2007); and J. David Woodard, *The New Southern Politics* (Boulder, CO: Lynne Rienner, 2006).

1.

1. Earl Black and Merle Black, *The Vital South* (Cambridge, MA: Harvard University Press, 1992).

2. Hastings Wyman, "Sarah Palin, the Republicans' Post-Election Superstar,"*Southern Political Report,* October 29, 2008, http://www. southernpoliticalreport.com/storylink_1029_639.aspx (accessed November 9, 2008).

3. Mark Hugo Lopez, "How Hispanics Voted in the 2008 Election," Pew Research, November 5, 2008, http://pewresearch.org/pubs/1024/exit-poll-analysis-hispanics (accessed November 9, 2008).

4. 2008 National Election Pool Exit Poll Data, *CNN.com,* http://www. cnn.com/ELECTION/2008/results/polls.main/ (accessed November 10, 2008).

5. 2004 National Election Pool Exit Poll Data, *CNN.com,* http://www. cnn.com/ELECTION/2004/pages/results/states/US/P/00/epolls.0.html (accessed November 10, 2008).

6. Earl Black and Merle Black, *Divided America* (New York: Simon & Schuster, 2007).

7. Black and Black, *Divided America.*

8. V. O. Key, *Southern Politics in State and Nation* (New York: Alfred A. Knopf, 1949).

9. U.S. Census Bureau, *Voting and Registration in the Election of November 2006* (Washington, D.C.: Government Printing Office, 2008).

10. Angus Campbell, Philip E. Converse, Warren E. Miller, and Donald E. Stokes, *The American Voter* (New York: John Wiley & Sons, 1960).

11. V. O. Key, *The Responsible Electorate* (Cambridge, MA: Harvard University Press, 1966), 7.

12. Edward G. Carmines and James A. Stimson, *Issue Evolution* (Princeton, NJ: Princeton University Press, 1989).

13. Carmines and Stimson, 12.

14. 2008 National Election Pool Exit Poll Data.

15. John R. Petrocik, William L. Benoit, and Glenn J. Hansen, "Issue Ownership and Presidential Campaigning, 1952-2000," *Political Science Quarterly* 118 (Winter 2003–4), 599–626.

16. Daniel A. Smith, Matthew DeSantis, and Jason Kassel, "Same-Sex Marriage Ballot Measures and the 2004 Presidential Election," *State and Local Government Review* 38 (2), 78-91.

17. Paul Allen Beck and Paul Lopatto, "The End of Southern Distinctiveness," in *Contemporary Southern Political Attitudes,* ed. Lawrence W. Moreland, Tod A.Baker, and Robert P. Steed, (New York: Praeger, 1982) 160-182.

2.

1. For an overview of the South's role in recent nomination campaigns, see John A. Clark and Audrey A. Haynes, "The 2000 Presidential Nomination Process," in *The 2000 Presidential Election in the South: Partisanship and Southern Party Systems in the 21st Century,* ed. Robert P. Steed and Laurence W. Moreland (Westport, CN.: Praeger, 2002), 23-35.

2. For an early example of the impact of delegate selection rules on nomination outcomes, see James I. Lengle and Byron Shafer, "Primary Rules, Political Power, and Social Change," *American Political Science Review* 70 (March 1976): 25-40.

3. The U.S. Supreme Court confirmed the authority of the national parties over delegate selection in *Cousins v. Wigoda* (1975) and *Democratic Party of the United States v. La Follette* (1981). See Leon D. Epstein, *Political Parties in the American Mold* (Madison: University of Wisconsin Press, 1986), 225-35.

4. Josh M. Ryan, "How to Get Superdelegates to Commit in the Democratic Primary: Win More Votes" (paper presented at the annual meeting of the Southern Political Science Association, New Orleans, LA, January 8-10, 2009).

5. See, for example, William G. Mayer and Andrew E. Busch, *The Front-loading Problem in Presidential Nominations* (Washington, D.C.: Brookings Institution Press, 2004).

6. The Democratic National Committee Rules Committee ruled in May that Michigan and Florida would be allowed to seat their delegations at the Democratic National Convention, but each delegate was awarded only half a vote. Once the nomination battle was over, the convention accepted a credentials committee recommendation that all delegates receive full voting rights.

7. David B. Magleby and William G. Mayer, "Presidential Nomination Finance in the Post-BCRA Era," in *The Making of the Presidential Candidates 2008,* ed. William G. Mayer (Lanham, MD: Rowman and Littlefield, 2008), 141-68.

8. Data obtained from the Campaign Finance Institute (http://www.cfinst.org).

9. John O'Connor, "Religion Influences Voters in South Carolina," *State,* (Columbia, SC), January 14, 2008.

10. Jim Morrill and Dan Huntley, "S.C. Primary Following Tradition of Raw Politics: Recent Tactic Uses Fake Phone Pollsters to Distort Candidates' Records," *Charlotte Observer,* Charlotte, NC, January 18, 2008.

11. Exit poll data obtained from http://www.cnn.com/ELECTION/2008/ primaries.

12. Adam C. Smith, "Crist Endorsement is Surprising, Risky," *Times,* (St. Petersburg, FL), January 28, 2008.

13. Recall that Florida's delegate allocation was cut in half by the Republican National Committee. With a full slate of delegates, the impact of McCain's narrow victory would have been even greater.

14. The expanded electorate made it difficult for pollsters to identify "likely voters" in preprimary surveys. See Bruce Ransom and J. David Woodard, "Explaining South Carolina's Presidential Primaries: Likely Voter Attitudes and

Voter Preferences" (paper presented at the 2008 Citadel Symposium on Southern Politics, Charleston, SC, March 6-7).

15. Roland S. Martin, "Commentary: Voters not Swayed by Racial Politics," CNN.com, January 27, 2008, http://www.cnn.com/2008/POLITICS/01/27/roland.martin/index.htm.

16. Anna Scott, "A Broken Promise, or Merely a Hello?: Sen. Clinton Thrills Some By Posing for Photos, But May Have Violated Her Pledge," *Herald-Tribune,* (Sarasota, FL), January 28, 2008.

17. Richard S. Dunham, "Texas Votes; Texas Does Little to Clear Up Battle," *Houston Chronicle,* March 6, 2008.

18. Brian Naylor, "Superdelegate Role Complicates Re-Election Bid," *All Things Considered,* National Public Radio, April 8, 2008, http://npr.org/template/story,php?storyId=89474042.

19. Michael Falcone, "Clinton Is Out $13 Million She Lent Campaign," *New York Times,* December 23, 2008.

20. Walter J. Stone and Alan I. Abramowitz, "Winning May Not Be Everything, but It's More Than We Thought: Presidential Party Activists in 1980," *American Political Science Review* 77 (December 1983): 945-56; Vincent L. Hutchings and LaFleur Stephens, "African-American Voters and the Presidential Nomination Process," in *The Making of the Presidential Candidates 2008,* ed. William G. Mayer (Lanham, MD: Rowman and Littlefield, 2008), 119-39.

21. The evidence on this point is by no means clear. For an opposing view, see Lonna Rae Atkeson, "From the Primaries to the General Election: Does a Divisive Nomination Race Affect a Candidate's Chances in the Fall?," in *In Pursuit of the White House 2000,* ed. William G. Mayer (New York: Chatham House, 2000), 285-312.

22. Barbara Norrander, *Super Tuesday: Regional Politics and Presidential Primaries* (Lexington: University Press of Kentucky, 1992); Charles D. Hadley and Harold W. Stanley, "Super Tuesday 1988: Regional Results, National Implications," *Publius: The Journal of Federalism* 19 (Summer 1989), 19-37; and Charles S. Bullock III, "The Nomination Process and Super Tuesday," in *The 1988 Presidential Election in the South: Continuity Amidst Change in Southern Party Politics,* eds. Laurence W. Moreland, Robert P. Steed, and Tod A. Baker (New York: Praeger, 1991), 3-19.

23. Ryan, "How to Get Superdelegates to Commit."

3.

1. The average vote in the last six Alabama gubernatorial elections has been 48.2 percent Democrat and 51.3 percent Republican.

2. Patrick R. Cotter, "Alabama: Commandments, Amendments, and Defendants, *American Review of Politics* 26 (Spring, 2005): 25–41.

3. John Davis, "Governor's Race a Wild One," *Advertiser,* (Montgomery, AL), June 4, 2006, 1A. Shortly after the primary Siegelman was convicted and immediately transported to federal prison. Sigeleman was later released on appeal and his case is still pending with one of the unresolved issues being

whether Republican political considerations entered into the decision to prosecute him (Adam Nossiter, "New Twist in Appeal of Ex-Alabama Governor," *New York Times,* November 22, 2008, http://www.nytimes.com/ 2008/11/22us/22siegelman.

4. Phillip Rawls, "Governor's Race Fundraising Trailing 2002," *Advertiser,* (Montgomery, AL), November 3, 2006, 3B; Jamie Kizzire, "Riley Wins Second Term," *Advertiser,* (Montgomery, AL), November 8, 2006, 1A.

5. After the 2006 election, Democrats held a sixty-two to forty-three majority in the state House and a twenty-three to twelve majority in the state Senate.

6. Kym Klass, "Primary Buzz Builds," *Advertiser,* (Montgomery, AL), January 6, 2008, 1A; Alvin Been, "Obama Electrifies Birmingham: Thousands Jam Arena to Hear Candidate," *Advertiser,* (Montgomery, AL), January 28, 2008, 1A; Charles J. Dean and Kent Faulk, "Bill Clinton, Huckabee, McCain in State Saturday." *News,* (Birmingham, AL), January 31, 2008, 6A.

7. Mary Orndorff, "State GOP All Aboard McCain Train—Finally," *News,* (Birmingham, AL), April 16, 2008, 1A; Charles J. Dean, "Democrats Turn toward Unity, Dismiss Old Malice," *News,* (Birmingham, AL), August 24, 2008, 6A; Ana Radelat, "Davis Talks to Alabama Delegates in Denver," *Advertiser,* (Montgomery, AL), August 26, 2008, 1A; Charles J. Dean, "Supporters Still Sore about Clinton Defeat," *News,* (Birmingham, AL), August 26, 2008, 6A; Charles J. Dean, "'My Crystal Ball Was Dim' About Obama, Reed Tells Delegates," *News,* (Birmingham, AL), August 29, 2008, 1A; Mary Orndorff, "State GOP Delegates Urge Return to Core Values," *News,* (Birmingham, AL), August 31, 2008, 1A, Mary Orndorff, "Huckabee Shows Up at Delegation's Hotel, Asks Voters to Pledge to McCain" *News,* (Birmingham, AL), September 3, 2008, 1A.

8. After the state's presidential primary, but before the party's nominating conventions, John McCain made a well-publicized tour of the state's poor black-belt region. He ended this tour at a thousand dollar-per-person fundraiser in Birmingham. Charles J. Dean, "In Black Belt, McCain Wins Hearts, Not Votes," *News,* (Birmingham, AL), April 22, 2008, 1A. At about the same time, Michelle Obama also attended a $1,000-per-person fundraiser in the Birmingham suburb of Mountain Brook. [Charles J. Dean, "Obama's Wife Drops by for Fundraiser," *News,* (Birmingham, AL), June 24, 2008, 1B.] Otherwise, neither party's presidential or vice presidential candidates campaigned in the state.

9. Sebastian Kitchen. "Voting Officials See Registration Spike," *Advertiser,* (Montgomery, AL), September 12, 2008, 1A. Phillip Rawls. "Blacks Registering to Vote at Faster Rate This Year," *Advertiser,* (Montgomery, AL), October 21, 2008, 1A; Sebastian Kitchen, "Record Numbers Expected to Vote," *Advertiser,* (Montgomery, AL), October 14, 2008, 1A; Kim Chandler, "Registration Closes with Record Numbers," *News,* (Birmingham, AL), October 25, 2008, 1D.

10. Shaila Dewan, "In Alabama, a Fight to Regain Voting Rights Some Felons Never Lost," *New York Times,* March 2, 2008, 21A; Kim Chandler, "ACLU Challenges State Denial of Felons' Vote," *News,* (Birmingham, AL), July 22, 2008, 1B; Kim Chandler, "Courts Say State May Bar Too Many Voters," *News,*

(Birmingham, AL), October 2, 2008, 1A; Kim Chandler, "Confusions Reigns in Alabama over Ex-felons' Ability to Vote," *News,* (Birmingham, AL), October 6, 2008, 1A.

11. Early indications are that even with the increased number of voters, the 2008 election may not have exceeded the 1992 contest in terms of the percentage of registered voters participating. Some caution, however, is required in the use of official voter registration figures. George Altman and Brian Lyman, "Voter Turnout Heavy, But Not Record Breaking," *Press-Register* (Mobile, AL), November 6, 2008, 1A; Kim Chandler, "Six Alabama Counties Have More Enrolled Voters than People of Voting Age," *News,* (Birmingham, AL), October 17, 2008, 1A.

12. Mary Orndorff, "Sparks Says He Won't Seek Senate Seat," *News,* (Birmingham, AL), June 13, 2007, 4B; Garry Mitchell, "Figures Says She Will Run against Sessions." *News,* (Tuscaloosa, AL), August 26, 2007, 1B.

13. Charles J. Dean, "Figures Faces Uphill Battle for Senate Seat," *News,* (Birmingham, AL), October 1, 2008, 1A; Sean Reilly, "Sessions Easily Captures Third Term," *Press-Register,* (Mobile, AL), November 5, 2008, 5A.

14. Mary Orndorff, "Everett to Retire from U.S. House," *News,* (Birmingham, AL), September 27, 2007, 1A; Kent Faulk, "Cramer Elects Not to Seek 10th Term,"*News,* (Birmingham, AL), March 14, 2008, 1C.

15. Patricia C. McCarter, "It's Parker vs. Parker in November Election," *Times,* (Huntsville, AL), July 16, 2008, 1B; Sebastian Kitchen and Jill Nolin, "Love Trumps Smith in GOP," *Advertiser,* (Montgomery, AL), July 16, 2008, 1A.

16. Sebastian Kitchen, "Congressman Campaigns for Jay Love," *Advertiser,* (Montgomery, AL), October 18, 2008, 1B; Rick Harmon, "Romney Campaigns for Love in Dothan," *Advertiser,* (Montgomery, AL), October 24, 2008, 1B; Bob Johnson, "Norquist Lauds Love for No New Tax Pledge," *Advertiser,* (Montgomery, AL), October 25, 2008, 1B; Sebastian Kitchen, "Support Flows for District 2," *Advertiser,* (Montgomery, AL), October 26, 2008, 1C; Patricia C. McCarter and Victoria Cumbow, "Cheney to Stand in for Bush," *Times,*(Huntsville, AL), September 18, 2008, 1A.

17. Sebastian Kitchen, "Bright Claims Victory in Close District 2 Race," *Advertiser,* (Montgomery, AL), November 5, 2008, 1A.

18. Patricia C. McCarter, "Democrat Takes Seat Vacated by Cramer," *Times,* (Huntsville, AL), November 5, 2008, 1B.

19. Mary Orndorff, "Rogers Faces Serious Challenge from Segall," *News,* (Birmingham, AL), October 23, 2008, 1B.

20. Markeshia Ricks, "Democrat Segall Gets National Party Support," *Advertiser,* (Montgomery, AL), October 16, 2008, 1B.

21. The Fourth District's Republican Robert Aderholt was the only other incumbent Alabama congressman to face opposition. Aderholt easily defeated his Democratic opponent, Nicholas Sparks, 74.9 to 25.1 percent.

22. Eric Velasco, "Supreme Court Hopefuls Shooting for Civility," *News,* (Birmingham, AL), September 19, 2008, 1A; Eric Velasco, "State Supreme Court Race Now U.S's Costliest," *News,* (Birmingham, AL), October 31, 2008, 1A; Phillip Rawls, "Shaw Wins State High Court Race," *News,* (Tuscaloosa, AL), November 13, 2008, 1A.

23. See, for example, V. O. Key Jr., *Southern Politics in State and Nation* (New York: Alfred A. Knopf, 1949); William Barnard, *Dixiecrats and Democrats: Alabama Politics 1942–1950* (Tuscaloosa: University of Alabama Press, 1974); Anne Permaloff and Carl Grafton, *Political Power in Alabama* (Athens: University of Georgia Press, 1995).

24. The role of race in the 2008 election has generated substantial speculation and commentary in the state and national media. See, for example, Adam Nossiter, "For South, a Waning Hold on National Politics," *New York Times,* November 11, 2008, 1A; Jamon Smith, "Race and Age Divided Electorate," *News,* (Tuscaloosa, AL), November 6, 2008, 1A; Jason Morton, "Voting on Issues, Not Race," *News,* (Tuscaloosa, AL), November 22, 2008, 1A. For recent scholarly examination of the role of race in electoral politics see, for example, Nicholas A. Valentino and David O. Sears, "Old Times There Are Not Forgotten: Race and Partisan Realignment in the Contemporary South," *American Journal of Political Science* 49 (July 2005): 672–88; Jonathan Knuckey, "Racial Resentment and the Changing Partisanship of Southern Whites, *Party Politics* 11 (January 2005): 5–28; Jonathan A. Cowden, "Southernization of the Nation and Nationalization of the South: Racial Conservatism, Social Welfare and White Partisans in the United States, 1956–92, *British Journal of Political Science* 31 (April 2001): 277–301; Byron E. Shafer and Richard Johnston, *The End of Southern Exceptionalism: Class, Race, and Partisan Change in the Postwar South* (Cambridge: Harvard University Press, 2006); and Alan I. Abramowitz and H. Gibbs Knotts, "Ideological Realignment in the American Electorate: A Comparison of Northern and Southern White Voters in the Pre-Reagan, Reagan, and Post-Reagan Eras," *Politics & Policy* 34 (March, 2006): 94–108.

25. Voting results from some of the state's almost totally white counties and some precinct analysis from Jefferson County (Birmingham) suggest, but do not definitely show, that Obama's support among white voters may have been greater than 10 percent. Jeff Hansen, "Blacks, Liberals Key to Obama Win in Jefferson County," *News,* (Birmingham, AL), November 7, 2008, 1C.

26. Mary Orndorff, "Davis Says Obama Win Will Hit Home," *News,* (Birmingham, AL), June 6, 2008, 3C.

27. Tom Gordon, "Davis Says a Black Candidate Can Win in Alabama," *News,* (Birmingham, AL), November 6, 2008, 1B.

4.

1. Aaron Gould Scheinin, "Democrats Deny Obama Cedes Georgia," *Atlanta Journal-Constitution,* September 8, 2008, 9A.

2. Aaron Gould Scheinin, "Obama TV Ad to Highlight McCain Link to Ralph Reed," *Atlanta Journal-Constitution,* August 21, 2008, 8A.

3. Jim Galloway and Aaron Gould Sheinin, "Obama to Trim Staff in Georgia," *Atlanta Journal-Constitution,* September 10, 2008, 1A.

4. Aaron Gould Sheinin, "Georgia Race is all About Volunteers," *Atlanta Journal-Constitution,* October 6, 2008, 6A.

5. *Insider Advantage/Poll Position,* September 11, 2008,

http://insideradvantagegeorgia.com/PollPosition%20Poll%201.pdf.

6. Aaron Gould Sheinin, "Tighter Race Brings Backup," *Atlanta Journal-Constitution,* October 25, 2008, 1A.

7. Aaron Gould Sheinin, "Georgia a Political Plum," *Atlanta Journal-Constitution,* November 9,2008, 10A.

8. Aaron Gould Sheinin, "Atlanta Event Raises Money, Profile," *Atlanta Journal-Constitution,* August 19, 2008, 7A.

9. Jim Galloway, "Campaign Turned Strategy on its Head," *Atlanta Journal-Constitution,* November 3, 2008, 7B.

10. The 25 percent vote share from blacks comes from a tabulation of turnout by race prepared by Georgia's Secretary of State. Comparable figures for 2008 had not been released when this was written.

11. Sheinin, "Georgia a Political Plum."

12. Jim Tharpe, "Senate Runoff Brings Big Spending," *Atlanta Journal-Constitution,* November 16, 2008, 3C.

13. Dick Morris and Eileen McCain, "Georgia Results Point out Strategy for Future," *DickMorris.com,* December 4, 2008; Robbie Brown, "Presidential Race is Still Alive in Georgia Runoff," *New York Times,* December 2, 2008.

14. "Chambliss Ahead by Four in Georgia Run-Off Race," Rassmussen Reports, http://www.rassmussenreports.com/public_content/politics/election_2008to/2008_senate.

15. Shannon McCaffrey, "Former Critics Rallying to Chambliss in Runoff," *Athens Banner-Herald,* November 16, 2008, 6A.

16. Blake Aued, "Pivotal Seat at Stake in Runoff," *Athens Banner-Herald,* November 16, 2008, 7A.

17. Aaron Gould Sheinin and Jim Tharpe, "Obama Lends Staff to Help Martin," *Atlanta Journal-Constitution,* November 12, 2008, 1C.

18. Robbie Brown and Carl Hulse, "Republican Wins Runoff for Senator in Georgia," *New York Times,* December 3, 2008.

5.

1. Richard M. Scammon, *America Votes: A Handbook of Contemporary American Election Statistics* (New York: Macmillan, 2004).

2. Charles D. Hadley "Louisiana" in *The 1984 Presidential Election in the South: Patterns of Southern Party Politics,* eds. Robert Steed, Laurence W. Moreland, and Tod A. Baker)New York: Praeger, 1986), 21- 44.

3. Louisiana Secretary of State, "State Wide Post Election Statistical Report," Louisiana Secretary of State,http://www400.sos.louisiana.gov/stats/Post_Election_Statistics/Statewide/2008_1104_sta.pdf (accessed November 6, 2008).

4. Robert E. Hogan, "Louisiana: Two-Party Growth and Increasing Party Polarization," *American Review of Politics* 24 (Spring 2003): 53–68.

5. Louisiana Democratic Party, "Louisiana Delegate Selection Plan for the 2008 Democratic National Convention," Louisiana Democratic Party,

http://www.lademo.org/ht/a/GetDocumentAction/i/1023474 (accessed May 4, 2007). *Green Papers: 2008 Presidential Primaries, Caucuses, and Conventions,* "Louisiana Democrat," Green Papers, http://www.thegreenpapers.com/P08/LA-D.phtml (accessed November 1, 2008).

6. Louisiana Republican Party, "LAGOP Releases Unofficial Results of Louisiana's Republican Caucuses," Louisiana Republican Party, http://www.lagoplcom (accessed November 1, 2008. Green Papers: 2008 Presidential Primaries, Caucuses, and Conventions, "Louisiana Republican," Green Papers, http://www.thegreenpapers.com/P08/LA-R.phtml (accessed November 1, 2008).

7. CNN 2008 Exit Poll Results, http://www.cnn.com/ELECTION/2008/results/polls.main/ (accessed November 5, 2008).

8. Paul Vitello and Michael Cooper, "For McCain, Losses Signal Challenges," *New York Times,* February 11, 2008.

9. CNN 2008 Exit Poll Results.

10. CNN 2008 Exit Poll Results.

11. Michael Cooper, "McCain Distances Himself from Bush and Jabs Obama," *New York Times,* June 4, 2008.

12. Rassmussen poll and Zogby poll results available at http://www.usaelectionpolls.com/2008/louisiana-2.html.

13. Center for Responsive Politics, "Louisiana Contributors to 2008 Presidential Candidates," http://www.opensecrets.org/pres08/presstatistics_cands.php?state=LA (accessed December 1, 1008).

14. Richard Rainey, "Demos Launch Massive Voter Drive," *Times-Picayune,* (New Orleans, LA) June 7, 2008.

15. Mary Foster, "Howard Dean's Tour Bus Rolls into New Orleans," Associated Press, July 18, 2008 http://www.wwltv.com/topstories/stories/wwl071708mldean.6a819d (accessed July 20, 2008).

16. Shaila Dewan, "A Vote Drive by Democrats in Louisiana Stirs Concern," *New York Times,* June 15, 2008.

17. Ian Urbina, "States' Actions to Block Voters Appear Illegal," *New York Times,* October 9, 2008.

18. Rasmussen poll results available at http://www.rasmussenreports.com/public_content/politics/election_20 082/2008_presidential_election/louisiana/election_2008_louisiana_president.

19. CNN, Election Coverage, http://www.cnn.com/ELECTION/2008/map/ad.spending/.

20. Melinda Deslatte, "Louisiana Shatters Record for Early Voting," Associated Press, October 29, 2008, http://www.2theadvocate.com/news/33487174.html (accessed November 1, 2008).

21. Louisiana Secretary of State, "State Wide Post Election Statistical Reports."

22. Louisiana Secretary of State, "State Wide Post Election Statistical Reports."

23. In 2007 the state's governor and other constitutional officers, along with the entire legislature, were up for election so the only major offices on the ballot in 2008 were those for Congress.

24. Will Sentell, "Kennedy, Landrieu on Attack," *Advocate*, (Baton Rouge, LA), October 13, 2008.

25. Campaign Finance Institute, "A First Look at Money in the House and Senate Elections," Campaign Finance Institute, http://www.cfinst.org/, November 6, 2008.

26. These were the first regular elections for Congress since the 1970s that did not use an open election system. Under the old system all candidates, regardless of party, ran against one another in a first-round election and if no candidate received a majority of the vote the two top vote-getters would proceed to a runoff. The legislature changed the open election system to a system of closed and semi-closed primaries for choosing nominees in advance of the general election. Such a system avoids the possibility of a runoff in December, which has created problems in the past for newly elected members in obtaining coveted committee assignments as the new Congress begins to organize.

27. Michelle Krupa and Frank Donze, "Anh 'Joseph' Cao Beats Rep. William Jefferson in 2nd Congressional District," *Times-Picayune* (New Orleans, LA), December 6, 2008.

28. CNN 2004 Exit Poll Results, http://www.cnn.com/ELECTION/2004/ (accessed November 6, 2008).

6.

1. Stephen D. Shaffer, David A. Breaux, and Barbara Patrick. "Mississippi: Republicans Surge Forward in a Two-Party State," *American Review of Politics* 26 (Spring 2005): 85-107.

2. Natalie Chandler, "With Dale Out, Hopefuls Will Dig for New Material," *Clarion-Ledger,* (Jackson, MS), August 9, 2007, 1A.

3. Figures from the Mississippi Secretary of State website: http://www. sos.state.ms.us/elections/2007.

4. "Editorials, Gov.: Barbour Best Choice Nov. 6," *Clarion-Ledger* (Jackson, MS), November 4, 2007, 4G.

5. "Lt. Gov: Bryant Best Choice Nov. 6," *Clarion-Ledger* (Jackson, MS), November 4, 2007, 4G. "Sec'y of State: Hosemann Best Choice Nov. 6," *Clarion-Ledger* (Jackson, MS), October 31, 2007, 8A.

6. For more discussion of the biracial legislative partnership, see Charles E. Menifield and Stephen D. Shaffer, ed. *Politics in the New South: Representation of African Americans in Southern State Legislatures* (Albany: State University of New York Press, 2005), 107-29.

7. See Mississippi Poll press releases at website http://www2.msstate.edu/~kauai/poll/poll.html.

8. "Pickering Joins McCain's Team," *Commercial Dispatch* (Columbus, MS), February 22,2007, 3A.

9. "Cochran Backs Romney Campaign," *Clarion Ledger* (Jackson, MS), January 24, 2008, 3A.

10. Natalie Chandler, "Obama Visits Metro to Mix, Mingle, Raise Money," *Clarion-Ledger* (Jackson, MS), June 16, 2007, 1B, 5B.

11. Ana Radelat, "Rep. Thompson Endorses Obama," *Clarion Ledger* (Jackson, MS), January 22, 2008, 1A.

12. Michael Newsom, "Clinton's Mississippi Comment Blasted," *SunHerald.com* (Jackson, MS), March 6, 2008 (accessed March 9, 2008).

13. Birney Imes, "Barack Obama Comes to Town," *Commercial Dispatch,* (Columbus, MS), March 11, 2008, 4A.

14. Kristin Mamrack, "Obama Tells Crowd in Columbus: 'I'm Not Running for Vice President,'" *Commercial Dispatch* (Columbus, MS), March 11, 2008, 1, 7A.

15. Mississippi Secretary of State's website, http://www.sos.state.ms.us/ elections/2008/Primary/Results.

16. See *CNN.com,* http://www.cnn.com/ELECTION/2008/primaries/results/ epolls/ (accessed March 12, 2008).

17. Emily Wagster Pettus, "Miss. Democrats Hope to Carry Primaries' Energy into November," *Starkville Daily News,* March 13, 2008, 3A.

18. Data are from a Mississippi State University survey. See http://www2. msstate.edu/~kauai/poll/Results08.htm.

19. Shelia Byrd, "McCain Back in Meridian Ahead of His 'Service' Tour," *Starkville Daily News,* March 31, 2008, 1A.

20. Kristin Mamrack, "McCain Walks Memory Lane in Meridian," *Commercial Dispatch* (Columbus, MS), March 31, 2008, 1A, 5A.

21. Natalie Chandler, "Meeting McCain: Mississippi Connections Touted," *Clarion-Ledger* (Jackson, MS), April 1, 2008, 1A, 4A.

22. "Editorials, Democrats: Biden No Stranger to Mississippians," *Clarion Ledger* (Jackson, MS), August 26, 2008, 6A.

23. Andy Taggart, "The Dems Race to the Left," *Clarion-Ledger* (Jackson, MS), August 27, 2008, 6A.

24. Natalie Chandler, "Conservative Views Expected to Play Well in Miss.," *Clarion Ledger* (Jackson, MS), August 30, 2008, 1A, 8A.

25. Elizabeth Crisp, "Campaigning Set to Rev up in Mississippi," *Clarion-Ledger* (Jackson, MS), September 7, 2008, 1A, 7A.

26. Brian Hawkins, "Local, State Democrats Echoing Call for Change by Obama," *Starkville Daily News,* September 14, 2008, 1A.

27. Natalie Chandler, "Democrats Challenge McCain on Reform," *Clarion-Ledger* (Jackson, MS), September 16, 2008, 1B.

28. Tim Pratt, "Republican Colom Publishes Book Urging Support of Democrat Obama," *Commercial Dispatch* (Columbus, MS), September 19, 2008, 7A.

29. Jerry Mitchell, "Who Will Win Mississippi: Turning Red State Blue a Difficult Assignment," *Clarion-Ledger* (Jackson, MS), September 21, 2008, 1A, 10A.

30. "Editorials, Debate '08: Neither Candidate 'Failed' Test," *Clarion Ledger* (Jackson, MS), September 27, 2008, 11A.

31. Jerry Mitchell, "Miss. Senator Supports McCain: About-face for Cochran as Election Nears," *Clarion Ledger* (Jackson, MS), October 14, 2008, 2B.

32. "Democrats Rally to Rock the Vote: Obama Supporters Seek Big Turnout in Mississippi," *WAPT.com* (Jackson, MS), October 19, 2008, (accessed October 21, 2008).

33. The Associated Press, "Mabus, Barbour Stumping for Candidates," *Clarion Ledger* (Jackson, MS), October 23, 2008, 3B.

34. "Editorials, Election '08: Obama Choice for Future," *Clarion Ledger* (Jackson, MS), November 2, 2008, 8G.

35. Jesse J. Holland, "Race for Trent Lott's Old U.S. Senate Seat Proving Competitive," *Starkville Daily News,* July 4, 2008, 7A.

36. Emily Wagster Pettus, "Wicker, Musgrove Race for Senate Intensifies," *Starkville Daily News,* October 16, 2008, 3A.

37. Ben Piper, "Governor Stumps for Wicker," *Hattiesburg American,* October 30, 2008, 2B.

38. Chris Todd, "2008 Senatorial Debate: Musgrove vs. Wicker, Mudslinging Match," *Clarion-Ledger* (Jackson, MS), October 4, 2008, 1A.

39. "Editorials, Election '08: Musgrove for Senate," *Clarion-Ledger* (Jackson, MS), October 26, 2008, 4G.

40. *Clarion-Ledger* and League of Women Voters, "The *Clarion-Ledger* and League of Women Voters Voter's Guide, 2008," *Clarion-Ledger* (Jackson, MS), March 9, 2008, 2G.

41. Emily Wagster Pettus, "Low Turnout Expected in Special Election in House Race," *Starkville Daily News,* April 22, 2008, 3A.

42. Patsy R. Brumfield, "Davis, McCullough Take off the Gloves," *Northeast Mississippi Daily Journal* (Tupelo, MS), March 5, 2008, http://www.djournal.com/pages/archive.asp?ID=267751&pub=1&div=News (accessed November 6, 2008).

43. Patsy R. Brumfield, "1st District Gets Notice for its Competitiveness," *Northeast Mississippi Daily Journal* (Tupelo, MS), April 12, 2008, 7A.

44. "Accusations Fly in House Race," *Clarion-Ledger* (Jackson, MS), April 18, 2008, 2B.

45. Editorial, "Our Opinions: Childers Best Choice, Consensus-Builder Stands Firmly in State Congressional Tradition," *Northeast Mississippi Daily Journal* (Tupelo, MS), April 18, 2008, 4B.

46. Emily Le Coz, "Childers, Davis Debate in Tupelo," *Northeast Mississippi Daily Journal* (Tupelo, MS), October 22, 2008, 2A.

47. Ana Radelat, "Mississippi Democrat Pushing for Gun Rights," *Clarion-Ledger* (Jackson, MS), September 14, 2008, 1B.

48. Leah Rupp, "Runoff Face Off: Underdog Draws Fervid Support despite Hurdles," *Clarion-Ledger* (Jackson, MS), March 31, 2008, 1A, 8A.

49. David Hampton, "Voters Narrow the Field for Congress," *Clarion-Ledger* (Jackson, MS), April 6, 2008, 4G.

50. Sid Salter, "Blognotes: Politics of Personal Relationships," *Clarion-Ledger* (Jackson, MS), April 3, 2008, 6A.

51. Shaffer, Breaux, and Patrick, "Mississippi: Republicans Surge Forward," 89, compares the Republican percentage of the two-party vote in Mississippi with the region and nation. The source of the 2008 preliminary results is the CNN website: http://edition.cnn.com/ELECTION/2008/results/president/ (accessed November 30, 2008).

52. Shaffer, Breaux, and Patrick, "Mississippi: Republicans Surge Forward," 100.

7.

1. See Robert P. Steed and Laurence W. Moreland, "South Carolina: Change and Continuity in the Palmetto State," in Charles S. Bullock III and Mark J.

Rozell, *The New Politics of the Old South: An Introduction to Southern Politics,* 3rd ed. (Boulder, CO: Rowman & Littlefield Publishers, 2007), 29– 48.

2. For a general discussion of the fortunes of Democratic presidential candidates in the South during its transition from Democratic to Republican successes, see Nicol C. Rae, *Southern Democrats* (New York: Oxford University Press, 1994), 46–64.

3. It was one of the three top-ranking Republican states in 1988, with 62.1 percent for George H. W. Bush over Michael Dukakis and again in 1992 with 48 percent for the incumbent President Bush to 39.9 percent to Bill Clinton. For a discussion of the 2000 election in South Carolina, see Laurence W. Moreland and Robert P. Steed, "South Carolina: Republican, Primarily," in Robert P. Steed and Laurence W. Moreland, eds. *The 2000 Presidential Election in the South: Partisanship and Southern Party Systems in the 21st Century* (Westport, CN: Praeger, 2002), 113–29.

4. See Cole Blease Graham Jr. and Samuel J. Wellborn, "Party Identification Among South Carolinians, 1990 to 2007," (paper presented at The Citadel Symposium on Southern Politics, Charleston, South Carolina, March 7, 2008).

5. Aaron Gould Sheinin, "Arizona Senator Leads Most S.C. GOP Polls, But Nine Others Are Hoping to Knock Him Off," *State,* (Columbia, SC), May 13, 2007. See Clemson University Palmetto Poll, for three interesting pre primary polls, the third of which showed that about half of Democrats were undecided in November 2007. The Clemson poll identified that Arkansas governor Mike Huckabee was closing in with 13 percent approval on the leaders at that time, with Romney at 17 percent and Thompson at 15 percent. McCain trailed at 11 percent.

6. James T. Hammond, "Political, Media 'Stars are Aligned' for S.C. State," *State* (Columbia, SC), April 26, 2007. The debate was held at South Carolina State University in Orangeburg. See als, Aaron Gould Sheinin, "Debate Expert Says S.C. Event's Format Favors Front-runners," *State* (Columbia, SC), April 26, 2007. The front-runners were Clinton, Edwards, and Obama. Veteran journalist David Broder thought the entire field showed promise, "Democratic hopefuls show political heft," *Washington Post,* April 27, 2007.

7. John O'Connor, "State Saved McCain's Primary-Campaign Hopes," *State* (Columbia, SC), November 2, 2008 and Gina Smith, "On Rough Primary Road, State Embraced Obama," *State,* November 2, 2008.

8. Gina Smith, "Obama's N.C. Staff Looks South," *State* (Columbia, SC), October 4, 2008. Obama did not concede South Carolina. His campaign asked his South Carolina volunteers to head to North Carolina, where polls at the time showed him in a dead heat with McCain. Obama eventually won North Carolina by a narrow margin.

9. Robert Behre, "SC Officials Predict Record Turnout," *Charleston Post and Courier,* November 4, 2008, and Jeff Wilkinson, "Record Numbers Cast Vote in State," *State* (Columbia, SC), November 5, 2008. In the 2004 presidential election, 1,631,148 South Carolinians voted.

10. Gina Smith, "SC Voters Full of Questions Headed into First Debate, *State,* September 26, 2008. See also Roddie Burris, "ETV Poll: Not-so-solid South" *State* (Columbia, SC), October 24, 2008.

11. A marginal seat requires a smaller change, or swing, in the next election for an opponent to win. Often a marginal seat is targeted by the out party with more campaign resources in an effort to reclaim the seat. The concept may more aptly apply to legislative elections than presidential elections. However, if states are viewed one at a time with respect to their Electoral College votes and the chances of winning them, the choice of the states in which to campaign takes on some of the tactics of a legislative election.

12. Aaron Gould Sheinin, "The Republican Label in South Carolina Means Different Things, Depending on Where You Live," *State* (Columbia, SC), November 5, 2007, referring to the Winthrop University/ South Carolina Educational Television poll, November 2007, conducted October 7– 28, 2007. See J. David Woodard, "The Republican Electoral Surge," in *The New Southern Politics* (Boulder, CO: Lynne Rienner, 2006), 249– 307, esp. 291–295. See also, http://www.cnn.com/2008/POLITICS/01/17/sc.guide/index.html (accessed January 18, 2008).

13. Winthrop University/ South Carolina Educational Television Polls. See, for example, http://www.scetv.org/index.php/winthrop/ for the October 2008 poll. There were also polls in August and February 2008 and in November, September, and May 2007.

14. See Alan Greenblatt, "Blueburbs" at http://ballotbox.governing.com/ 2008/11/bluburbs.html, November 6, 2008.

15. See Earl Black and Merle Black, *Divided America: The Ferocious Power Struggle in American Politics* (New York: Simon and Schuster, 2007), 12–18.

16. Yvonne Wenger, "Graham Easily Defeats Conley for 2nd Term," *Charleston Post and Courier*, November 5, 2008.

17. Wayne Washington, "S.C. Has Always Been a Key Political Player," *State* (Columbia, SC), November 2, 2008.

18. Robert Behre, "State Democrats Hope to Build on Obama's Showing," *Charleston Post and Courier*, November 5, 2008, and Yvonne Wenger, "GOP Chair Speaks Out about Republican Success in SC," *Charleston Post and Courier*, November 5, 2008.

19. Dan Hoover, "Dawson Touts State's Success in GOP Chairmanship Bid," *Greenville News*, November 25, 2008.

20. Wayne Washington, "Clinton, Obama Sign on for Rally," *State* (Columbia, SC), January 3, 2008. Roddie Burris, "Rally Putting Focus Back on King Day," *State* (Columbia, SC), December 12, 2008.

8.

1. For a discussion of the important role of the rural swing counties in 2004, see Jay Barth and Janine Parry, "Arkansas: Still Swingin' in 2004," *American Review of Politics* 26 (Spring & Summer 2005): 133-54.

2. Andrew DeMillo, "Arkansas Democrats Pin Their Hopes on Another Clinton," *Associated Press*, June 22, 2007.

3. DeMillo, "Arkansas Democrats."

4. Andrew DeMillo, "Hillary Hopes to be Regular Ark. Presence," *Associated Press*, August 25, 2007.

5. DeMillo, "Hillary Hopes."

6. Andrew DeMillo, "Clinton Thanks Neighbor Who Saved Her from Christmas Tree," *Associated Press*, January 30, 2008.

7. Associated Press, "Obama to Open Presidential Campaign Office in Little Rock," *Associated Press*, January 18, 2008.

8. Tara M. Manthey, "Arkansas Democrats Pledge Allegiance to Clinton," *Arkansas Democrat-Gazette* (Little Rock, AR), December 9, 2007.

9. "Arkansas Gov. Huckabee Says He's Thinking of GOP Presidential Run," *Associated Press*, September 16, 2005.

10. Andrew DeMillo, "Huckabee Touts Support for White House Bid Among Ark. Republicans," *Associated Press*, November 7, 2007.

11. Andrew DeMillo, "Ark. Primary May Highlight Huckabee's Strains Within GOP," *Associated Press*, February 4, 2008.

12. Campaign finance data from *New York Times* website, http://elections.nytimes.com/2008/president/campaign-finance/map.html.

13. Leslie Wayne, "Huckabee's Stature Rises, Mobilizing Tax Critics," *New York Times*, December 2, 2007.

14. Jake Bleed, "State Democrats to Push Case for Early Presidential Primary," *Arkansas Democrat-Gazette* (Little Rock, AR), April 20, 2006.

15. John Lyon, "Huckabee, Clinton Win Arkansas," *Arkansas News Bureau*, February 6, 2008.

16. For exit poll results, see http://www.abcnews.go.com/images/PollingUnit/ARDemHorizontal.pdf and http://www.abcnews.go.com/images/PollingUnit/ARRepHorizontal.pdf.

17. Arkansas's voters typically do not register by party and may participate in either party's primary no matter their partisan registration.

18. John M. Broder, "McCain, Supporters Slam Clark and Obama Campaign," *New York Times*, June 30, 2008.

19. Andrew DeMillo, "McCain Hopes to Build Support in Ark. with Fund-raising Swing," *Associated Press*, April 24, 2008, and Andrew DeMillo, "McCain: He'll Seek Votes of 'Clinton Democrats,'" *Associated Press*, August 11, 2008.

20. Matthew S. L. Cate, "Obama Campaign Planning to Open State Head-quarters," *Arkansas Democrat-Gazette* (Little Rock, AR), September 10, 2008.

21. Andrew DeMillo, "Ark. Wants to be Wooed by Obama," *Associated Press*, August 9, 2008, and Shaila Dewan, "A Southern Democratic State, But an Uneasy Fit for Obama," *New York Times*, August 16, 2008, 14A.

22. Janine A. Parry and Bill Schreckhise, *The Arkansas Poll, 2008* (Fayetteville: Diane D. Blair Center of Southern Politics and Society, University of Arkansas, 2008). Dataset available upon request.

23. Matthew S. L. Cate, "Obama Ancestors Found a Home in State in 1840s," *Arkansas Democrat-Gazette* (Little Rock, AR), July 30, 2008.

24. Dewan, "A Southern Democratic State."

25. Matthew S. L. Cate, "Sen. Clinton: Cure is Obama," *Arkansas Democrat-Gazette* (Little Rock, AR), October 11, 2008.

26. See http://www.vimeo.com/2448474.

27. Arkansas's sharp rightward turn earned the state a smattering of national media attention. See, for example, Adam Nossiter, "For South, a Waning Hold on National Politics," *New York Times* November 11, 2008, 1A.

28. Diane D. Blair and Jay Barth, *Arkansas Politics and Government,* 2nd ed. (Lincoln: University of Nebraska Press, 2005): 91-94.

9.

1. For a detailed analysis of the emergence of Florida as battleground state since 1992, see William E. Hulbary, Anne E. Kelley, and Lewis Bowman, "Florida: A Muddled Election" in *The 1992 Presidential Election in the South: Current Patterns of Southern Party and Electoral Politics,* ed. Robert P. Steed, Laurence W. Moreland and Tod A. Baker (Westport, CT: Praeger 1994): 119–37; Kathryn Dunn Tenpas, William E. Hulbary, and Lewis Bowman, "Florida: An Election With Something for Everyone," in *The 1996 Presidential Election in the South: Party Politics in the 1990s,* ed. Laurence W. Moreland and Robert P. Steed (Westport, CT: Praeger 1997): 147–63; Steven Tauber and William E. Hulbary, "Florida: Too Close To Call" in *The 2000 Presidential Election in the South: Partisanship and Southern Party Systems in the 21st Century,* ed. Robert P. Steed and Laurence W. Moreland (Westport, CT: Praeger 2002); and Susan A. MacManus, "Florida: The South's Premier Battleground State," *American Review of Politics* 26 (Summer 2005): 155–84.

2. Harry S Truman of Missouri, who carried Florida in 1948, is considered an "honorary" southern Democrat given that he hailed from a border state.

3. For a discussion of how Florida may become increasingly Democratic, see John B. and Ruy Teixeira, *The Emerging Democratic Majority* (New York: Scribner, 2002).

4. Steve Bousquet and Alex Leary, "Crist Cruises," *St. Petersburg Times,* November 8, 2006, 1A.

5. Abby Goodnough, "Republicans Seem to Rally in Run for Seat Foley Quit," *New York Times,* November 2, 2006, 23A.

6. The congressional level vote in the presidential elections is taken from Polidata, http://www.polidata.us/pub/reports/12a0a2a.pdf (accessed November 9, 2008).

7. Abby Goodnough, "Seeking an Edge, Florida Changes its Primary Date," *New York Times,* May 4, 2007, 1A.

8. Adam C. Smith, "Florida Primary Will Not Count, Dean Warns," *St. Petersburg Times,* June 13, 2007, 6A.

9. Adam C. Smith, "Clinton Alone in Push for Fla. Delegates," *St. Petersburg Times,* January 26, 2008, 5B.

10. See Table 9.3 for the counties that constitute each region.

11. Florida would later have its full voting rights restored at the Democratic National Convention.

12. Adam C. Smith, "Crist: McCain is Best Choice," *St. Petersburg Times,* January 27, 2008, 13A.

13. Data are from the Florida Republican Primary Exit Poll, http://www. cnn.com/ELECTION/2008/primaries/results/epolls/index.html#FLREP (accessed February 1, 2008).

14. For this and all other references to Real Clear Politics polling averages in

Florida, see http://www.realclearpolitics.com/epolls/2008/president/
fl/florida_mccain_vs_obama-418.html (accessed December 1, 2008).

15. Adam C. Smith, "It's Time for Obama to Shout Hello, Fla." *St. Petersburg Times,* May 13, 2008, 1A.

16. Adam C. Smith "Crist Hangs Out at McCain Ranch," *St. Petersburg Times,* May 25, 2008, 3B.

17. Adam C. Smith "Obama's Campaign Signs Star Strategist," *St. Petersburg Times,* June 17, 2008, 1B.

18. Adam C. Smith "Obama Backers to Blitz Florida," *St. Petersburg Times,* June 10, 2008, 1A.

19. Jonathan Weisman and Robert Barnes, "Both Presidential Campaigns Make it Clear that Florida Matters," *Washington Post*, August 3, 2008, 14A.

20. Beth Reinhard, Lesley Clark, and Jennifer Lebovich "Democrats Determined to Win Florida," *Miami Herald,* October 11, 2008, http://www.miamiherald.com/460/story/735894.html (accessed October 25, 2008).

21. Jim Stratton, "Many Republicans Ask: Where's McCains TV Presence?," *Orlando Sentinel*, October 12, 2008, http://www.orlandosentinel.com/news/politics/orl-prezmedia1208oct12,0,372728.story (accessed October 15, 2008).

22. "Joe the Plumber" was invoked by McCain during the final presidential debate to attack Obama on taxes. In fact the individual, Samuel Joseph Wurzelbacher, was neither named "Joe" nor did he actually possess a plumbing license in Toledo, Ohio. Wurzelbacher had told Obama during a campaign event that Obama's small business tax plan would keep him from buying the plumbing business that employed him.

23. Mary Ellen Klas and Marc Caputo "Florida Republicans Cast Blame as McCain Trails in Polls," *Miami Herald*, October 12, 2008,http://www.miamiherald.com/news/florida/story/722731.html (accessed October 13, 2008).

24. Campaign appearance statistics are taken from *Washington Post*, http://projects.washingtonpost.com/2008-presidential-candidates/tracker/states/fl/ (accessed November 12, 2008).

25. Obama may have been helped, ironically, by the decision of Governor Crist to extend early voting hours to twelve hours a day from eight hours a day, and a total of twelve hours over the weekend.

26. As of August 2008, 41 percent of registered voters held Democratic Party registration, 37 percent Republican party registration, and 22 percent "other" or no party registration; http://election.dos.state.fl.us/NVRA/history.asp (accessed December 5, 2008).

27. Beth Reinhard "Obama to Visit Florida to Encourage Early Voting," *Miami Herald*, October 19, 2008, http://www.miamiherald.com/front-page.html (accessed October 20, 2008).

28. Alex Leary, "Gore Returns to Palm Beach," *St. Petersburg Times,* November 1, 2008, 3A.

29. Alex Leary, Janet Zink, and Adam C. Smith, "McCain, Obama Battle in Florida," *St. Petersburg Times*, October 30, 2008, 1A.

30. Adam C. Smith, David DeCamp, and Alex Leary, "Tight Race Surges to Finish Line," *St. Petersburg Times*, November 2, 2008, 1B.

31. The voting-eligible population measure of turnout is used as a more valid measure of voter turnout than the voting age population as the latter includes non-citizens and felons. On this point see Michael P. McDonald and Samuel L. Popkin, "The Myth of the Vanishing Voter," *American Political Science Review* 95 (December 2001): 963–74. Voter-eligible population data for 2008 were taken from the United States Election project, http://elections.gmu.edu/preliminary_vote_2008.html (accessed December 1, 2008).

32. Indeed, Obama's vote was also highly correlated with that of both Al Gore in 2000 (r = .89) and Bill Clinton in 1996 (r = .78), reflecting a continuity in the county-by-county structure of the vote in Florida. On this point, more generally, see Jonathan Knuckey, "The Structure of Party Competition in the South: The Case of Florida," *American Review of Politics* 25 (Spring 2004): 41–65.

33. The 2004 exit poll did not control for race for the relationship between age and vote choice, so a direct comparison with the patterns in 2008 cannot be made.

34. A separate exit poll was conducted for the vote on Amendment 2 vote; see http://edition.cnn.com/ELECTION/2008/results/polls/#val=FLI01p1 (accessed November 12, 2008).

35. District-level party registration data were obtained from the Florida Secretary of State, Elections Division, http://election.dos.state.fl.us/voter-registration/statistics/pdf/2008/2008genCongDist.pdf (accessed December 1, 2008).

36. See http://www.crewsmostcorrupt.org/summaries/feeney.phpndeed (accessed December 1, 2008).

37. Mark Schlueb and Rachael Jackson, "Democrats Kosmas, Grayson Defeat GOP Veterans Keller, Feeney," *Orlando Sentinel*, November 5, 2008, http://www.orlandosentinel.com/news/local/state/orl-electcong0508nov05,0,6414743.story (accessed November 8, 2008).

38. Christopher Lee, "Scandal Embroils Congressman; Fla. Democrat Accused of Paying Ex-Mistress to Keep Quiet," *Washington Post*, October 14, 2008, 15A.

39. David Rieff, "Will Little Havana Go Blue?," *New York Times*, July 13, 2008, http://www.nytimes.com/2008/07/13/magazine/13CUBANS-t.html) accessed August 6, 2008).

40. An Obama victory in 2012 in Florida would mark the first time since 1948 that the state would have voted Democratic in two consecutive presidential elections.

10.

1. For discussions of recent electoral politics in North Carolina see Charles Prysby, "North Carolina: Continued Two-Party Competition," in *The 2000 Presidential Election in the South,* ed. Robert P. Steed and Laurence W. Moreland (Westport, CT: Praeger, 2002), 169–80; Charles Prysby, "North Carolina: The Development of Party Organizations in a Competitive Environment," *American Review of Politics,* 24 (Spring and Summer, 2003): 145–64; Charles Prysby, "A Civil Campaign in a Competitive State: The 2002

North Carolina U.S. Senate Election," in *Running on Empty? Campaign Discourse in Congressional Elections,* ed. by L. Sandy Maisel and Darrel West (Lanham, MD: Rowman and Littlefield, 2004), 215–28; Charles Prysby, "North Carolina: Color the Tar Heels Federal Red and State Blue," *American Review of Politics,* 26 (Spring and Summer, 2005): 185–202; Charles Prysby, "North Carolina: Two-Party Competition Continues Into the Twenty-First Century," in *The New Politics of the Old South: An Introduction to Southern Politics,* 3rd ed., ed. by Charles S. Bullock III and Mark J. Rozell (Landham, MD: Rowman and Littlefield, 2007), 161–86; and Charles Prysby, "The Reshaping of the Political Party System in North Carolina," in *The New Politics of North Carolina,* ed. Christopher A. Cooper and H. Gibbs Knotts (Chapel Hill: University of North Carolina Press, 2008), 61–84.

2. Three of the last six Senate elections were midterm elections, which are not shown in Table 10.1. In 1990, Republican Jesse Helms was reelected. In 1998, Democrat John Edwards defeated incumbent Republican Lauch Faircloth. In 2002, Republican Elizabeth Dole won the seat of the retiring Helms.

3. Gallup Poll, "Bush Job Approval at 25%, His Lowest Yet," news release, October 6, 2008, http://www.gallup.com (accessed November 18, 2008).

4. Responses to other exit poll questions display a similar relationship between disapproval of Bush's policies and support for Obama. For example, slightly over one-half of the respondents disapproved of the Iraq war, and nearly 80 percent of this group voted for Obama. Obama also did extremely well among those who strongly disapproved of Bush's performance as president.

5. Mark Farinella (who helped to direct the Obama campaign in North Carolina), telephone interview with the author, December 22, 2008.

6. The North Carolina Republican Party also had a strong organizational effort, although it lagged behind what the Democrats were able to do. The Republican Party had thirty field offices, with forty paid staffers in these offices (plus staff in Raleigh). Their Victory '08 fund was approximately nine million dollars. Like the Democrats, the Republicans used a mixture of phone calling, direct mailing, and door-to-door contacting to mobilize likely Republican voters. Their effort was especially concentrated in the seventy-two hours prior to election day, when they contacted about five hundred thousand voters. The 2008 effort was superior to what the party put forth in 2004. (Chris McClure (executive director of the North Carolina Republican Party), telephone interview with the author, December 22, 2008.)

7. Registration figures came from the North Carolina State Board of Elections website, http://www.sboe.state.nc.us (accessed December 11, 2008).

8. American voter turnout increased from 60.1 to 61.6 percent of the eligible population. The turnout rates for North Carolina and the United States are based on the voter-eligible population, defined as adult citizens who are not ineligible to vote due to a felony conviction. All turnout data come from the United States Election Project website, http://elections.gmu.edu/voter_turnout.htm (accessed December 20, 2008).

9. The figures on population change were calculated from data presented in Office of State Budget and Management, "Population Estimates and

Projections," Office of State Budget and Management, http://www.osbm. states.nc.us (accessed November 29, 2008).

10. Obama also did well in most other counties with major cities. He won 59 percent of the vote in Guilford County (Greensboro), 55 percent in Forsyth County (Winston-Salem), and 76 percent in Durham County (Durham), which are the other counties in the state that contain a city with a population of more than two hundred thousand.

11. The National Election Pool exit poll in North Carolina included interviews of election day voters at the polling places along with telephone interviews of those who voted early or by absentee ballot. Fewer than 50 percent of the voters cast a ballot on election day, so including interviews with early voters was essential for a representative sample. About 2,150 voters were interviewed on election day. Telephone interviews were conducted with about 650 early voters. The telephone interviews were weighted to match the proportion of early voters in the electorate. Joe Lenski (Executive Vice President, Edison Media Research), personal communication with the author, December 7, 2008.

12. The poll also showed that 56 percent of respondents were satisfied with Dole's representation of the state. Elon University Poll, conducted April 18, 2008, http://www.elon.edu/e-web/elonpoll/ (accessed November 18, 2008).

13. Shaila Dewan, "A Republican Incumbent Finds a Once-Safe Race Less So," *New York Times,* October 16, 2008, 16A.

14. Through September 30, 2008, Dole had raised $13.8 million, compared to just $5.3 million for Hagan. However, the Democratic Senate Campaign Committee spent $6.6 million on ads on behalf of Hagan, whereas the National Republican Senatorial Committee spent only $2.8 million on behalf of Dole. Expenditures for the fourth quarter of 2008 were not available at the time of this writing.

15. Dewan, "A Republican Incumbent."

16. "Ad Attacks Dole's Work on Banking Committee," *Charlotte Observer,* October 24, 2008, http://www.charlotteobserver.com/politics/story/ 274094.html (accessed Oct. 28, 2008).

17. Lisa Zagaroli, "'Godless' Ad Sets off War of Words between Hagan, Dole," *Charlotte Observer,* October 30, 2008, http://www.charlotteobserver. com/politics/story/287745.html, (accessed October 28, 2008).

18. The exit poll data in Tables 11.3 and 11.4 also show that Hagan's sources of support were very similar to Obama's. Hagan did slightly better than Obama among conservatives and Republicans, which helped her to run somewhat ahead of Obama. Hagan also did better than Obama among whites and men. She also won 31 percent of the vote of white evangelicals, which is almost identical to Perdue's support from this group, and this is some evidence that the Dole "Godless" ad discussed above did not resonate that well among religious conservatives.

19. Gary D. Robertson, "Tax Cuts Still on Minds of NC Governor Candidates," *News and Observer,* (Raleigh, NC), October 21, 2008, http://www.newsobserver.com/2102/v-print/story/1263137.html (accessed October 23, 2008).

20. Rob Christensen, "Ads Stake Campaign Territory," *News and Observer*

(Raliegh, NC), September 14, 2008, http://www.newsobserver.com/622/v-print/story/1218084.html (accessed November 6, 2008).

21. Mark Johnson, "Ad: McCrory's Charlotte Looms over Rest of N.C.," *Charlotte Observer*, October 23, 2008, http://www.charlotteobserver.com/politics/story/271678.html (accessed October 25, 2008).

22. These figures come from the political committee disclosure reports filed by the candidates with the North Carolina State Board of Elections, http://www.app.sboe.state.nc.us (accessed October 27, 2008).

11.

1. Earl Black and Merle Black, *The Vital South: How Presidents are Elected*, (Cambridge: Harvard University Press, 1992).

2. Peter F. Nardulli, "The Concept of a Critical Realignment, Electoral Behavior, and Political Change," *American Political Science Review* 89 (March 1995): 10–22.

3. V. O. Key, Jr., *Southern Politics in State and Nation*, (Knoxville, TN: University of Tennessee Press, 1949), 59.

4. Key, 75.

5. Michael Nelson, "Tennessee: Once a Bluish State, Now a Reddish One," in *The New Politics of the Old South, 3rd edition*, Charles S. Bullock III and Mark J. Rozell, eds. (Boulder, CO: Rowman and Littlefield Press, 2007).

6. Nardulli.

7. Black and Black.

8. David M. Tucker, *Memphis Since Crump* (Knoxville: University of Tennessee Press, 1980).

9. Factor analysis using varimax rotation, conducted by author, based on data compiled by Jerome M. Clubb, William H. Flanigan, and Nancy H. Zingale, *Electoral Data for Counties in the United States: Presidential and Congressional Races, 1840–1972* ICPSR Study No. 8611, 1978, updated by author.

10. John Lyman Mason, "Tennessee: Politics and Politicians Who Matter Beyond State Borders," in *The New Politics of the Old South, 2nd edition*, Charles S. Bullock III and Mark J. Rozell, eds. (Boulder, CO: Rowman and Littlefield Press, 2003).

11. David Brodsky, "Tennessee: Genuine Two-Party Politics," in *The New Politics of the Old South*, Charles S. Bullock III and Mark Rozell, eds. (Boulder, CO: Rowman and Littlefield Press, 1998), 169.

12. Jennings Perry, *Democracy Begins at Home* (Philadelphia: J. P. Lippencott, 1944).

13. Ronald Keith Gaddie, "Testing Some Key Hypotheses of Voter Turnout" (paper presented at the meeting of the Southern Political Science Association, Atlanta, GA, November 2000).

14. Gaddie.

15. Key, 63.

16. Brodsky.

17. Ronald Keith Gaddie and Michael D. Jones, "Tennessee: A Quiet Sort of Inequality," in *New Voices of the Old South: How Women and Minorities Influence Southern Politics*, Todd G. Shields and Shannon G. Davis, eds. (Tallahassee: Florida State University John Scott Daily Florida Institute of Government, 2008).

18. Association of Religion Data Archives, "Religions, Congregations, and Membership Study,"(Counties File, 2000), http://www.thearda.com (accessed June 29, 2009).

19. Gaddie and Jones.

20. The Texas primary was won by Hillary Clinton. However, the Texas rules also contain a caucus component, which allowed Obama to walk away with most of the Lone Star State's delegates.

21. "Why Mr. Obama is Surging," *Chattanooga Times Free Press*, October 23, 2008, 6B.

22. Charles S. Bullock III and Ronald Keith Gaddie, *The Triumph of Voting Rights in the South* (Norman: University of Oklahoma Press, 2009).

23. Bullock and Gaddie.

24. In order to understand the Tennessee presidential election and the Obama candidacy, I specified a series of three weighted least squares regression equations to estimate the role of race and religion in structuring the vote for Obama in 2008, John Kerry in 2004, and also to estimate the structure of the change in vote at the county level from Kerry to Obama. Electoral data for the analysis were obtained from the Tennessee State Division of Elections. County-level racial data came from the United States census. Data on religious denominations were obtained from the Association of Religion Data Archive. The weighted least squares estimation is weighted by the size of the electorate in each county. This approach is used to control for potential heteroskedasticity arising from the use of aggregated data of units with widely varying populations.

25. See, for a similar argument about Oklahoma, Jim McKinley, "Where Tuesday's Tide Was All Republican," *New York Times*, November 7, 2008.

12.

1. After the 1976 election, Texas had two Republicans representing it in the U.S. House, three (out of thirty-one) in the Texas state Senate, and nineteen (out of one hundred fifty) in the Texas House of Representatives.

2. It was pretty clear that Democrats were only "renting" this seat. This was Tom DeLay's seat, but since he was already the Republican nominee, no Republican's name was on the ballot. Despite having a write-in unfriendly hyphenated name, Republican Shelly Sekula-Gibbs garnered 61,938 votes, 41.8 percent of the total cast in 2006. Throughout the 2008 cycle, Nick Lampson was considered the most endangered Democratic House incumbent.

3. For a list of Texas general election polls, go to http://www.pollster.com/polls/tx/08-tx-pres-ge-mvo.php.

4. Bennet Roth, "Clinton Racks up Victories in Texas, Ohio," *Houston Chronicle*, March 5, 2008, 1A.

5. Jay Cost, "How Obama Won Wisconsin," Real Clear Politics, February 20, 2008, http://www.realclearpolitics.com/horseraceblog/2008/02/how_obama_won_wisconsin.html (accessed November 19, 2008).

6. Michael Luo, "Remarks that Led to Hand-Wringing in Clinton Camp May Have Paid Off." *New York Times,* March 6, 2008.

7. Pollster.com, "2008 Texas Democratic Primary," *Pollster.com,* http://www.pollster.com/polls/tx/08-tx-dem-pres-primary.php (accessed November 17, 2008).

8. Brian Arbour, "Early Returns in Texas," *Monkey Cage,* February 27, 2008, http://www.themonkeycage.org/2008/02/early_returns_in_texas.html (accessed November 17, 2008).

9. Andrew Gumbel, "Clinton Faces Her Own Alamo as She Battles Obama in Texas," *Independent on Sunday* (London, England), March 2, 2008. The ad showed a red phone ringing near a bed, presumably located in the White House. A narrator is then heard stating, "It's three a.m. and your children are safe and asleep. But there's a phone in the White House, and it's ringing. Something's happening in the world. Your vote will decide who answers that call. Whether it's someone who already knows the world's leaders, knows the military—someone tested and ready to lead in a dangerous world." The TV ad concludes with Senator Clinton, who is wearing reading glasses, picking up the phone.

10. See the Real Clear Politics average for the Texas primary at http://www.realclearpolitics.com/epolls/2008/president/tx/texas_democratic_primary-312.html#polls, or the Pollster.com average at: http://www.pollster.com/polls/tx/08-tx-dem-pres-primary.php.

11. "Clinton's Red-phone Resurgence," *Boston Globe,* March 6, 2008.

12. Texas primary exit poll results are available online at http://www.cnn.com/ELECTION/2008/primaries/results/epolls/#TXDEM (accessed November 17, 2008).

13. Rural Texas is defined as those counties that are not part of any metropolitan area, as designated by the U.S. Census Bureau. These counties proved crucial to Clinton's primary victory. Clinton defeated Obama by a margin of 113,998 there, overcoming Obama's 13,740 vote margin in the rest of the state.

14. For comparison purposes, that number is 111 percent greater than the number of votes cast in the Republican primary.

15. Turnout numbers are from the Elections Division of the Texas Secretary of State, http://www.sos.state.tx.us/elections/historical/70–92.shtml (accessed November 17, 2008).

16. Paul Burka, "Almost Blue." *Texas Monthly,* May 2008, 18–22.

17. Included in the visit to Dallas was a separate meeting with oil billionaire T. Boone Pickens, discussing issues relating to natural gas and wind power.

18. George Washington University, "The Travels of Senator Joe Biden—September 2008," George Washington University, http://www.gwu.edu/~action/2008/obama/bidencal0908.html (accessed June 28, 2009).

19. R. G. Ratcliffe, "Texas Donations; $206 Million; Residents Put 31 Percent More into This Election than in 2004," *Houston Chronicle,* November 9, 2008, 3B.

20. While the exit polls asked many voters if they supported expanded offshore drilling, this question was not asked to exit poll respondents in Texas.

21. "Texas Statewide Survey" (October 15–22, 2008), Department of Government, University of Texas, http://www.laits.utexas.edu/txp_media /htm/poll/files/200810-summary.pdf (accessed June 28, 2009).

22. Stewart M. Powell and Kyle Pendergast, "Campaign 2008; Once-Key Issues Vanish from Race," *Houston Chronicle,* November 3, 2008, 1A.

23. The Texas sections in the *Almanac of American Politics* over the last two decades cover the effectiveness of the state's different districting plans.

24. *Lulac v. Perry,* 548 U.S. 399 (2006).

25. Nathan L. Gonzalez, "Texas 22: Top of the List," June 22, 2007, http://rothenbergpoliticalreport.blogspot.com/2007/06/new-print-edition-missouri-6-texas-22.htm (accessed January 30, 2009).

26. Fund-raising numbers are available from OpenSecrets.org.

27. All historical election results in this paper come from the Congressional Quarterly Voting and Elections Collection, http://www.cqpress.com/product/ CQ-Voting-and-Elections-Collection.html (accessed June 28, 2009).

28. For political scientists, the 1976 Texas campaign is most famous for the story of Ford biting into a tamale—husk and all—at a market in San Antonio. The story is told in the opening of Samuel Popkin's seminal book *The Reasoning Voter* (Chicago: University of Chicago Press, second edition, 1994).

29. We defined rural as counties that were not part of metropolitan area as defined by the U.S. Census Bureau. The urban counties are those at the center of a metropolitan area. So Bexar (the home of San Antonio) is the urban county in the San Antonio metropolitan area. We included both Dallas and Tarrant (Fort Worth) counties as urban. Counties that are part of a metropolitan area, but are not the center of the urban area, are coded as suburban.
This is of course a crude definition. For examples, both authors grew up in Harris County, which we code as urban. But both authors would identify their neighborhoods as suburban. But since county is the unit of measurement for votes going back historically, we use this crude, if instructive, measure.

30. Karl Rove, "History Favors Republicans in 2010," *Wall Street Journal,* November 13, 2008, http://online.wsj.com/article/SB122653996148523063.html (accessed June 28, 2009).

31. Paul Burka, "State of Play," *Texas Monthly,* August 2008, 128–33.

32. Nate Silver, "Dean Defends Lieberman Decision, Speaks of 'Mandate for Reconciliation,'" *FiveThirtyEight.com,* November 18, 2008, http://www. fivethirtyeight.com/2008/11/dean-defends-lieberman-decision-speaks.html.

33. Peter Wallsten, "Democrats Set Sights on Texas: Some Believe Latinos Can Help Change the State from Red to Blue," *Los Angeles Times*, November 9, 2008.

34. Again, Obama won among all age eighteen to twenty-nine voters in the state 54 to 45 percent. He won this group because minorities make up approximately 44 percent of young voters, and he won nearly all African American young voters, and two-thirds of young Latinos.

35. It should be noted that small town voters nationally did not just bitterly cling to the Republican Party. Nationally, McCain gained 3 points among small-town voters over George W. Bush in 2004.

36. East Texas is defined as east of Interstate 35 to San Antonio, and north of Interstate 37, which runs from San Antonio to Corpus Christi. This separates East Texas from West Texas (west of I-35, north of I-10) and South Texas (south of I-10 and I-37).

37. See the map from the *New York Times,* available online at http://elections. nytimes.com/2008/results/president/map.html.

38. Population data come from the Texas State Data Center and Office of the State Demographer, and are available at http://txsdc.utsa.edu/.

13.

1. See, for instance, Howard Fineman, "The Virginians; Want to Know How The Campaigns Ahead Will Unfold," *Newsweek,* December 26, 2005, 70.

2. John McGlennon, "Virginia: The Triumph of Experience over Hope," *The American Review of Politics* 26 (Summer, 2005) 245–65.

3. Michae Shear,, "'Macaca Moment' Marks Shift in Momentum," *Washington Post,* September 3, 2006, 1C.

4. Anne E. Kornblut, "A Tightening Potomac Primary?" *Washington Post,* February 6, 2008, 22A.

5. "Profile of the Virginia Primary Voters," *New York Times,* http://politics. nytimes.com/election-guide/2008/results/vote-polls/VA.html?scp=3&sq= virginia%20primary%20exit%20polls&st=Search (accessed November 25, 2008).

6. V. O. Key, *Southern Politics in State and Nation,* (Knoxville: University of Tennessee Press, 1984) 20.

7. "McCain VP Vetters Eye Virginia's Cantor," *Washington Times,* August 3, 2008, 1A.

8. Ben Smith and Amie Parnes, "Kaine 'Very, Very High' on VP Shortlist," *Politico,* July 28, 2008, http://www.politico.com/news/stories/0708/12115.html (accessed January 2, 2009).

9. Michael Muskal, and Peter Nicholas, "Obama Fires Back at McCain Camp for Seizing on His 'Lipstick on a Pig' Comment," *Los Angeles Times,* September 11, 2008, http://articles.latimes.com/2008/sep/11/nation/ na-campaign11(accessed January 3, 2009).

10. Karen Tumulty, "In Battleground Virginia, a Tale of Two Ground Games," *Time,* October 12, 2008, http://www.time.com/time/politics/article/ 0,8599,1849422,00.html (accessed December 29, 2008).

11. For these and other preelection polling results reported here, see *Pollster.com,.* Virginia polls, http://www.pollster.com/polls/va/08-va-pres- ge-mvo.php (accessed December 29, 2008).

12. University of Wisconsin Advertising Project, "Obama Outspending McCain 3 to 1 on TV: Nearly 75% of Presidential Ad Spending in Red States," news release, October 31, 2008.

13. Curtis Gans, "African-Americans, Anger, Fear and Youth Propel Turnout to Highest Level Since 1960," Center for the Study of the American Electorate, Washington, D.C., December 17, 2008.

14. Tim Craig, "Rush to Register Swells Va. Rolls by 10%," *Washington Post,* October 16, 2008, 1B, 5B.

15. Registration figures for the state as a whole and individual localities was drawn from information available on the Virginia State Board of Elections site,http://www.sbe.virginia.gov/cms/Election_Information/Index.html

16. Craig, 5B.

17. All exit poll data drawn from CNN's website, http://www.cnn.com/ELECTION/2008/results/polls/#VAP00p1, http://www.cnn.com/ELECTION/2008/results/polls/#val=VAP00p2 , and http://www.cnn.com/ELECTION/2008/results/polls/#val=VAP00p3 (accessed December 26, 2008).

18. McGlennon, 258.

Conclusion

1. Thomas F. Schaller, *Whistling Past Dixie: How the Democrats Can Win Without the South* (New York: Simon and Schuster, 2006).

2. Thomas F. Schaller, "The South Will Fall Again," *New York Times,* July 1, 2008, http://www.nytimes.com/2008/07/01/opinion/01schaller.html?n=Top/News/U.S./U.S.%20States,%20Territories%20and%20Possessions/Mississippi (accessed January 4, 2009).

3. Adam Nossiter, "For South, a Waning Hold on Politics," November 12, 2008, http://delong.typepad.com/egregious_moderation/2008/11/adam (accessed January 3, 2009).

4. Jack Bass, "In Dixie, Signs of a Rising Biracial Politics," *New York Times,* May 11, 2008, http://www.nytimes.com/2008/05/11/weekinreview/11bass.html?pagewanted=print (accessed January 4, 2009).

5. Jose Antonio Vargas, "Obama Raised Half a Billion Online," *Washington Post,* November 20, 2008, http://voices.washingtonpost.com/the-trail/2008/11/20/obama_raised_half_a_billion_on.html (accessed January 4, 2009).

6. Thomas F. Schaller, "Do Democrats Need the South?"*Salon.com,* November 14, 2006, http://www.salon.com/opinion/feature/2006/11/14/no_south/.

7. Frances Fox Piven and Richard A. Cloward, *Why Americans Don't Vote* (New York: Pantheon Books, 1988) and Robert Erickson, "State Turnout and Presidential Voting: A Closer Look," *American Politics Research* 23 (1995): 387–96.

8. Michael McDonald, United States Elections Project, http://elections.gmu.edu/index.html (accessed January 4, 2009).

9. McDonald.

10. David S. Broder, "The GOP Goes South," *Washington Post,* December 28, 2008, http://www.washingtonpost.com/wp-dyn/content/article/2008/12/26/AR2008122601129.html (accessed January 4, 2009).

11. Broder.

12. Christopher Cooper and H. Gibbs Knotts, "Defining Dixie: A State-Level Measure of the Modern Political South," *American Review of Politics* 25 (Summer 2004): 25–39.

13. Bass.

14. Earl Black and Merle Black, *Politics and Society in the South* (Cambridge: Harvard University Press, 1987), 13.

15. Associated Press, "Census: Blacks Moving Back to the South at Record Pace," *St. Petersburg Times,* October 31, 2003, http://www.sptimes.com/2003/10/31/Worldandnation/Census__Blacks_moving.shtml (accessed January 4, 2009).

16. Associated Press.

17. Kurt Badenhausen, "The Best States for Business," *Forbes,* August 16, 2006, http://www.forbes.com/2006/08/15/best-states-business_cz_kb_0815 beststates.html (accessed January 4, 2009).

18. Robert Atkinson and Scott Andes, "The 2008 State New Economy Index: Benchmarking Economic Transformation in the States," Information Technology and Innovation Foundation, November 18, 2008, http://www.itif.org/index.php?id=200.

19. V. O. Key, *Southern Politics in State and Nation* (Knoxville: The University of Tennessee Press, 1984), 4.

20. Matt Lassiter, *Suburban Politics in the Sunbelt South* (Princeton: Princeton University Press, 2006).

21. See Michael W. Giles, "Percent Black and Racial Hostility: An Old Assumption Revisited," *Social Science Quarterly* 58 (December 1977): 412–17, and Marylee C. Taylor, "How White Attitudes Vary with Racial Composition of Local Populations: Numbers Count," *American Sociological Review* 63 (August 1998): 512–35.

22. Christopher Cooper and H. Gibbs Knotts, "Reflections on the 2008 Election," UNC Press blog, November 13, 2008, http://uncpressblog.com/2008/11/13/reflections-on-the-2008-election/ (accessed January 4, 2009).

Contributors

Branwell DuBose Kapeluck is an associate professor of political science at The Citadel. A codirector of The Citadel Symposium on Southern Politics since 2004, he is the coauthor of "Southern Governors and Legislatures," a chapter in *Writing Southern Politics*.

Laurence W. Moreland is a professor of political science at The Citadel. He is codirector of the Citadel Symposium on Southern Politics and is the author and editor of a number of publications, including *The 2000 Presidential Election in the South* and *Writing Southern Politics: Contemporary Interpretations and Future Directions*.

Robert P. Steed is a professor of political science at The Citadel. He is codirector of the Citadel Symposium on Southern Politics and is the author and editor of a number of publications, including *Eye of the Storm: The South and Congress in an Era of Change* and *Writing Southern Politics: Contemporary Interpretations and Future Directions*.

Scott E. Buchanan is an assistant professor of political science at The Citadel and director of the Citadel Symposium on Southern Politics. He has written articles on partisan realignment in the South. In addition, he has been involved in oral histories of Georgia political figures of the 1950s and 1960s. Buchanan is also a past president of the Georgia Political Science Association.

John A. Clark is a professor of political science at Western Michigan University. He has written numerous articles that have appeared in journals such as *Legislative Studies Quarterly* and the *American Political Science Review*. He has also contributed chapters to numerous edited works and was coeditor most recently of *Southern Political Party Activists: Patterns of Conflict and Change, 1991–2001*.

Patrick R. Cotter is a professor of political science at the University of Alabama. His past affiliations with the Capstone Poll at the University of Alabama and the National Network of State Polls have focused much of his research and publication on public opinion and political behavior, especially in the South, but he has also done research on such topics as social services and the aging and voting behavior in Central America. He was a recent cocontributor to the edited work *Southern Political Party Activists: Patterns of Conflict and Change, 1991–2001*.

Charles S. Bullock III is the Richard B. Russell Professor of Political Science at the University of Georgia. His areas of research include policy analysis, interest groups, legislative politics, and southern politics. He is the author of several books, including *Runoff Elections in the United States*, which was the winner of the 1993 V. O. Key Award. He has published in a wide array of journals including the *American Political Science Review, Journal of Politics*, and, most, recently the *Georgetown Journal of Law and Public Policy*.

Robert E. Hogan is an associate professor of political science at Louisiana State University. He studies various aspects of American electoral politics. In particular his research interests focus on campaigns, political parties, and interest groups at the state level. He is the author of numerous articles appearing in journals such as *Journal of Women, Politics, and Policy*; *American Review of Politics*; and *American Journal of Political Science*. He has also contributed chapters to a number of edited works, including most recently *Southern Political Party Activists: Patterns of Conflict and Change, 1991–2001*.

Eunice H. McCarney graduated from Louisiana State University in May 2009 with a degree in political science.

David A. Breaux is a professor of political science at Mississippi State University. His research focuses on legislative process, both state and national. He has written numerous book chapters on southern politics, most recently in *Southern Politics in the 1990s*. His work has appeared in journals such as *Legislative Studies Quarterly* and the *American Review of Politics*.

Stephen D. Shaffer is a professor of political science at Mississippi State University. He has published extensively on Mississippi party organizations and political campaigns, as well as on national public opinion and federal elections. Shaffer directs the Mississippi Poll. He coauthored the book *Mississippi Government and Politics*, the 2006 V. O. Key award winning book; *Politics in the New South: Representation of African Americans in Southern State Legislatures*; and has published in such journals as *American Journal of Political Science, Western Political Quarterly*, and *Social Science Quarterly*.

Cole Blease Graham is a professor of political science at the University of South Carolina. His major fields of specialization are public administration and public management and American state-local government and politics, with an emphasis on South Carolina politics. His publications include a coauthored book on public organization management, a coauthored book on South Carolina government and politics, and a coedited book on court administration. He is also the author of numerous book chapters and articles in journals such as the *Southeastern Political Review* and *Southern Cultures*.

Jay Barth is an associate professor of political science at Hendrix College. He was the 2000–1 recipient of the American Political Science Association's Steiger Congressional Fellowship. He is the author of numerous book chapters, with a particular focus on Arkansas politics and southern politics. His most recent chapter appeared in *Southern Political Party Activists: Patterns of Conflict and Change, 1991–2001*. He has also published a number of journal articles, which have appeared in such journals as *State Politics and Policy* and *Political Psychology*. Most recently, he has coauthored the second edition of *Arkansas Politics and Government: Do the People Rule?*

Janine A. Parry is an associate professor of political science at the University of Arkansas. She is also the director of the Arkansas Poll. She has published work in such journals as *State Politics and Policy Quarterly, Journal of Black Studies,* and *Political Behavior.* She has also published a number of chapters in edited books, most recently *New Voices in the Old South: How Women and Minorities Influence Southern Politics.* Her latest work was as coeditor of *Readings in Arkansas Politics and Government.*

Todd Shields is a professor of political science at the University of Arkansas. He is also the associate director of the Fulbright Institute of International Relations and the director of the Diane D. Blair Center of Southern Politics and Society. His research interests lie broadly in campaigns and elections. He also has research interests in political psychology, political communication, and research methods, publishing many journal articles in these areas and a book examining the likely effects of campaign finance referendums on congressional elections. He is the coauthor of *Money Matters: The Effects of Campaign Finance Reform on Congressional Elections* and the coeditor of *The Clinton Riddle: Interdisciplinary Perspectives of the 42nd President.*

Jonathan Knuckey is an associate professor of political science at the University of Central Florida. His research interests include Southern politics, political parties, campaigns and elections, and religion and politics. He is the author of many journal articles appearing in journals such as *Political Research Quarterly, Social Science Quarterly,* and the *American Review of Politics.* He is also the author of several book chapters, the latest appearing in *Southern Political Party Activists: Patterns of Conflict and Change, 1991–2001.*

Charles Prysby is a professor of political science at the University of North Carolina at Greensboro. His principle research interests are in elections, voting behavior, political parties, contextual analysis, and southern politics. He is the coauthor of two books, *Political Choices* and *Political Behavior and the Local Context.* He is the coeditor of and a contributor to *Southern Political Party Activists: Patterns of Conflict and Change, 1991–2001.* He has contributed numerous chapters to edited books and is the author of many journal articles. His scholarly articles have appeared in journals such as the *Journal of Politics* and the *Journal of Political Methodology.*

Ronald Keith Gaddie is a professor of political science at the University of Oklahoma. His chief research interests are in elections, southern politics, environmental politics, and redistricting and representation. He is the author, coauthor, or coeditor of fourteen books. In 2009, he published *Georgia Politics in a State of Change* and *The Triumph of Voting Rights in the South.* His current research project is a book-length examination (with Charles S. Bullock III) of the legal and political strategies associated with the Texas redistricting fight and the subsequent appellate legal battle. The book is titled *Delayed Democracy: The Texas Redistricting War of 2001–2006.* He has contributed book chapters to numerous books as well as published articles in journals such as *Political Research Quarterly* and *Public Budgeting and Finance.*

Brian K. Arbour is an assistant professor of political science at City University of New York, John Jay College of Criminal Justice. He has published several articles in journals such as *American Politics Research, Journal of Political Marketing*, and the *American Review of Politics*. He also serves as a member of the Fox News Decision Desk staff, interpreting exit poll results and calling elections.

Mark McKenzie is an assistant professor of political science at Texas Tech University. He also received his J.D. from the University of Texas School Of Law in 1998. His current research focuses on judicial politics, elections, and political behavior, and his research has appeared in *American Politics Research*.

John J. McGlennon is a professor at the College of William and Mary. He specializes in United States politics with a special focus on the South and Virginia. He has many publications to his credit, including two coauthored books: *The Life of the Parties: A Study of Presidential Activists* and *Party Activists in Virginia*.

H. Gibbs Knotts is associate professor at the Western Carolina University. He has written a number of articles in refereed journals such as *Social Science Quarterly* and the *Journal of Politics,* many of which have focused on southern politics. Along with numerous book chapters, Gibbs is the coeditor of *The New Politics of North Carolina*.

Index

Aaron, Hank, 51
abortion, 53
Abramoff, Jack, 53, 157
ACORN, 73
Aderholt, Robert, 39
age and the 2008 election in the South, 5, 6–7
Aistrup, Joseph, xix
Alabama: comparison with national voting, 46; down-ticket elections in, 38–41; gender and voting in, 42–43; income voting patterns in, 42–43; nomination process in, 27, 37–38; race and voting in, 42–47; recent political history in, 36–37; regional voting in, 41–43; 2008 results in, 6, 38–39; voting patterns in, 41–46
Al-Qaeda, 146, 219
Alexander, Lamar, 191
Allen, George, 216, 231
Altmire, Jason, 28
American Review of Politics, xix
American Voter, The, 9
Anderson, Gary, 84
Archer, Bill, 202
Arkansas GOP Leadership Team, 121
Arkansas: campaign in, 122–24; age and voting in, 132; the Clinton factor in, 133; down-ticket elections in, 134–36; ethnicity and voting in, 132; gender and voting in, 129–31; ideology and voting in, 132–33; income and voting in, 132; issues in, 132; nomination process in, 27, 120–22; party identification and voting in, 132–33; primary turnout in, 123; 2008 results in, 125–29; race and voting in, 132; state lottery in, 135–36; turnout in, 133–34; voting patterns in, 129–34
Arkansas Politics and Government: Do the People Rule?, xv
Arkansas Travelers, 121
Atwater, Lee, 100
Austin American-Statesman, 199
Axelrod, David, 237
Ayers, William, 145, 219

Baker, Richard, 81
Baker, Tod A., xviii
Baldwin, Chuck, 39, 93, 104, 126, 224
Barbour, Haley, 83, 84–85, 86, 88, 89, 94

Barr, Bob, 39, 56, 57, 62, 93, 104, 126, 224
Barrett, J. Gresham, 104, 113
Bass, Jack, 236
Baxley, Bill, 36–37
Baxley, Lucy, 36–37, 41
Beasley, David, 116
Beebe, Mike, 120, 124
Berry, Marion, 126
Biden, Joe, 4, 25, 29, 87, 93, 104, 126, 148, 199, 218
Big Mule-Black Belt coalition, 41
bin Laden, Osama, 146, 219
Bipartisan Campaign Reform Act of 2002 (BCRA), 21
Bishop, Sanford, 51
Black, Earl, xiii, xix, 4, 7
Black, Merle, xiii, xix, 4, 7, 65
Blair, Diane Divers, xiv, xix, 129
Bloomberg, Michael, 233
blueburbs, 106
Bonilla, Henry, 202
Boozman, John, 126, 134
Boston Globe, 198
Boucher, Rick, 224
Bright, Bobby, 39, 40
Brimer, Kim, 197
Brock, Bill, 181
Brodsky, David, 180, 181
Brown, Henry, 104, 113
Bryant, Phil, 84, 91, 94
Buchanan, Bruce, 201
Buckley, Allen, 64
Bumpers, Dale, xv
Burka, Paul, 199
Bush, George H. W., 3, 68, 86, 202, 204
Bush, George W., 68, 89, 101, 151, 215, 241: effect on 2008 campaign, 3, 69, 79–80, 85, 94, 112, 124, 137, 149, 227; and Texas politics, 195–213
Bush, Jenna, 232
Bush, John Ellis "Jeb," 138, 141, 146

Campbell, Angus, 9
Campbell, Carroll, 100
Cantor, Eric, 218, 224
Cao, Joseph, 81
Caraway, Hattie, xv
Cardenas, Al, 141
Carmines, Edward, 9
Carter, Jimmy, 68, 99, 195, 204, 205

Carville, James, 237
Cassidy, Bill, 81
Castle, Darrell L., 93, 104, 126
Castro, Raul, 143
Cavanaugh, Twinkle Andress, 41
Cazayoux, Don, 81
Chambliss, Saxby, 60–65
Cheney, Dick, 80
Childers, Travis, 90, 91, 92, 93, 97
Citizens for Responsibility and Ethics in
    Washington, 157
Civil Rights Act of 1964, 15
civil rights movement, xiii, xix, 99, 178
Civil War, xix, 99
Clarion Ledger, 84, 88
Clark, Wesley, 122–23
Cleland, Max, 63
Clement, Frank, 181
Clemente, Rosa, 93, 104, 126
Clinton, Bill, xiv, xv, xx, 25, 26, 41, 63,
    68, 70, 86, 102, 120, 124, 137, 138,
    146, 198, 204, 237, 238
Clinton, Chelsea, 86, 120
Clinton, Hillary: and Alabama, 37; and
    Arkansas, 120–24; and Florida, 140,
    143, 146; and Georgia, 50–51; and
    Louisiana, 69–71; and Mississippi, 86;
    and North Carolina, 164; and South
    Carolina, 102–3; and Tennessee,
    183–85; and Texas, 198, 210; and
    Virginia, 217–18; and the 2008
    nomination, 17–31; nomination
    strategy, 28–29
Clyburn, James, 88, 101, 104, 114, 116
Cobb, Sue Bell, 37
Cochran, Thad, 85, 88, 91, 92, 93
Cohen, Steve, 191
Colom, Wilbur, 88
Community Voters Project, 221
congressional contests: historical trends,
    241; south wide, 241–42
Conley, Bob, 104, 112
Connelly, John, 100
Connolly, Gerald, 224, 233
Cook, Richard, 92, 93
Corden, Paul, 104, 114
Corker, Bob, 177
Cornyn, John, 196, 197, 202
Cowart, Daniel, 186
Cramer, Bud, 39
Crist, Charlie, 23, 74, 138, 139, 141,
    143–45
Crump, E.H., 178, 179, 180, 181–82
Cuban American National Foundation,
    158
Culberson, John, 196, 197, 202

Dale, George, 84
Dallas Morning News, 199
Dardenne, Jay, 73
Davis, Artur, 37, 45, 47
Davis, Greg, 90–91, 93
Davis, Jim, 138
Davis, Tom, 232, 233
Davis, Wendy, 197
Dawson, Katon, 115
Day, Bill, 224
Dean, Howard, 21, 73, 87, 208
DeLay, Tom, 201
DeMint, Jim, 23, 101, 114
Democratic Attorney General Association,
    84
Democratic Blue Dog Coalition, 90, 91, 92
Democratic Congressional Campaign
    Committee, 157, 158
Democratic nomination race, 24–28
Democratic Senatorial Campaign
    Committee, 61, 64
Diane D. Blair Center of Southern Politics
    and Society, xiv, xix
Diaz-Balart, Lincoln, 148, 157
Diaz-Balart, Mario, 148, 157–58
Dixiecrat Revolt, xvii, 99, 181
Dodd, Chris, 25
Doggett, Lloyd, 203
Doherty, Larry Joe, 197, 202
Dole, Bob, 204
Dole, Elizabeth, 163, 168, 170
Dortch's Law, 180
Douglas, Stephen, 218
Dowdy, Wayne, 87
Drake, Joshua, 126
Drake, Thelma, 224, 233
Dukakis, Michael, 238, 239
Dyer, Jane Ballard, 104, 113

early voting, 55
economic concerns: in Arkansas, 132; in
    Georgia, 59; in Louisiana, 79; and
    regional voting patterns, 11–12; in
    South Carolina, 110–11; in Texas, 200
economic environment, 244–45
Edwards, James, 100
Edwards, John, 21, 25, 26, 69, 85, 101,
    102, 140, 162, 165, 183, 238
Eisenhower, Dwight D., xviii, 68, 203
election of 1928, xvii, 203
election of 1948, xvii, 99, 181
election of 1952, 68, 99, 203
election of 1956, 99, 203
election of 1960, 99
election of 1964, 4, 40, 68, 99, 179, 181,
    212, 216
election of 1968, 99

election of 1972, 68, 99, 204
election of 1976, 68, 99, 147, 195, 204
election of 1980, 68, 204
election of 1984, xviii, 68, 212
election of 1988, 68, 94
election of 1992, 68, 86
election of 1996, 3–4, 68, 204; compared
    to 2008, 41, 147;
election of 2000, 68, 101, 139; compared
    to 2008, 4, 21, 41, 119, 125–26, 137,
    196, 230
election of 2004, 68, 83, 101; compared to
    2008, 4, 6, 7, 41, 55–58, 75, 82, 94,
    119, 125–26, 133, 167, 189–91, 196,
    199, 206–7, 223, 228, 230
Ellis, Tyrone, 87
Ellisor, Michael, 113
Ellmore, Mark, 224
Equal Rights Amendment, xiv
Everett, Terry, 39

Falwell, Jerry, 23, 221
Feder, Judy, 224
Federal Election Campaign Act of 1974,
    19
Feeney, Tom, 141, 148, 157
Figures, Vivian Davis, 38, 39
Fimian, Keith, 224
Fleming, Eric, 92, 93
Florida: age and voting in, 151–54;
    campaign in, 142–47; down-ticket
    elections in, 148, 156–58; gender and
    voting in, 151, 152; ideology in, 153,
    155; income and voting in, 152,
    154–55; issues in, 156; nomination
    process in, 23, 24, 26, 52, 140,
    139–42; party identification in, 153,
    155; race and voting in, 150–51, 152,
    159; recent political history in, 138–39;
    regional voting in, 147–50; 2008
    results in, 147; voting patterns in,
    147–56; voter turnout in, 147
Foley, Mark 138, 157
Folsom, Jim, Jr., 37
Forbes, 244
Forbes, Randy, 224
Ford, Gerald, 204
Ford, Harold, Jr., 177, 188, 191, 245
Fordice, Kirk, 89
Fort Worth Star-Telegram, 199
Franks, Jamie, 87
Fredrick, Jeffrey, 219, 232
Freedom Watch, 64
frontloading, 19, 139–40

Garcia, Joe, 148, 158
gay rights: in Arkansas, 14; in Florida, 14

gender and the 2008 election in the South,
    5, 8–9
Georgia: campaign in, 53–55; comparison
    with national voting, 58–59; down-
    ticket elections in, 60–65; nomination
    process in, 27, 50–53; race and voting
    in, 59; 2008 results in, 53–59; voting
    patterns in, 56–59, 62–63
Gephart, Dick, 101
Gill, Joel L., 91, 93
Gilmore, James, 217, 224, 231, 232, 234
Giuliani, Rudy, 22, 23–24, 30, 63, 102,
    141
Goldwater, Barry, 40, 68, 99, 179, 181,
    239
Gonzalez, Matt, 93, 104, 126
Goode, Virgil, 224, 233
Goodlatte, Bob, 224
Gore, Al, Jr., xx, 41, 63, 101, 125, 137,
    149, 146, 183, 196, 238
Gore, Al, Sr., 181
Graham, Lindsey, 101, 104, 112–13
Gramm, Phil, 202
Gravel, Mike, 140
Grayson, Alan, 148, 157
Griffith, Parker, 39, 40
Gwatney, Bill, 123

Hagan, Kay, 168, 170, 173–74
Hager, John, 232
Harper, Gregg, 91, 92, 93
Harrelson, Nancy, 104, 114
Harris, Katherine, 138
Hartke, Anita, 224
Havard, William, xviii
Hayes, Robin, 171
Helms, Jesse, 245
Herring, Jim, 88
Hispanics, 4–5, 9
Hodges, Jim, 116
Hollings, Ernest F., 114
Hood, Jim, 84
Hope and Recovery Summit, 69
Hosemann, Delbert, 84
Houston Chronicle, 199
Huckabee, Mike, 22, 23, 24, 30, 37, 52,
    63, 68, 69, 71–72, 86, 102, 121, 122,
    141, 184, 217
Hunter, Duncan, 69, 102
Hurricane Gustav, 81
Hurricane Ike, 13, 199
Hurricane Katrina, 37, 69, 82, 84, 242

income and the 2008 election in the South,
    5, 7
Inglis, Bob, 104, 114
Insider Advantage, 54

invisible primary, 19, 30
Iowa caucuses, 19, 22, 25, 52, 139, 140
issues: key ones in 2008, 9–16; related to
    regional voting patterns, 10–14

Jackson, Jesse, 26
Jennings, Toni 141
Jim Crow, xiii, xix
Jindal, Bobby, 67, 74
Joe the Plumber, 145
Johnson, Hank, 51
Johnson, Lyndon B., 4, 138, 212, 216,
    228, 233, 239
Jones, Bob, III, 23
Jones, Vernon, 60

Kaine, Timothy, 216, 217, 218, 219, 234
Kefauver, Estes, 181
Keller, Ric, 148, 156
Kennedy, John, 80, 99
Kennedy, Rebekah, 126
Kerry, John, 21, 25, 41, 55, 82, 84, 101,
    125, 137, 139, 149, 151, 154, 167,
    183, 196, 215, 228, 238, 239
Ketner, Linda, 104, 112
Key, V.O., Jr., xvii, xviii, 9, 15, 178, 180,
    217
King, Martin Luther, Jr., 181
Kissel, Larry, 171
Klein, Ron, 139
Kosmas, Suzanne, 148, 157
Ku Klux Klan, 186, 192

Lamis, Alexander P., xix
Lampson, Nick, 196, 197, 201, 202
Landrieu, Mary, 69, 80, 82
Larson, Lyle, 197, 202
La Riva, Gloria, 126
Lehman Brothers, 144
Lewis, John, 51
Lincoln, Abraham, 218
literacy test, 180
Los Angeles Times, 208
Lott, Trent, 85, 89, 92
Louisiana: age and voting in, 76; campaign
    in, 72–74; comparison with national
    voting, 76–79; down-ticket elections in,
    80–81; gender and voting in, 76–77;
    income voting patterns in, 76; ideology
    and voting in, 77–78; nomination
    process in, 27, 69–72; race and voting
    in, 76–77; recent political history in,
    68–69; regional voting in, 76–77;
    religion and voting in, 76; 2008 results
    in, 74–81; voting patterns in, 71–72,
    75–79
Love, Jay, 39, 40

Lublin, David, xix
Ludacris, 63

Mabus, Ray, 86, 88
Mahoney, Tim 139, 148, 157
Maine caucuses, 24
Marshall, Robert, 232
Martin, Jim, 60–65
Martinez, Mel, 23, 141
Martinez, Raul L., 148
Mason, John Lyman, 180
McCain, John: and Alabama, 35–47;
    and Arkansas, 119–36; and Florida,
    137–59; and Georgia, 49–65; and
    Louisiana, 67–82; and Mississippi,
    83–97; and North Carolina, 161–75;
    and South Carolina, 99–116; in
    Tennessee, 177–93; and Texas,
    195–213; and Virginia, 215–34; and
    the 2008 election, xx, 3–16; and the
    2008 nomination, 17–31; nomination
    strategy, 30
McCaul, Michael, 196, 197, 202
McCay, John, 92, 93
McCrory, Pat, 163, 173
McCullough, Glenn, 90
McDonald, Bubba, 63, 65
McEnulty, Frank, 93
McFarland, Deb, 126
McKinney, Cynthia A., 93, 104, 126, 224
Michigan primary, 19, 22, 26
Miller, Andrea, 224
Miller, Rob, 104, 113
Mississippi: biracial coalition in, 85, 97;
    campaign in, 87–88; comparison with
    national voting, 92; congressional
    campaigns in, 89–92; gender and voting
    in, 95–97; ideology and voting in,
    94–95; income and voting in, 95–96;
    nomination process in, 85–87; party
    identification and voting in, 94–95; race
    and voting in, 95–96; recent political
    history in, 83–85; religion and voting
    in, 94–95; 2008 results in, 92–97;
    voting patterns in, 94–97
Mondale, Walter, xiii, 238, 239
Montana primary, 28, 142
Moore, Roy, 36
Moran, James, 224
Mounger, Billy, 91
Mountain Republicanism, 179
Mumpower, Jason, 191
Musgrove, Ronnie, 83, 89, 90, 93

Nader, Ralph, 39, 93, 104, 126, 224
Naifeh, Jimmy, 191
Nardulli, Peter, 178

National Republican Congressional
Committee, 232
National Republican Senatorial Campaign
Committee, 216
National Republican Trust, 64
National Rifle Association, 91
National Right to Life Committee, 23
Nelson, Bill, 138
Nevada caucuses, 23, 140
New Hampshire primaries, 19, 22, 24, 25,
139, 140
Nixon, Richard M., 99, 204
nomination process (2008): in Alabama,
27, 37–38; in Arkansas, 27, 120–22; in
D.C., 50; in Florida, 19, 22, 26, 52,
139–42; future reforms, 30–31; in
California, 26, 50; in Georgia, 27,
50–53; in Iowa, 19, 22, 25, 52,102,
121, 139, 140; in Louisiana, 24, 69–72;
in Michigan, 19, 22, 25, 26; in
Mississippi, 85–87; in Montana, 28,
142; in New York, 26, 50; in Nevada,
23, 140; in New Hampshire, 19, 22,
25, 50, 102, 139, 140; in North
Carolina, 164; in Ohio, 27, 197; in
Rhode Island, 27, 197; rules, 18–21; in
South Carolina, 23, 24, 25–26, 101–3,
121, 140; in South Dakota, 28, 142;
south wide, 17–31; in Tennessee, 27; in
Texas, 27–28, 196–98; in Vermont, 27,
197; in Virginia, 27, 216–18; in
Wisconsin, 198; in Wyoming, 19, 22
Noriega, Rick, 197
Northeast Mississippi Daily Journal, 90
North Carolina: age and voting in, 169;
campaign in, 164–65; comparison with
2004 election, 167; comparison with
national voting, 166; down-ticket
elections in, 168–73; gender and voting
in, 167, 169; ideology and voting in,
167–68; nomination process in, 164;
party identification and voting in,
167–68; population change in, 167;
race and voting in, 167, 169; recent
political history in, 161–63; registration
effort in, 166; religion and voting in,
169; 2008 results in, 169; voting
patterns in, 167–69, 173
Nossiter, Adam, 236
Nye, Glenn, 224, 233

Obama, Barack: and Alabama, 35–47; and
Arkansas, 119–36; and Florida,
137–59; and Georgia, 49–65; and
Louisiana, 67–82; and Mississippi,
83–97; and North Carolina, 161–75;
and South Carolina, 99–16; and

Tennessee, 177–93; and Texas,
195–213; and Virginia, 215–34; and
the 2008 election, xiv, xx, 3–16; and
the 2008 nomination, 17–31;
nomination strategy, 28
Obama, Michelle, 218
Ohio primary, 27
Olson, Pete, 196, 197, 202

Palin, Sarah, 4, 29, 53, 63, 87, 93, 104,
126, 145, 148, 199, 218
Pang, Wally, 93
Parker, Wayne, 39, 40
Paseur, Deborah Bell, 41
Paul, Ron, 22, 102, 121, 232
Pelosi, Nancy, 91
Perdue, Beverly, 163, 172–73
Perdue, Sonny, 55, 63
Perriello, Tom, 224, 233
Perry, Jennings, 180
Perry, Rick, 201
Pfotenhauer, Nancy, 248
Pickering, Chip, 85, 91, 92
Plouffe, David, 237
poll tax, 180
population change in the South, 242–45
Potomac Primary, 217
poverty tour, 86
Powell, Jim, 63
presidential contest (2008): historical
perspective, 237–39; key issues, 237;
south wide, 236–39; voter turnout
trends, 239–40
Presidential Republicanism, 40
Prill, Ted, 90
Project Vote, 73
Pryor, David, xv
Pryor, Mark, 126, 135
Puryear, Eugene, 126

race: and the 2008 election in the South,
4–5, 7–9; in Alabama, 42–47; in
Florida, 4, 150–51, 152, 159; in
Georgia, 59; in North Carolina, 167,
169; in the South, 245–247; in South
Carolina, 106–8; and the 2008 nomination in the South, 29–30; in Tennessee,
180–81, 186–88; in Texas, 4, 209–11;
in Virginia, 4, 223, 225
racial change, 243
racial diversity, 242–44
racial threat hypothesis, 246–47
Rasoul, Sam, 224
Reagan, Ronald, xiii, 3, 68, 100, 204, 212
Real Clear Politics, 54, 60
realignment, xiii, xviii, 68, 136, 178, 179,
195, 215–16, 234

Reconstruction, xix, 68, 195
redistricting, 84
Reece, Carroll, 179
Reed, Joe, 37
Reed, Ralph, 53
Reeves, Tate, 84
religion and the 2008 election in the South, 5, 7
Republican nomination race, 21–24
residency (type), 5, 7
Responsible Electorate, The, 9
Richardson, Bill, 25
Riley, Bob, 36, 37
Rhode Island primary, 27
Robertson, Pat, 23
Rodriguez, Ciro, 196, 197, 202
Rogers, Mike, 39, 40
Romney, Mitt, 21, 22, 23, 24, 30, 37, 52, 63, 70, 71, 74, 85, 101, 121
Rooney, Tom, 148, 157
Roosevelt, Franklin D., 3
Root, Wayne A., 93, 104, 126
Ros-Lehtinen, Ileana, 148, 157, 158
Ross, Charlie, 91
Ross, Mike, 120, 126
Rove, Karl, 80, 206
rural swing counties (Arkansas), 120

San Antonio Express-News, 199
Sanders, Bernie, 86
Sanford, Mark, 116
Schale, Steve, 143
Schaller, Thomas, 235
Schlafly, Phyllis, xiv
Schlesselman, Paul, 186
Schuler, Heath, 171
Scott, David, 51
Scott, Robert, 224
Segal, Joshua, 39, 40
Sekula-Gibbs, Shelly, 201
Service to America Tour, 86
Sessions, Jeff, 38, 39
Sharpton, Al, 101
Shaw, E. Clay, 139
Shaw, Greg, 41
Siegelman, Don, 37
Silent Hattie Speaks: The Personal Journal of Senator Hattie Caraway, xv
Skelly, Michael, 197, 202
Smith, Al, 203
Snyder, Vic, 126
Solid South, xiii
South Carolina: age and voting in, 108–10; campaign in, 103; down-ticket elections in, 112–15; ideology and voting in, 109, 111; income and voting in, 109–11; nomination process in, 24, 52, 101–3, 121, 140; party identification patterns in, 100–101; party identification and voting in, 109, 111; race and voting in, 106–8; recent political history in, 99–101; regional voting in, 105–6, 107; religion and voting in, 110–12; 2008 results in, 103–15; voting patterns in, 106–12; voter registration in, 103–5
South Dakota primary, 28, 142
Southern Politics in State and Nation, xvii, xviii
southern strategy, 181, 237
Sparks, Nicholas B., 39
Spencer, Albert F., 104, 114
Spratt, John, 104, 114
Stanley, Ralph, 230
Stevenson, Adlai, 99
Stimson, James, 9
Strong, Donald S., xvii
Suits, Daniel, 126
superdelegates, 18, 28, 31, 70
Super Tuesday, 19, 26–27, 31, 50, 52, 68, 70, 121, 122, 139, 140, 142, 183, 186, 197
Symington, Stuart, xiv

Taggart, Andy, 87
Tancredo, Tom, 102
Tanenblatt, Eric, 55
Taylor, Gene, 92, 93
Taylor, Mark, 55
Tennessee: down-ticket elections in, 191–92; geographical regions in, 178–79; nomination process in, 27, 183–85; political history of, 178–82; race relations in, 180–81; race and voting in, 186–88; religion and politics in, 182–83, 192; 2008 election results in, 185–88; voting patterns in, 184, 186–91
Texas: age and voting in, 206; changes in, 203–5; down-ticket elections in, 201–3, 208–9; ideology and voting in, 211–12; issues and voting in, 200–1; nomination process in, 27, 196–98; race and voting in, 209–11; recent political history in, 195–96; Republican strengths in, 208–13; residential voting patterns in, 204–5, 210–11; 2008 election results in, 196; turnout in, 198–99; urban voting in, 206–7; voting patterns in, 206–12
Texas Monthly, 208
Thompson, Bennie, 86, 92, 93
Thompson, Fred, 22, 23, 30, 52, 85, 101–2
Thurmond, Michael, 51

Thurmond, Strom, 99, 100, 112, 181
Times Press, 186
Tinker, Nikki, 191
Tomlinson, Abel Noah, 126
Tower, John, 195
Truman, Harry S, 3, 138, 178, 204
Tuck, Amy, 84
Tuke, Bob, 191

United Mine Workers Union, 230

Vermont primary, 27
Virginia: absentee voting in, 221; age and
    voting in, 223–26; campaign in,
    218–20, 227–28; down-ticket elections
    in, 231–33; gender and voting in, 223,
    225; ideology and voting in, 225, 227;
    income and voting in, 225–26; issues
    and voting in, 225, 227; nomination
    process in, 27, 216–18; party identifica-
    tion in, 225, 227–28; polling in,
    219–20; race and voting in, 223, 225;
    recent political history in, 215–16;
    regional voting in, 226, 228–30;
    registration drives in, 220–21; religion
    and voting in, 225, 227; turnout in,
    222; 2008 results in, 222–30; voting
    patterns in, 222–230
Vitter, David, 69
Voting in Power, 73
voting patterns (2008): Alabama, 41–46;
    Arkansas, 129–34; Florida, 147–56;

Georgia, 56–59, 62–63; Louisiana,
    71–72, 75–79; Mississippi, 94–97;
    North Carolina, 167–69, 173; South
    Carolina, 23, 106–12; south wide,
    5–14; Tennessee, 184, 186–91; Texas,
    206–12; Virginia, 222–30
Voting Rights Act of 1965, 114, 181, 184,
    202

Wages, John M., 93
Waggoner, Frank, 104, 114
Wallace, George C., 99, 235
Walters, C. Faye, 104, 114
Warner, John, 217, 231, 232
Warner, Mark, 216, 217, 218, 224, 231,
    232
Webb, James, 216, 218, 231
Weill, Ted C., 93
*Whistling Past Dixie: How Democrats Can
    Win Without the South*, 235
White, Brad, 88
Whitten, Jamie, 90
Wicker, Roger, 86, 89, 90, 92, 93
Wilder, L. Douglas, 234
Wilson, Joe, 104, 113
Winfield, Paul, 87
Wisconsin Advertising Project, 143
Wittman, Robert, 224
Wolf, Frank, 224
Wright, Fielding, 181

Young, Andrew, 51

BRANWELL DUBOSE KAPELUCK is associate professor of political science at The Citadel. LAURENCE W. MORELAND and ROBERT P. STEED are professors of political science at The Citadel and editors of the Presidential Election in the South series that began in 1984 in conjunction with the biennial Citadel Symposium on Southern Politics. *A Paler Shade of Red* was developed with support from the Diane D. Blair Center of Southern Politics and Society at the University of Arkansas.